NATALIE WATERSON, who is bilingual in English and Russian, was born in London in 1922. She was educated at Aylesbury Grammar School, Buckinghamshire, and the University of London. In 1948, after studying at the School of Slavonic and East European Studies and at University College, she took an honours degree in Russian with subsidiary French. She was then awarded a Governing Body Postgraduate Studentship for two years to study phonetics and linguistics at the School of Oriental and African Studies. Among the lectures which she attended during that time were those of J. R. Firth. In 1950 she was appointed Lecturer in Phonetics at SOAS, becoming Senior Lecturer in 1982. She is an active member of various learned societies, in particular of the International Association for the Study of Child Language, of which she was President from 1978 to 1981. She has also made many valuable contributions to international symposia on child language and related topics over the years. Natalie Waterson has published articles in books and journals on various aspects of prosodic phonology, child language development, speech perception, speech therapy, Turkish, Uzbek and Georgian. She is at present writing a book on child language. Her publications include *The Development of Communication* (which she co-edited with C. E. Snow) and *An Uzbek-English Dictionary*.

PROSODIC PHONOLOGY

PROSODIC PHONOLOGY
THE THEORY AND ITS APPLICATION TO LANGUAGE ACQUISITION AND SPEECH PROCESSING

Natalie Waterson
Senior Lecturer in Phonetics,
School of Oriental and African Studies,
University of London

Grevatt & Grevatt
Newcastle upon Tyne

Published by Grevatt & Grevatt, 9 Rectory Drive, Newcastle upon Tyne NE3 1XT

 Natalie Waterson 1987

Designed and set by Grevatt & Grevatt.
Printed in Great Britain by Jasprint Ltd., 12 Tower Road, Glover District 11, Washington, Tyne and Wear NE37 2SH.

British Library Cataloguing in Publication Data:

Waterson, Natalie
  Prosodic phonology: the theory and its
  application to language acquisition and
  speech processing.
  1. Prosodic analysis (Linguistics)
  I. Title
  414   P217.3
ISBN 0-947722-02-5

Price: £12.95 net plus carriage charge:
  UK: 15% (single-copy orders) or 10% (multiple-copy orders)
  Overseas: 30%. Extra £1.00 bank charges with non-sterling
            payments
  $33\frac{1}{3}$% trade discount plus above p & p to UK booksellers only

All Grevatt & Grevatt books are non-commercially published and priced. This book may be bought direct from the publisher or through general distributors.

The publisher gratefully acknowledges the kind co-operation of the following in advertising this publication:
  The International Association for the Study of Child Language
  The International Society of Applied Psycholinguistics
  The Linguistics Association of Great Britain
  AILA Commission on Pscholinguistics Newsletter
  British Linguistic Newsletter
  Child Language Bulletin

In memory of my husband, Ernest Alfred Waterson,
and
to my children, Patrick and Elaine: to them
I owe my deep and abiding interest in first language acquisition.

CONTENTS

	Abbreviations, Notations, and Typographical Conventions	x
	Acknowledgments	xii
	Introduction	1
1	Prosodic Phonology: An Introduction to the Theory	4
2	Prosodic Phonology: Illustration of Analysis	15
3	Child Phonology: A Prosodic View	25
4	Perception and Production in the Acquisition of Phonology	53
5	Growth of Complexity in Phonological Development	88
6	A Tentative Developmental Model of Phonological Representation	108
7	Patterns as Units of Speech Perception	121
8	Summary	134
	References	143
	Index of Personal Names	150
	Index of Subjects	152

ABBREVIATIONS, NOTATIONS, AND TYPOGRAPHICAL CONVENTIONS

The number after each entry refers to the page where that entry is first used.

General

( )^2 parentheses with 2 as superscript: reduplicated syllable, e.g., $(CV)^2$, 17

(C-)^2 partial reduplication, i.e., the consonant is reduplicated but the vowel is not, 31

( )^3 parentheses with 3 as superscript: 'triplicated' syllable, e.g., $(PVP)^3$, 92

C_1 first consonant in a series, e.g., C_1VC_2, 12
C_2 second consonant in a series, e.g., C_1VC_2, 12

{ }   brace brackets: sentence structure, 93
{ }^{2} brace brackets with 2 as superscript: reduplicated sentence structure, 93
{{ }{ }}   brace brackets within brace brackets: sentence structure consisting of a sequence of sentence structures, 93
[ ]   square brackets: (1) phonetic transcriptions in IPA, 9
                   (2) enclose author's interpolations, 5

Pitch contours are represented as follows: ─── ─── ·· ─── ·

i.e., high level stepping down to low and then rising, 130

Age is represented as follows: 1;11.21 = 1 year, 11 months, 21 days, 16

───   horizontal line: stressed syllable, 130; see also pitch contours above
-   short dash in place of an example: no recorded form, 29
·   bold dot: unstressed syllable, 130; see also pitch contours above

LR1   first level of representation, 109
LR2   second level of representation, 109
MLU   mean length of utterance, 107
P   the author's child who was the subject of some of the phonological studies, 26; see also P under **Syllabic and non-syllabic systems**
T   English past tense morpheme, 11
VOT   voicing onset time, 124

Syllabic and non-syllabic systems

C   consonant system, 8
V   vowel system, 8
ə   (schwa) syllabic system, 10; see also ə under **Prosodies**
F   fricative system, 12
K   continuant system, 29
L   liquid system, 66
N   nasal system, 12; see also N under **Acoustic**
P   stop/plosive system, 12; see also P under **General**
S   sibilant system, 12
P̂L   stop system with liquid release, 56
P̂S   stop system with sibilant release, 56
F̂L   fricative system with liquid release, 111
F̂S   fricative system with sibilant release, 111

Abbreviations, notations, and typographical conventions   xi

$\widehat{SP}$ checked sibilant system, 56

α   low V grade, 18
ε   middle V grade, 18
ι   high V grade, 11
     (see also y, w, ə under **Prosodies**)

A   relatively more open V grade, 65
I   relatively more close V grade, 65

Prosodies

The smaller superscript form as used in formulae is given in brackets.

y (y) exponents: frontness, non-rounding, 11
w (w) exponents: backness, generally accompanied by lip-rounding, 11
ə (ə) exponents: neutral as to exponents of y and w, 11
     The values of α, ε, ι (see also **Syllabic and non-syllabic systems**) depend on the position of y, w, ə in relation to α, ε, ι within the syllable, e.g., w preceding $\bar{\alpha}$, viz., $^w\bar{\alpha}$: the exponent is [ɑ:], 21; w following $\bar{\alpha}$, viz., $\bar{\alpha}^w$: the exponent is [au], 21.

     y, w, ə are also used to mark prosodic contrasts between syllables when V grades are not specified, e.g., $^yCV^wCV$, 124.
h (h) exponents: breathiness and absence of voice, 11
h̲ (h̲) non-h exponents: non-breathiness and possibility of voice, 11
r (r) exponents: lip-rounding or lip protrusion, 123
r̲ (r̲) non-r exponents: absence of lip-rounding and lip protrusion, 123
‾   long syllable length, e.g., $\overline{Cι^wC}$, 11; see also $C\bar{V}$, 20
˘   short syllable length, e.g., $C\breve{V}$, 18; see also $(C\breve{\iota}^w)^2$, 18

Terms of C systems

The smaller subscript form as used in formulae is given in brackets.

p (p) labial exponent: labial place of articulation, 12
t (t) apical exponent: alveolar place of articulation, 12
k (k) dorsal exponent: velar or palatal place of articulation, 12

Subscript numerals are used to mark the number of contrasting terms in C and V systems, e.g., P_3 = P system with a contrast of three terms, 12; V_2 = V system with a contrast of two terms, 20; see also C_1, C_2 under **General**.

Acoustic

F1   first formant, 23
F2   second formant, 23
F3   third formant, 23
Hz   Herz, 74
K   Kiloherz, e.g., 1K, 2K, 79
Int   intensity trace, 74
N   nasal trace, 76; see also N under **Syllabic and non-syllabic systems**
M   mouth trace, 76
Osc   oscillogram, 74

ACKNOWLEDGMENTS

It is a pleasure to acknowledge my debt to my colleagues in the Department of Phonetics and Linguistics at the School of Oriental and African Studies. Their contribution to the development of prosodic phonology in the form of publications, seminar papers, and discussions, helped me to work out my own particular brand of the theory. My biggest debt is to Eileen Whitley, formerly Reader in Phonetics, whose course on the prosodic analysis of English I had the privilege of attending, and with whom I had many valuable discussions in connection with my work on child phonology. Her influence on my understanding of the theory has been profound.

For permission to reproduce Papers 1-7, in some cases with major revisions, grateful acknowledgments are due to the following:

The Danish Association of Speech Therapists and *Nordisk Tidsskrift for Logopedi og Foniatri* (Papers 1 and 2);
Cambridge University Press and *Journal of Linguistics* (Paper 3);
Swets Publishing Service and Swets & Zeitlinger (Paper 4);
John Wiley & Sons Ltd. (Paper 5);
North-Holland Publishing Company (Paper 6);
Wattana Suksamai, Dean of the Faculty of Humanities, Chiangmai University (Paper 7).

My grateful thanks are also due to Grevatt & Grevatt, who undertook the task of publishing this book, with all the problems inherent in the production of the abstract formulations of prosodic phonology. I owe a particular debt to Siew-Yue Killingley, who encouraged me to put the book together and then did all the editorial and production work. The attractive format and general appearance of the book are due to her painstaking work.

The interpretation of prosodic phonology is my own view of the theory and I do not claim that it is necessarily shared by all members of the London school. The content is thus entirely my own responsibility.

London   N. W.
February 1986

INTRODUCTION

After a long period during which the emphasis in linguistics was on the development of syntactic theory, recent years have seen a considerable rise in interest in phonological theory. A growing awareness of the limitations of linear segmental phonologies, such as phonemic phonology and generative phonology, has resulted in attempts to develop phonologies of a non-linear kind in order to handle phenomena of a suprasegmental nature more satisfactorily and, hopefully, to shed more light on the processing of speech. This has reawakened an interest in prosodic phonology and it therefore seems appropriate at this time to try to give a more explicit account of the theory, and to make some of the latest developments more readily available, so as to provide an opportunity for its merits and demerits to be considered alongside those of other developing non-linear theories.

What is very much needed today, if full advantage is to be gained from the technological advances of our time, is a phonological theory which is viable in relation to other disciplines associated with speech, such as psychology, physiology, and neurology. With a theory of such a nature we can hope to get fuller insights into how speech is processed. For a theory to be maximally relevant for other disciplines, its units, though of an abstract nature, must be relatable to what is known about language and speech at the acoustic, auditory and articulatory levels as far as possible, and also to what is known of brain function for speech. Segmental phonology has failed in these respects: speech is continuous, with a great deal of overlapping from one articulation to another, with consequent acoustic overlapping; the segmentation into successions of consonants and vowels, therefore, does not accord with the articulatory and acoustic facts. For this reason it has not proved possible to find clear-cut acoustic correlates for phoneme segments. Phoneticians are now seeking new theoretical approaches where the unit of speech perception is no longer the phoneme segment, but a larger unit such as syllable, word, phrase, or sentence. A useful review of some such approaches is given in Bond (1981). Non-linear phonological theories seem much more promising. Prosodic phonology was the first non-linear theory and the more recent ones, viz., autosegmental phonology and metrical phonology (see Hulst and Smith 1983), appear to derive from prosodic phonology, which was multidimensional from the start. This is seen particularly clearly in Henderson (1949). The theory has its origins as far back as the 1930s when J. R. Firth reacted against the structuralist view that phonology and transcription were to be encompassed within a single theory. Firth felt that linguistic description should be separated from questions of transcription and broke away from the phoneme tradition in phonological description. As a result, the phoneme segment has no place in prosodic phonology and the theory is therefore free from the limitations of phoneme theory. In prosodic phonology the emphasis is on whole units: on whole syllables, words, pieces, and sentences; on syntagmatic as well as paradigmatic relations. This takes into account articulatory overlapping and its consequences. These factors, expressed in terms of prosodies and phonematic units, are more easily relatable to the acoustic, auditory, and articulatory facts than are phoneme segments. The descriptive units of prosodic phonology may therefore be claimed to have some physical reality, and hypotheses of speech processing based on this theory are thus more likely to find support in other disciplines, such as psychology and neurology. The social component of the theory, the context of situation (see Paper 1), ensures that the linguistic analysis takes the context of language use into account. This is important as context plays an important part in the interpretation of speech (see Papers 6 and 7).

Firth was very much of the opinion that the study of language acquisition would bring valuable insights to linguistic theory and he greatly regretted the dearth of such studies in his day. In 1935 he wrote: 'Our greatest difficulty at present is the absence of any really well-documented work on how we acquire our speech as we grow up' (Firth 1935: 27-8). He then refers to the study of child language as 'a vast field of research' in what he called the 'biographical study of speech' (Firth 1935: 29). Fifteen years later, writing about the value of the personal for linguistic studies, he again makes a plea for child language research:

> Individual linguistic biographies should also be attempted through the seven ages of man. There may be such biographical studies of language in existence, based on adequate documentation of the learning of speech and language by children and young persons—but I have not seen them. (Firth 1950: 188)

The papers reprinted in this volume were selected to show how a theory of speech processing has been developed through the application of prosodic theory to the study of the acquisition of phonology. This use of prosodic theory has been acknowledged to have certain advantages over other theories of phonological development, thus justifying Firth's expectations. In his review of theories of the acquisition of phonology, Mowrer writes: 'Many questions, unanswerable by other theories, find explanations using prosodic theory' (Mowrer 1980: 20; see also Ferguson and Garnica 1975). One may add that further development of the theory, from 1981 to 1986 (Papers 6, 7 and Summary), offers plausible explanations for certain aspects of speech processing in child and adult, and can account for problems such as normalization and the rapidity with which speech is processed.

The papers included in this volume span a period of fifteen years, from 1971 to 1986. The first paper outlines the background to prosodic theory and attempts to explain the main principles, concepts, and terms used. Paper 2 gives an illustration of the application of prosodic phonology to a child's first words, showing an analysis into structures and systems as well as a comparison of phonological development at different stages. The other papers illustrate different aspects of the development of a theory of speech processing through the study of child phonology. Paper 3 is probably the best known of all the papers and is the first account of the learning of phonology by pattern recognition. It is the whole-unit or holistic approach of prosodic phonology which brought to light the patterned relationships between a child's hardly recognizable words and the adult models and thus made it possible to explain the somewhat bizarre forms of early words, as well as why sounds that children are capable of producing are not used in all the contexts in which they occur in adult forms. Paper 4 considers the relation between perception and production in language acquisition and proposes, on the evidence of longitudinal development, that many changes in the child's forms of words are related to increasing perceptual discrimination, attention first being given mainly to auditorily salient parts of adult words and then gradually to the less salient, until the child's forms eventually match the adult forms. Acoustic evidence in the form of mingograms and spectrograms is provided to illustrate greater and lesser salience in the adult forms.

The subject of Paper 5 is the relation of phonological development to other areas of language development: to syntactic development, vocabulary growth and to amount of language use. The description of a child's forms acquired over a period of time, taking into account the syntagmatic relationship of the structures of syllables comprising word structures and word structures comprising sentences, makes it possible to show how the level of language complexity gradually increases. The same sort of processes are shown to be at work in the development of one-syllable, two-syllable, and multi-syllable words as in one-word, two-word, and multi-word sentences. It is also shown that progress does not take place at the same time and pace at all the levels of language considered. When there is progress at one level, other levels may stand still. These insights are possible because of the holistic approach of prosodic phonology in that whole units are considered—syllables in relation to words, words in relation to the sentence or piece. This is one of the major advantages of prosodic phonology.

Paper 6 is an attempt to work out a form of internal representation of the phonological system in terms of the type of patterns used to describe a child's phonology. The internal representation consists of two levels, a phonetic level and a phonological level. The levels are shown to be constructed by the child over a period of time, beginning with the early spontaneous vocalizations and gradually developing into a complex network via babbling, the protolanguage and first words. Changes in a child's form of a word are related to restructuring at the levels of representation. The importance of context in aiding the recognition of patterns is emphasized. The patterns are shown to be invariant and thus offer an explanation for normalization in speech.

In Paper 7 the theory of speech processing by pattern recognition is developed more fully and is illustrated in relation to both child and adult speech. More detailed discussion of the concept of invariant auditory pattern is presented and a proposal is made as to how it may function in the interpretation of continuous speech.

Finally, in the Summary at the end of the book, the theories of the acquisition of phonology and speech processing are summarized, and supporting evidence from other disciplines is brought together.

These papers are not merely reprints of the original publications. Papers 1 and 2 have been completely revised. Papers 4 and 6 have been given some revision, while Papers 3, 5, and 7 have been changed only in minor ways. The Summary is completely new.

PROSODIC PHONOLOGY: AN INTRODUCTION TO THE THEORY

First published in *Nordisk Tidsskrift for Logopedi og Foniatri*. (July 1981). 26-35. A paper presented at the Annual Conference of the Danish Speech and Hearing Therapists at Fünen, Denmark in 1980.

Background

Prosodic phonology is the phonological component of a theory of linguistic description that John Rupert Firth was developing between the 1930s and 1950s.

Firth was the first professor of linguistics in Great Britain. He held the Chair in the University of London from 1944 until his retirement in 1957. Firth had a forceful personality; he was a creative thinker, and he had a great enthusiasm for his subject. His influence on the way linguistics developed in this country was tremendous and it is due to him that the study of linguistics owes its well-established position in British universities today.

Firth had strong ideas about what the field of linguistics should encompass. At the time he was working on his theory, structuralism was dominant in linguistics, and for the structuralist, semantics and phonetics were peripheral to the study of linguistics. Furthermore, the general thinking was that each level of linguistic description should be autonomous, that phonological description should not make use of grammatical information and vice versa. In Firth's new theory semantics was to have the central role, and the description of phonetics, phonology, syntax and semantics was to be closely integrated: any congruence between the levels was to be stated and full use was to be made of information gained at one level to establish categories at another.

During this period considerable progress was being made in research in acoustic and articulatory phonetics, and this revealed much overlapping of acoustic features and articulatory processes in speech. Phoneme theory, being essentially transcription orientated, required that speech should be segmented into successions of consonants and vowels, and this was seen not to accord with the facts. There was therefore a general recognition of the inadequacy of phoneme theory. American linguists tried to overcome the problem by introducing concepts such as juncture phonemes and long components, but Firth preferred a radical change. The British tradition in phonetics had always been strong and Firth was himself a skilled phonetician. He was very aware of the importance of phonetics and felt there should be a clear separation between the needs of transcription and phonological theory. What he saw as necessary for phonological description was an emphasis on whole units instead of segmentation: analysis of words, pieces (i.e. groups of words), and sentences as *wholes*. Firth also laid great stress on the syllable as an element of structure of the word:

> The phonological analysis of the word must take into account the syllabic structure, and that involves the recognition of the constituents of the syllable itself. These constituents are sonants [i.e. syllabics] and consonants, and may be termed phonematic constituents of the syllable and of the word also.
> (Firth 1948: 146)

To handle the overlapping features that extend beyond the segment or have relevance to syllables, words, pieces, and sentences, he introduced the concept of prosodies:

> Syllables as constituents of words can be said to have *features* such as stress, quantity, nasalization, aspiration, tone, and a number of other attributes. These may be termed 'prosodic features' or simply prosodies.   (Firth 1948: 146)

One of the functions of prosodic phonology was thus to provide the means for handling overlapping features. The analysis into prosodies and phonematic units is both analytic and synthetic. It shows how the unit under analysis is segmented, and through the statement of prosodies, it also shows how it is held together or synthesized. One may note that Henderson's paper, 'Prosodies in Siamese' (Henderson 1949), which is one of the earliest and neatest applications of prosodic theory to a language, has the sub-title 'A study in synthesis'.

Another aspect in which Firth differed fundamentally from the structuralist linguists of his time was that he saw linguistics not just as the abstract study of speech and language but as involving man in his social environment; linguistics was to be concerned with the use of language in communication within the social context: the communicative aspects of language were all-important.

Language in society

In a paper in which Firth welcomes the development of linguistics as a new science (i.e. as descriptive linguistics, separate from comparative and historical philology), he sounds a note of warning:

> Though we are prepared for the development of linguistics as a group of sciences, we are anxious not to lose sight of man. We wish to avoid the kind of linguistics which appears to leave out as much of man and personality as possible.
> (Firth 1948: 141)

Firth thus had a strong sociolinguistic element in his linguistics before sociolinguistics had come into being. He kept emphasizing the importance of man and society: 'My intention is to link language studies with social human nature, to think of persons rather than individuals...', and in the same paper: 'Linguistics...is mainly interested in persons and personalities as active participants in the creation and maintenance of cultural values, among which languages are its main concern' (Firth 1950: 186).

Firth's foresight may also be seen in his interest in language acquisition. At the time when child language was not recognized as a relevant field of study for linguistics, he was propagating the idea that such studies would bring useful insights to linguistic theory (Firth 1935: 27-9; 1950: 188).

Meaning through contextualization

As stated earlier, for Firth, meaning was the core of linguistic theory. He used the term 'meaning' in a rather wide sense. When he first sets out the basic principles of his linguistic theory (Firth 1935), he equates meaning with function:

> I propose to split up meaning or function into a series of component functions. Each function will be defined as the use of some language form or element in

relation to some context. Meaning, that is to say, is to be regarded as a complex of contextual relations, and phonetics, grammar, lexicography, and semantics each handles its own components of the complex in its appropriate context.

(Firth 1935: 19)

Firth sums up his proposals at the end of the paper as follows:

By this time we are accustomed to the subdivision of meaning or function. Meaning, then, we use for the whole complex of functions which a linguistic form may have. The principal components of this whole meaning are phonetic function,—which I call a 'minor' function—the major functions—lexical, morphological, and syntactical (to be the province of a reformed system of grammar), and a function of a complete locution in the context of situation, or typical context of situation, the province of semantics. (1935: 30)

Meaning at the different levels of analysis was to be arrived at through the study of the linguistic elements in context: contextualization was a key concept. This is also seen in Firth's development of the concept of collocation, i.e., that part of the meaning of a word is its characteristic use with certain other words or phrases (Firth 1951).

In order to relate language to the social environment, Firth developed the construct of 'context of situation'. He described it as 'a convenient abstraction at the social level of analysis' and as forming 'the basis of the hierarchy of techniques for the statement of meanings' (Firth 1950: 183). Briefly the context of situation brings into relation three categories (Firth 1950: 182):

1) the participants and their verbal and non-verbal actions
2) the relevant objects
3) the effect of the verbal actions.

Contexts of situation are grouped and classified on the basis of the recurrent behaviour of members of a society in their different roles and thus represent a system of what is typical. As much of the exemplification of the theory in this book will be made in relation to child language, examples of some contexts of situation that would be relevant to a study of child language development will be used for illustration. These would be the repetitive routines in which the majority of children are involved with their mother or other caretaker every day—such as greeting on the child's awaking, picking up, feeding, nappy changing, bathing, playtime, bedtime. In such contexts of situation, the participants may be further specified as mother, father, grandmother, friend, stranger. The child may be specified as infant, toddler, male, female. Such specification is necessary because the sort of interaction that takes place, both verbal and non-verbal, will differ, depending on who the participants are; for instance, interaction between mother and baby will be very different from that between stranger and baby. Relevant objects will be things like food, toys, books, items of clothing, items of furniture (high chair, cot, bath, pram). In the early stages of language learning most communication has reference to what is present and what is going on, i.e., to the 'here and now', and the objects and activities involved in a child's daily life are clearly relevant. The effect of the verbal action is to produce some response—or no response; for instance, a young child may reply, or imitate what was said or ignore the attempts at communication. Such a framework as the context of situation is very useful for identifying what the child is trying to communicate, particularly at the one-word utterance stage and when the child's first words are not easily recognizable by their phonetic form.

In making use of the construct of context of situation in linguistic analysis, the first abstraction is to isolate a text, e.g., from the verbal process, in the context of situation; the analysis then proceeds in a way that Firth likened to the dispersion of light of mixed wave-lengths into a spectrum:

> The technique of syntax is concerned with the word process in the sentence. The technique of phonology states the phonematic and prosodic processes within the word and sentence. The phonetician links all this with the processes and features of utterance. The sentence must also have its relations with the processes of the context of situation. (Firth 1950: 183)

Firth was not committed to a 'top-down' or 'bottom-up' strategy but allowed both:

> To make statements of meaning in terms of linguistics, we may accept the language event as a whole and then deal with it at various levels, sometimes in ascending order, beginning with social context and proceeding through syntax and vocabulary to phonology, even phonetics, and at other times in the opposite order,...
> (Firth 1951: 192)

Prosodic phonology should thus be viewed as one of the levels of analysis in a theory of integrated linguistic description that Firth was developing: the statement of meaning at the phonological level. Phonological analysis is linked to phonetics in the relationship of exponence, i.e., phonetic realizations of phonological units, and to grammar, in that separate phonological descriptions are made for different grammatical classes, e.g., for nouns and for verbs, and in that phonological units are used to help establish grammatical categories. Examples of this may be seen in Bendor-Samuel (1960) and Palmer (1955).

As far as linguistic universals are concerned, Firth stated explicitly that he was not aiming at universals in his theory:

> Such linguistic theory as may appear in the papers is not intended as an attempt to establish universals for general linguistic description, but rather as an approach to general linguistic theory to be applied to the particular description of specific language material... (Firth 1957: xii)

Nevertheless, his theory may be viewed as universalist in a weak form.[1] The theory implies the belief that the phonology of every language can be described at the most general level in terms of (1) a finite set of structures composed of sequences of C and V units, (2) systems at C and V places in the structures, viz., phonematic units, and (3) units which have relevance to the whole or part of the structures, viz., prosodies. The language-specific aspects are the particular set of structures and the particular prosodies and phonematic units functional in the language.

Prosodic phonology has been developed by Firth's colleagues in London; his semantic theory was worked out to a degree, but unfortunately he died before he was able to develop his ideas on syntactic analysis. Halliday's systemic grammar is considered by some to be the nearest to

---

1 I am grateful to my colleague R. J. Hayward for drawing my attention to this.

Firth's approach (Halliday 1973; Berry 1975). Looking back to the early days of descriptive linguistics, Firth's views emerge as being far ahead of his time. Much of what he was proposing about thirty years ago, which was against the prevailing trends of his time, is now generally accepted: the importance of semantics in linguistic theory; the need for the syllable in phonological description; the advantages of a non-linear phonological theory; the requirement of the statement of the relationship between phonology and grammar; the social communicative function of language, and the relevance of the study of first language acquisition for linguistic theory. To this one may add his interest in discourse analysis and stylistics. Firth's contribution to the field of descriptive linguistics deserves wide recognition and it seems that it is beginning to get its due, e.g., Robins (1983), Robins and Fromkin (1985).

Prosodic phonology

Before proceeding to more detailed discussion of prosodic phonology, consideration will be given to the key concepts and terms used in prosodic analysis; they are as follows:
1) restricted language and renewal of connection
2) multistructural
3) the piece
4) polysystemic
5) prosodies and phonematic units: system and structure
6) partial analysis.

1) Restricted language and renewal of connection

The notion of *restricted language* means that the field of study is to be defined, and the description is then made within the limits stated. The many social roles a person has to play in his society claimed Firth's attention and the concept of restricted language made it possible to give descriptions of these roles as separate languages, the roles being related to different contexts of situation.

The description of the phonological system of one style of speech of one speaker is considered to be a viable representation of the usage within the language community because the social function of speech is recognized. The speech of one speaker must be reasonably representative of the speech of the community or he would not be able to communicate. The validity of the description made can be tested by 'renewal of connection', i.e., by comparing the system set up for the one speaker with those of other speakers belonging to the same community. It brings to the fore what is common to the community and what is idiosyncratic to the one speaker. This may be illustrated in relation to a study of a child's phonological development. The child, in becoming a member of a particular linguistic community, passes through a learning process that every native speaker goes through, allowing of course for a measure of individual difference. The particular English child's language development that I studied has much in common with that of other English children, as those who have worked in this field will immediately recognize. For example, the start with single word utterances and gradual increase to longer utterances of two, three, and more words; the omission of function words (e.g. 'in', 'on', 'is') and of inflections (e.g., plural endings, 3rd person singular endings, possessive -s); the large number of reduplicated word patterns like [mama], [dada], [bæbæ], [tɪtɪ]; the consonant harmony of CVC monosyllables like [bʌp] for 'cup' and [gʌk] for 'duck'; the absence of consonant clusters as in [dɔp] for 'stop' and [nəu] for 'snow'; the early acquisition of a well-differentiated vowel system and of nasals [m, n] and plosives [p, b, t, d, k, g] as the first consonants to be used systematically. This particular child's early language development is thus typical in many ways, and it is therefore possible to make generalizations on the basis of the findings while making allowance for individual variation. Such generalizations as are made then need to be tested by 'renewal of connection' with data of other English children, with the expectation that there will be much in common.

The concept of *restricted language* in my studies is used to describe the child's phonological development as a series of phonological systems related to stages. Each stage has a restricted language which is viewed as a total system, and which differs from the systems of the preceding and following stages, although there are, of course, degrees of overlap. (See Papers 2 and 3.)

2) **Multistructural**

Multistructural in prosodic phonology refers to the convention that linguistic units of like structure are handled together, and those of unlike structure are handled separately; for instance, words of one syllable are dealt with together, and apart from words of two and three syllables. Further subdivisions of one-syllable words are then made; for example, into those with open endings, e.g., CV and V, and those with closed endings, e.g., VC and CVC, and so on. This is because the system of contrasts functioning within the different types of structure often differs. Words of the same grammatical class are similarly handled together and separately from words of different classes, e.g., separate phonological systems are set up for nouns and for verbs. This makes it possible to account for phonological differences of different word classes: for instance, where nouns have inflections which differ in form from those of verbs, the type of junction between stem and inflection may be different.

In my study of the acquisition of the phonological system of English, there are striking differences in structure and in usage of words with one, two, three, and more syllables in the course of language acquisition, and an analysis that did not take this into account would fail to give an adequate description of the course of the child's language development. (For examples see Paper 5.)

The multistructural approach also makes it possible to show the different degrees of complexity of the phonological systems at the various stages. For instance, one-syllable words attain a higher degree of differentiation earlier than two-syllable words. Two-syllable words had only open syllables, e.g., CV and V at the time when one-syllable words had both open and closed syllables, e.g., V, CV, CVC, and VC. Three-syllable words were rare in the early stages, but as they began to be used, their structure was seen to be similar to a combination of a one-syllable word and a two-syllable word, e.g., CV + CVCV. Later, three-word utterances are similarly shown to consist of a combination of a familiar one-word utterance with a familiar two-word utterance, e.g., the frequently used utterance 'gone' with the also often used 'Mama glove' (Mama's glove), giving 'Mama glove gone' (Mama's glove's gone).

3) The piece

Piece is used when it is not required to define a structure grammatically; it is thus a generalized term which relates to the whole or part of a syllable, word, phrase or sentence. The phonological characteristics of a piece are described in the same way as those of other phonological units, e.g., the syllable and word. In my child language studies, I need to make phonological analyses of utterances of one and more words long, and to consider words in the context of the utterance in which they occur. For this the concept and term *piece* is used. This concept provides a framework within which to study the phonological structure of utterances of more than one word, and makes it possible to show that early on, the larger pieces are made up of smaller pieces which are already established as independent units in the language system. The use of the concept of piece also provides an additional means by which one can show the increase in complexity of the phonological system at different stages, for instance, by taking into account the number of words in the piece and considering how far the piece is composed of familiar, well-established words, and how far it consists of newly-acquired words. In the earliest stages, the piece is composed mostly of familiar, well-established words; in later stages it is a combination of established and new; and in the last stage the piece has the possibility of consisting of new words only (Paper 5).

4) Polysystemic

Polysystemic is another essential term. Prosodic theory is polysystemic in three senses: firstly, in that emphasis is given to differences between systems at different places in structure. For instance, in a PVP structure, the P (plosive) system at word initial is recognized as differing from the P (plosive) system at word final. A recognition of the differences in the form of the plosion in different contexts at the level of phonetic exponence is implicit, e.g., voiceless plosives in English, [p, t, k], are quite strongly aspirated in an initial stressed syllable but there is little or no aspiration when the plosives are in final position, and they are relatively weakly articulated. In my child phonology studies differences of this kind at the acoustic and auditory levels are shown to account for some of the differences between the child's forms and the adult's. For example, the child produced two-syllable words with a plosive at the onset of each syllable where the adult had plosives, such plosives being auditorily salient, e.g., [be:be:] for [bɪskɪt] 'biscuit', but the child did not produce the final plosives which are less salient in two-syllable words, e.g., he did not produce the final [t] of 'biscuit'. Prosodic theory provides a suitable framework within which to describe such relationships.

From what has already been said under the heading of *multistructural*, it follows that prosodic phonology is also polysystemic in a second sense: in that different phonological systems may be set up for different grammatical classes. For instance, it is necessary to treat function words in English (e.g., pronouns, prepositions, auxiliaries, conjunctions) as having different phonological structures from content words (e.g., nouns, adjectives, adverbs, verbs). Function words have prosodic function and a ə unit as opposed to the obligatory V unit and the non-obligatory ə unit of content words. Different structures also need to be set up for suffixes, as opposed to stems. Stems have V as an obligatory element but suffixes can have the possibility of C alone as a structure, for example, the regular past tense suffix in English. This may be represented by T with h, h̲ and ə prosodic links with the stem—e.g., h with h-final stems: [wɔːk] 'walk', [wɔːkt] 'walked'; h̲ with h̲-final stems: [wɔːm] 'warm', [wɔːmd] 'warmed'; and ə with P_t-final stems whether they are h or h̲: [weɪt] 'wait', [weɪtɪd] 'waited', [weɪd] 'wade', [weɪdɪd] 'waded', respectively.

The third sense in which *polysystemic* is used is that different strata in a language, such as native words, loan words and onomatopoeic words are described as constituting different phonological systems within the one language. A good example of this is Henderson (1951). The analysis of my child language data revealed that many of the first attempts at new articulations and more complex word forms were made in direct repetitions after adults, in onomatopoeic words, and in what may be termed language games, that is to say, in interaction with the parents in the recitation of stories, nursery rhymes, counting, and the alphabet. Such repetitions or direct imitations are relatively complex in form in comparison with the child's everyday language use, e.g., the child's [ʔevm̩] 'heaven' at the time when he had only simple structures with no consonant clusters. The polysystemic approach allows for the separate treatment of these two different types of language use, where the phonology of the everyday language may be classed as the major system, and the different phonology of the more restricted language of language games may be classed as a peripheral system—peripheral in that it is not yet part of the more widely used everyday system.

5) Prosodies and phonematic units: system and structure

The elements of structure of prosodic phonology, prosodies and phonematic units, will be considered together with the terms *system* and *structure*. A distinction is made between syntagmatic and paradigmatic contrasts and functions. The syntagmatic contrasts are carried by features that extend over stretches of speech larger than the consonant or vowel segment, for instance, lip-rounding and backness in the English word 'boot' [buːt]. Lip-rounding and backness start with the bilabial closure for [b] and continue throughout the vowel.[2] When such features have contrastive function (the rounding and backness in 'boot' contrast with the lip-spreading and frontness in 'beat' [biːt]) they are allotted to prosodies so that the structures of 'boot' and 'beat' are symbolized as CV^wC and CV^yC respectively. Prosodies are elements which are capable of extension over sequences of phonematic units and which have relevance to syllables, words and larger units such as the piece and the sentence. They are 'unplaced'. Phonematic units occupy places in structure in sequence and are thus 'placed'.

The distinction between syntagmatic and paradigmatic relations involves the use of the terms *structure* and *system*. Syntagmatic relates to structural aspects of phonological patterns, and *paradigmatic* relates to systems. These latter are set up at different places in structure. Structure is stated in terms of C and V units, and also ə where required. C, V and ə are mutually exclusive and are arranged in a sequential relation. V is an obligatory element in stressed and accented syllables; V or ə is obligatory in unaccented and unstressed syllables. A syllable

---

[2] 'Backness' is represented by the raising of the back of the tongue towards the velum (soft palate) in the position for the vowel [uː].

cannot consist of a C element alone. At the most general level then, syllable and word structures are stated in terms of C, V and ə. Examples of some syllable structures are: CV, CVC, VCC, Cə. The statement of word structures may consist of single syllables, e.g., CV, CVC, CCV, VCC, or it may consist of two, three, or more syllables which are composed of sequences of syllables of various kinds, for instance: CVCV, CəCVC, CVCə, CCVCV, CVCCVCV, CVCVCVCVC. It follows that sentence structures may consist of sequences of words of various structures. Accent placement is included in the statement of structure as opposed to system. Such statements relate to units larger than a segment—e.g., to a syllable, word, or piece, and are thus prosodic statements defining the structure of the syllable, word, or piece. Prosodies may relate to contrasts at the initials (i.e., onsets) and finals (i.e., endings) of structures such as words and syllables, e.g., open and closed onset and ending of syllables: open onset, VC, in contrast with closed onset, CV; open ending, CV, in contrast with closed ending, VC. Features extending over the whole or part of a structure, such as palatalization, velarization, aspiration and nasalization have all been treated as prosodies where they have been found to have contrastive function. Thus syntagmatic relations within structures which have contrastive or demarcative function are treated prosodically. Because of the recognition of the interrelationship of phonology and grammar, features with morphophonological value may also be treated as prosodies, e.g., n, y, and zero word prosodies as markers of first, second and third person in Terena (Bendor-Samuel 1960).

Phonematic units represent systems, the paradigmatic relations that are functional in structures. Systems are set up to give values to C and V elements at different places in structure. Several contrasting systems may be set up at C places. These often have manner of articulation as phonetic exponents—for instance, at one C place in structure, e.g., C_1 in C_1VC_2, there may be, say, four systems: P, N, F, and S systems. Within each system, a further contrast of terms must be described. These frequently have place of articulation as phonetic exponents. For example, in the initial P system of English, three terms need to be specified to account for the bilabial, alveolar and velar contrast. Three examples will serve for purposes of illustration: [pæd] 'pad', [kæd] 'cad', [dæd] 'Dad'. The structure is CVC; the systems at C are P, i.e., PVP. The initial P system has a three-term contrast, P_3, 3=p, t, k or $P_{p/t/k}$. Final P has one term only, P_t. The contrast of breathy onset of 'cad' and 'pad' and the non-breathy onset of 'Dad' needs to be treated prosodically as this is a functional contrast in English: ^{h}PVP 'pad' and 'cad' and $\underline{h}$PVP 'Dad'.

At V places, systems have to be set up to account for contrasts carried by tongue height, i.e., open, middle, and close, to account for differences such as are found in, for instance, [pæn] 'pan', [pen] 'pen' and [pɪn] 'pin'. The analysis of vowels is dealt with in Paper 2 but meanwhile it should be noted that the systems at C and V places and their terms constitute the phonematic units.

An important tenet of prosodic theory is that the systems set up at various places in structure are not equated. For instance, in a CVC structure, some of the systems set up for initial and final Cs may appear to be the same—they are represented by the same symbols. A hypothetical example will suffice here for the sake of simplicity (but see Henderson

1949 for actual language examples): in a CVC structure there is a contrast of four systems at initial C, viz., P, N, F, and S, but only three at final C, viz., P, N, and S. In such a case, P, N, and S systems are considered to have different values in the two places in structure. In the initial place, they are part of a commutation set of four whereas in final place they belong to a set of three. Initial and final systems are thus not identified, that is to say, the initial P system is not equated with the final P system. It will be seen that the question of neutralization does not arise. The fact that P initial is considered to be different from P final shows a recognition of a difference at the level of phonetic exponence. However, the fact that differences are recognized does not mean that no importance is attached to the phonetic similarity between the exponents. It is, of course, sometimes necessary to recognize that there is some sameness. There is a closer relationship between the systems at onset and ending of a PVP structure than between those at the onset and ending of a PVF structure, and PVP is relatively less complex than PVF because at the level of phonetic exponence there is a similarity in manner of articulation at the onset and ending which is absent in a PVF structure. For example, in child language, at a certain stage of development, there are words like [gʌk] 'duck', [bʌp] 'cup', and [beɪm] 'plane', in which the initial and final consonants harmonize: they have same manner and place of articulation or same place of articulation. The number of articulatory contrasts within such words is very limited compared with those found in their adult counterparts. Such harmonized forms are easier to produce than, say, PVF words like 'beef' [biːf] and 'tooth' [tuːθ], where there is a difference of manner and place of articulation at onset and ending.

Syntagmatic contrasts of the kind described above, viz., contrasts of systems as well as contrasts of terms within a structure, proved to be an important dimension in the description of a child's developing phonological system, and this relationship needs to be taken into account in order to demonstrate some of the aspects of the growth of complexity in the child's phonology as time goes on. In my study, the child's early word and piece structures contained a relatively small number of syntagmatic contrasts and the number of such contrasts increased gradually. For instance, in the early stages, the number of syntagmatic contrasts within two-syllable words was minimal, with only P systems or N systems within the structure, e.g., PVPV and NVNV.[3] Later a contrast of P and N systems within a structure became possible, e.g., PVPVN. This dimension can be handled by prosodic theory, and such contrasts, having relevance to the whole structure, are classed as prosodic. Paper 5 gives a full account of the growth of complexity of a child's phonological system using this theoretical approach.

6) Partial analysis

Prosodic theory has the advantage of allowing partial analyses to be made so that only the particular focus of interest needs to be handled at any one time. For example, at some point in the description, only prosodic contrasts may be dealt with, as when different types of syllable structure are considered; at another point, C systems may be the main

---

[3] There was an exception: the form [biːnə] 'Bina' which has the structure PVNV. It was the name of the girl who helped to look after the child.

concern, as when examining the paradigmatic contrasts of C systems in a CVC structure. This has proved useful in the study of child language development, where it is necessary to draw attention to particular aspects of the developing phonological system. For example, V systems usually develop ahead of C systems in the case of English children, so that in the early stages more attention needs to be focused on the former, and in the later stages it is the C systems which need to be dealt with in more detail.

Through the use of prosodic theory, with its emphasis on the syntagmatic, synthetic aspects of language, it is possible to focus on different relationships within structures in the child's phonological system at different stages of development and to show different kinds of relationship between the child's and adults' forms and structures than have been shown before, and thus to offer solutions to some problems of language acquisition for which no explanation had previously been found (Ferguson and Garnica 1975: 172-4; Mowrer 1980: 22).

An outline has now been given of the background to the development of prosodic phonology and the concepts and terms used. From the account given, it will be seen that prosodic theory is not process orientated—there are no underlying forms and no derivational processes; the formulations are related directly to their phonetic exponents. Furthermore, the phonological structures stated for a language represent all and only the possible structures of that language and exclude structures that do not occur. Only a few isolated examples have been given in illustration so far. Fuller exemplification is provided in Paper 2 in the form of an analysis of a child's phonological systems at two different stages of development.

Useful accounts of prosodic phonology to supplement the one given here may be found in Palmer 1970 (Introduction) and in Robins (1957); also Lass (1984). Palmer (1970) contains a bibliography of publications of Firth and his colleagues from the 1940s to the 1960s (pp. 253-6).

In the papers that follow, it will be seen how the use of prosodic theory for the study of child phonology has led to a theory of speech processing which offers a plausible explanation for the normalization of variables in speech and the rapidity with which speech is processed.

2
PROSODIC PHONOLOGY: ILLUSTRATION OF ANALYSIS

Original title: 'Prosodic phonology: further illustration'. Paper presented at the Annual Conference of the Danish Speech and Hearing Therapists at Fünen, Denmark in 1980. Not previously published, to the author's knowledge.

Two aspects of a child's acquisition of the phonological system of English will be used to illustrate analysis in terms of prosodic phonology:
1) the progress of a reduplicated two-syllable word to a match with the adult form, and
2) a comparison of the child's vowel systems at different stages of language acquisition.

The child's reduplicated word and its changing forms will first be described in relation to the adult form in phonetic terms. This description will form the basis for the phonological description where the changes will be expressed in terms of prosodic phonology. The example to be considered is [pupu], the child's word for *pudding*. Other words progressed in a similar way but this one was selected, as several interesting records were available for it.

The first step is to examine the child's [pupu] and see what has to be achieved in order to match the adult form [pudɪŋ]. The place of the accent was correct from the start, i.e., on the first syllable, so accent will not be considered further. The child's first syllable, [pu], is already a close match, so no changes are needed there. The onset has complete closure at the bilabial place, and the back of the tongue is raised fairly high towards the soft palate; this tongue position is maintained after the release of the labial closure, and there is lip-rounding throughout the syllable. The second syllable, [pu], has certain features in common with the adult's second syllable [dɪŋ]. [p] and [d] are both plosives but the place of closure differs: the child's is bilabial, but the adult's is alveolar. [u] of [pu] is a half-close vowel as also is [ɪ] of [dɪŋ] but the vowel in [pu] is in a lip-rounded syllable with backness, as opposed to the one in [dɪŋ] which is in a syllable with spread lips and frontness.[1] The child's syllable is open (i.e., it ends in a vowel) and has no final nasal consonant; the adult's is closed (i.e., it ends on a consonant) and ends in a velar nasal. The child thus needs to unround and front his second syllable, to change the place of closure from bilabial to alveolar, and to add a final nasal with velar closure. These changes take place over a time span of about two months (see overleaf).

The child started off with [pupu]. In the first attempt to match the model more closely, he adds a final (palatal) nasal, and begins to unround

---

[1] In the child's reduplicated patterns, the vowels of both syllables regularly matched the vowels of the adult models in degrees of openness (i.e., close, mid, open) and the child only had reduplicated plosive patterns where the adult models had a plosive at the onset of both syllables (see Waterson 1970 and Paper 3 for examples). There was only one exception to this—the word 'busy' [bɪzɪ] for which the child had [bɪbɪ].

Age	Child's forms
1;6	[pupu]
1;7	[bubaɪɲ/bubuɪɲ]
1;7	[pupəɲ/bupəɲ]
1;8	[budun]
1;8	[pudun]
1;8	[pudɪŋ]

the second syllable. In doing so, he uses a more open, long vowel, [aɪ], in one of the forms. He also uses voiced, lax plosives although he previously used voiceless, tense plosives. Voiced sounds at the beginning of words and syllables were the regular early usage of the child, and he appears to find this more familiar production easier when he attempts something new, as it reduces the number of contrasts to be made (viz., the contrast between tense, voiceless articulations and lax, voiced ones) and this makes it possible for him to concentrate his efforts on what needs his extra care and attention.

In the next two forms, [pupəɲ] and [bupəɲ], he appears to have mastered the production of the contrast of a rounded syllable followed by an unrounded one, and has gone back to using the tense, voiceless onset which he apparently recognized as the correct onset from the start. In the [bupəɲ] form, he makes a contrast of a voiced onset in the first syllable followed by a voiceless one in the second. This is the opposite of what he needs to do to match the model, but he is managing to make a contrast of this type of onset within a two-syllable word.

The next step is a change in place of articulation—from bilabial place at the onset of both syllables to bilabial at the onset of the first and alveolar at the onset of the second. He again uses voiced, lax onsets, and in addition, uses backness and rounding in both syllables, as in his first form [pupu]. Again the use of the familiar is used to reduce the number of contrasts to be made while something new is being attempted. In [budun], the child now has a bilabial-alveolar contrast, and the closure for the final nasal is now made at the alveolar place, the same place of articulation as for [d] at the onset of the syllable, so there are still only two place-of-articulation contrasts within the word. The next form, [pudun], has the new place contrasts: bilabial-alveolar-alveolar, within the familiar features of backness and rounding, but now he is using his earlier acquired ability to make a contrast of voiced and voiceless syllable onsets within a word, this time in the correct sequence. Finally he produces [pudɪŋ], a close match to the adult form. Now he uses all the contrasts that he has learnt: rounding versus non-rounding (or lip-spreading), voiceless versus voiced syllable onsets, bilabial versus alveolar place contrast, and now an additional contrast of velar place of articulation in final position. He is thus making all the articulatory contrasts required to match the adult model.

It is important to note that the skill to make contrasts was acquired gradually and that what was learnt was not put to use all at once but was eventually combined. This shows, along with many other examples in child language, that in the early stages of learning, the number of operations a child can carry out at a time is very limited. Prosodic phonology can handle the acquisition of such contrasts in terms of prosodies and phonematic units.

This development from a simple reduplicated pattern to a match with the adult model will now be represented in terms of the theory. Partial analysis enables us to deal with different aspects of progress separately instead of trying to describe them at the same time, and this makes the analysis more manageable. The C systems will be considered first. C systems are considered in relation to the type of syllable in which they function, viz., h prosodic and h̲ prosodic syllables; this is because type of syllable onset is very relevant to the description of the systems.

As noted above, the child's form is [pupu] and he has to achieve [pudɪŋ]. The structure is a reduplicated monosyllable, an open CV syllable: (CV)[2]. The syllable is h prosodic: ^{h}CV (tense, voiceless, breathy onset) and w prosodic: ^{w}CV (back, rounded); the latter will be considered with the V systems. The system at C is P (plosive), i.e. PV. The P system has one term, p (labial), P_pV.[2] The phonological representation of [pupu] is thus (^hP_pV)[2]. There are no syntagmatic contrasts between the two syllables.

The phonological representation of [pudɪŋ] shows a number of syntagmatic contrasts within the structure. Syllable structure is CVCVC, a contrast of open syllable, CV, with a closed syllable, CVC. The first syllable is h prosodic, the second h̲ prosodic (lax, non-breathy onset): ^{h}CV$^h̲$CVC, a contrast of h and h̲ prosodic syllables. There is also a contrast of w prosody of the first syllable and y prosody of the second; this will be considered with the V systems. The systems at the onsets of the first and second syllables are P, and at the ending of the second syllable is N: PVPVN, a contrast of P and N systems. The terms of the P systems are p and t, and of the N system, k: P_pVP_tVN_k, a contrast of three terms. There are thus five different types of syntagmatic contrast in the adult structure. The child's structure therefore needs to undergo changes if it is to match that of the adult. The changes that take place are illustrated below.

The first changes bring the child's structure closer to the adult structure. The forms [bubaɪɲ] and [bubuɪɲ] have the structure CVCVC, as in adult [pudɪŋ], but both syllables are h̲ prosodic: $^h̲$CV$^h̲$CVC. This is in accord with the vast majority of the child's structures with P onsets at this time. The C systems are now PVPVN; contrasts of P and N systems are as in the adult structure, but the terms are different: there is a syntagmatic contrast of terms, p and k: P_pVP_pVN_k. It should be noted that the exponents of the dorsal term k differ—the adult's is velar, while the child's is palatal.

The next change is in the type of syllable onsets: [pupəɲ]. Both syllables are now h prosodic, ^{h}CV^{h}CVC, the first syllable matching the adult structure: ^{h}CV. A contrast of h̲ and h is sometimes found, though not in the same sequence as in the adult structure, i.e., in the form [bupəɲ]: h̲ CV^{h}CVC.

A change in the syntagmatic contrast of terms of the C systems follows next: the example is [budun]. There is now a contrast of terms at the

---

[2] In the child's phonological system the P system had 3 terms: p, t, k, to account for contrasts such as [pæpæ] 'Patrick', [tɪtɪ] 'Kitty' and [kukuː] 'cuckoo'.

P systems, p and t; and the term of the N system, t, matches the t term at the onset of the syllable in which it functions: $P_p VP_t VN_t$. There is thus a new contrast of p and t terms, a contrast nearer to that of the adult structure. However, both syllables are h prosodic: ʰCVʰCVC, as was the case when syllable structure changed from (CV)² to CVCVC, with a contrast of P and N systems, i.e. PVPVN. The number of contrasts is thus less than it would otherwise have been.

In [pudun] the h and h̄ prosodic contrast is functional: ʰCVh̄CVC.

Finally, in [pudɪŋ], the final contrast is present: a syntagmatic contrast of three terms, as in the adult structure: p, t and k: $P_p VP_t VN_k$.

The V systems will now be described in another partial analysis. They are examined in relation to syllable prosodies y, w, ə, and length, which are particularly relevant to their description. It should be noted that the prosodies are characteristics of the syllable, not of the V systems. A three-grade contrast, high ɪ, middle ɛ, and low α, is required to describe the child's V systems right from the start, as illustrated in the latter part of this paper, but in the particular example considered here, viz., the changes from [pupu] to [pudɪŋ], only two grades (ɪ and α) are involved.

In [pupu], the V grade is ɪ in both syllables; syllable length is short, CV̆; syllable prosody is w, and as noted earlier, the structure is a reduplicated monosyllable: (Cɪ̆ʷ)². This structure has to change to that of [pudɪŋ], in which the V grade is ɪ in both syllables, with short length: Cɪ̆Cɪ̆C, and there is a contrast of w prosody in the first syllable and y prosody in the second: Cɪ̆ʷCɪ̆ʸC. The structure of the first syllable of [pupu] is Cɪ̆ʷ, the same as that of [pudɪŋ], so no change of V grade or prosody is required. The structure of the second syllable of [pupu], Cɪ̆ʷ, has some elements in common with the second syllable of [pudɪŋ], viz., [dɪŋ], Cɪ̆ʸC. The V grade is ɪ, and length is short, ɪ̆. What is required is y prosody in place of w prosody.

A change of prosody in the second syllable is seen in the structure of the next four forms, viz., [bubaɪɲ], [bubuɪɲ], [pupəɲ] and [bupəɲ]. In the structure of [bubaɪɲ], a change to y prosody in the second syllable is accompanied by a change in V grade from ɪ to α, and from short to long length, viz., Cɪ̆ʷCā ʸC. These last two changes are the opposite of what is needed for [dɪŋ], Cɪ̆ ʸC. In the structure of [bubuɪɲ], the V grade of the second syllable is correct, i.e., ɪ, but the length is long instead of short: CɪCɪ̄C. The prosody is wy instead of y: Cɪ̆ʷCɪ̄ʷʸC. The structure of the two forms that follow, viz., [pupəɲ] and [bupəɲ], has the correct V grade and length in the second syllable: Cɪ̆Cɪ̆C, but the prosody is əy, so it is not quite correct: Cɪ̆ʷCɪ̆ə ʸC. The structure of [budun] and of [pudun] has the correct V grade and length, as in the case of the two preceding forms, viz., Cɪ̆Cɪ̆C, but the prosody is now w throughout instead of w in the first syllable and əy in the second syllable. This can be explained when seen in relation to changes in the C systems which have been described earlier, viz., a simplification of structure when something new is added. Finally, the V grade, length, and other prosodies of the structure match those of the adult structure, with a contrast of w and y prosodies of the first and second syllables: Cɪ̆ ʷCɪ̆ ʸC.

Having completed the analysis of C systems, V systems, and prosodies, they can be looked at together to see how, for instance, changes in the C systems relate to changes in the V systems. For example, the absence of contrast of V systems and prosodies in the two syllables is found at the time when the syntagmatic contrasts of C systems are developing in the structure, as in the form [budun]. The analysis of V systems yielded $\check{Ci}^w\check{Ci}^wC$, and of C systems $\underline{h}P_pV\underline{h}P_tVN_t$. This may be illustrated by putting all the samenesses of the two syllables in one formula and the differences in another:

    samenesses: $\underline{h}\check{Ci}^w\underline{h}\check{Ci}^wC^3$ differences: $P_pVP_tVN_t$

So far V systems have been considered in syntagmatic contrasts. They will now be considered in relation to paradigmatic contrasts. For this, part of the data of stage I of an English child will be analysed, i.e., the first words from 0;10.14 to 1;2.21, and then comparison of the V systems will be made with those of stage II, 1;2.21 to 1;4.10. It will be remembered that prosodic analysis is multistructural, and one of the meanings of this is that like structures are analysed together and separately from unlike structures. For instance, one-syllable words are analysed separately from two-syllable words, and one-syllable words are further subdivided in accordance with type of syllable structure.

The data for stage I are given below, and are divided into monosyllabic and multi-syllabic utterances.

Data for stage I

Monosyllables

[neɪ] → [nəu] 'no'[4]   [bæŋ] bang (onomatopoeic)

[dɛə] there   [ba:] Bob

[ʌp] up   [nau] now

[gud] good   [bəun] bone

[æn] Anne   [nɪə] near (repetition)

Multisyllables

[mama] Mama   ['ɪn 'dɛə] in there (repetition)

[dada] Dada   ['nəu 'nəu] no, no

[bi:nə] Bina   ['gu 'weɪ] go away

[kuku:] cuckoo   [pɔp pɔp pɔp] pop, pop, pop (onomatopoeic)

[gu'naɪ] goodnight (repetition)   [dɪə dɪə dɪə] dear, dear, dear (repetition)

Because of considerations of space, only the one-syllable words will be examined.

The first level of analysis is in terms of C and V. The data can be

---

[3] The structure of the syllables is different: CV and CVC, but there is a convention that prosodies are shown in relation to syllable structure.

[4] [neɪ] was the first form used but it soon changed to [nəu].

analysed into open ending, CV, and closed ending, VC and CVC, words:

CV	VC	CVC
[dɛə]	[ʌp]	[gud]
[ba:]	[æn]	[bæŋ]
[nɪə]		[bəun]
[neɪ] → [nəu]		

In stage I there are thus three types of structure: CV, VC, and CVC.

In order to save repetition, the way contrasts at V places are handled in stages I and II will be explained first and then an analysis of the two stages will be given separately. To handle contrasts at V places, a threefold contrast of V grade needs to be set up. The three grades are α, ɛ, and ι. The vowel sounds that are the exponents of these three grades vary in tongue height from open to close. Exponents of α have tongue height between open-mid and open: [æ, a:, ɑ:] and the starting points of [aɪ] and [au]. Exponents of ɛ vary from close-mid to open-mid: [ʌ, ə:, ɔ, ɔ:] and the starting points of [eɪ] and [ɛə]. Exponents of ι vary from close to half-close [i:, u:, ɪ, ʊ] and the starting point of [ɪə]. The systems set up at V places are thus α, ɛ, ι. These function in syllables having different prosodic elements, viz., y, w, ə, and length. The same prosodic contrasts, and the same three V grades are required to describe the adult V system, so the child can be shown to have these basic contrasts of the adult phonological system from the start, but they are used in a much more limited way in the child's system—he does not have the full range of combinations that are found in the adult phonology.

Monosyllables of stage I

The V systems within the different structures will now be considered, together with the prosodic elements which characterize them. In accordance with the principle of multistructuralism, separate analyses will be made for different structures. There are open syllable structures, CV, and closed syllable structures, CVC and VC.

Open syllable structure: CV

One of the examples is a direct repetition, viz., [nɪə]. As the analysis is polysystemic, words that are functional in the child's system will be treated separately from repetitions which are not functional in the child's speech. There are four examples without the repetition: [dɛə], [ba:], [nau], [neɪ] → [nəu]. Here there is a contrast of two grades, V_2, $2 = α$, ɛ, and syllable length is long.

Examples with $\bar{α}$: [ba:], [nau]; examples with $\bar{ɛ}$: [dɛə], [neɪ, nəu].
α grade: contrast of prosodies w and ə; length is long, $C\bar{V}$

$C\bar{α}^w$ [nau] now $C\bar{α}^ə$ [ba:] Bob

ɛ grade: contrast of prosodies y and ə, length long, $C\bar{V}$

$C\bar{ɛ}^y$ [neɪ] no $C\bar{ɛ}^ə$ [dɛə] there

Very soon there was a change of prosody in 'no' from y to w: $C\bar{ɛ}^y$ to $C\bar{ɛ}^w$. This type of description captures the relation between [neɪ] and [nəʊ]. It shows that the structure was like the adult's apart from the prosody.

If the direct repetition [nıə] which has the ι grade is now considered, a contrast of a third grade is added.

ι grade: the structure has a ə prosodic ending, syllable length is long, $C\bar{V}$

$C\bar{\imath}^ə$ [nıə] near

One may say that there is a three-grade contrast in the child's CV structures but that it is not yet fully operational.

Closed syllable structures: CVC and VC

A three-grade V system operates here (even if the onomatopoeic example, [bæŋ], is excluded as a special usage): V_3, 3=α, ε, ι.

α grade: y prosody is the only possibility; length is short, $\check{V}C$

$y\check{α}C$ [æn] Anne

ε grade: length is long in $C\bar{V}C$, short in $\check{V}C$. Long length is associated with w prosody and short length with ə prosody:

$C\bar{\varepsilon}^w C$ [bəʊn] bone $\check{\varepsilon}^ə C$ [ʌp] up

ι grade: length is short, $C\check{V}C$. The one example is related to a w prosody:

$C\check{\imath}^w C$ [gʊd] good.

There is a direct repetition, [ın] in ['ın 'dɛə] 'in there', with y prosody:

$\check{\imath}^y C$ [ın] in.

Monosyllables of stage II

The data show that there is an increase in the number of monosyllables,[5] 19 (and 4 repetitions) compared with 9 (and 1 repetition) in stage I (see overleaf).

There is a big increase in the number of prosodic contrasts of monosyllables. In fact, the child has acquired nearly all the combinations of the adult system. There is also a new open syllable structure, V. The child's system now has two open syllable structures, CV and V, and two closed syllable structures, CVC and VC. A three-grade V system, α, ε, and ι, now functions in open syllable structures, compared with a two-grade system, α, ε, in stage I.

Open syllable structures, CV and V

α grade: α grade now functions with four contrasts, $\bar{α}^w, \bar{α}^ə, {}^w\bar{α}, y\check{α}$ (five if the repetition 'I' is included: $\bar{α}^y$), and length is long or short. There were only two contrasts in stage I, $\bar{α}^w$ and $\bar{α}^ə$, and length was long:

length: **long,** $C\bar{V}, \bar{V}$

    $C\bar{α}^w$ [naʊ] now $C\bar{α}^ə$ [baː] Bob
    (both acquired in stage I)

    ${}^w\bar{α}$ [ɑː] the letter *r* $\bar{α}^y$ [aı] I (repetition)

---

[5] There was also an increase in multisyllabic utterances but they are not being considered here, so the data are not given.

Data for stage II

Monosyllables

[əu] the letter *o*   [bu] book
[u:] the letter *u*   [bɔ:] ball
[ɑ:] the letter *r*   [bæ] bag
[ʌ] the letter *a*   [dau, daun] down
[aı] I (repetition)   [mæ̃, mæn] man
[hʌ] the letter *h*   [mɔ:] more
[hæ, hæt] hat   [mɯ] me (nursery rhyme)
[dɔ] dog   [gɔn] gone
[du:] two   [gaun] dressing-gown (repetition)
[du:] cockadoodledoo (repetition)   [kot] coat
[bəu] boat   [də:t] dirt (repetition)
[bʌ] the letter *b*

---

short, CV̌

Cγᾰ [bæ] bag

ε grade: ε grade functions with five prosodic contrasts, Ē^ə, Ē^w, ^wĒ^w, ^wĔ, Ĕ^ə, with long and short length, compared with two with long length only in stage I, first Ē^y and Ē^ə, then Ē^w and Ē^ə.

length: **long, CV̄**

CĒ^ə [dɛə] there   CĒ^w [bəu] boat   C^wĒ^w [bɔ:] ball
(acquired in stage I)   (essential lip-   (essential lip-rounding
                                rounding at   throughout)
                                ending)

short, CV̌

C^wĔ [dɔ] dog (essential lip-rounding   CĔ^ə [bʌ] the letter *b*
   at start)

ı grade: functions with w prosody with a contrast of long and short length, Ī^w, Ĭ^w (with ə also if the nursery rhyme example is included). In stage I the only example was in a direct imitation, Ī^ə.

length: **long, CV̄**

CĪ^w [du:] two

short, CV̌

CĬ^w [bu] book   C^əĬ [mɯ] me (this is not found in the
                                              system of adult English)

Closed syllable structures, CVC and VC

A three-grade V system operates, as in stage I, α, ε, ɩ.

α grade: There is a contrast of two, ā^w and ᵞă, compared with only one possibility, ᵞă, in stage I.

length: **long,** CV̄C

  Cā^wC [daun] down

  short, V̆C

  ᵞăC [æn] Anne (acquired in stage I)

ε grade: There are three prosodic contrasts (four if the example of the direct repetition 'dirt' is included) ε̄^w, ε̆ᵊ, ε̆^w (and ᵊε̄), i.e., long and short length with w and ə, compared with long length with w and short length with ə in stage I.

length: **long,** CV̄C

  Cε̄^wC [bəun] bone   CᵊεC̄ [də:t] dirt (repetition)
  (acquired in stage I)

  short, CV̆C and V̆C

  C^wε̆C [gɔn] gone   ε̆ᵊC [ʌp] up (acquired in stage I)

ɩ grade: There is only one possibility, with short length, as in stage I, ĭ^w:

  Cĭ^wC [gʊd] good (but in stage I there was also a repetition with y, viz., ĭʸ)

It has now been demonstrated how the child started off with the three V grades required by the adult system but with few prosodic contrasts, and that he gradually acquired more contrasts. In this type of analysis it can be shown clearly that the structure of monosyllables in stage I is much simpler than in stage II, and that progress takes the form of the acquisition of prosodic contrasts in association with the three V grades. The sort of features that are the exponents of the various prosodies are: lip-rounding, lip-spreading, and their absence; backness, which is usually associated with lip-rounding; frontness, generally associated with lip-spreading, and central quality. Short and long syllable quantities are exponents of the length prosody. The exponents of V grades are degrees of openness of vowel. These various features have acoustic correlates, that is to say, they have some reality. To take some examples: the degrees of openness of vowel relate to F1; the backness, frontness, and central quality, lip-rounding and spreading, relate to F2 and F3; breathy and non-breathy syllable onsets relate to voicing onset time, which can be demonstrated instrumentally. The use of such features in the phonetic description and as a basis for the phonological description is thus more satisfactory than describing speech in terms of phoneme segments which have no one-to-one correlates at the acoustic level. Prosodic analysis, having a sound physical basis, is more likely to lead to a greater understanding of speech perception and how speech is processed in general. It should also provide useful insights for speech therapy. Some insights gained from this type of analysis have been used in a pilot scheme for remedial work with two deaf subjects (Waterson 1978; Buffery and Waterson 1980).

It has now been shown how prosodic theory works in relation to a type of English—how analysis is made of the word as a whole unit, taking into account its constituent syllables; the analysis is analytic in that the units being described are shown to be made up of several elements, and it is synthetic in that it shows how the units are held together by other elements. The prosodic approach is thus very different from the segmental type analyses of phonemic and generative phonological theories.

3
CHILD PHONOLOGY: A PROSODIC VIEW

First published in *Journal of Linguistics* 7 (1971). 179-211.

During the past few years linguists have begun to express doubts about the validity of segmental analysis for the study of child language and have come to feel that it is probable that a child perceives spoken language differently from an adult, e.g. Bellugi and Brown (1964: 113); Ingram (1966: 218); Ladefoged (1967: 148-9); Lenneberg (1967: 279-81); Weir (1962: 30). They are also beginning to realize the importance of treating a child's language as having its own independent system (Carroll 1961: 332; Fry 1966: 194). To date, however, investigators of child speech have made their analyses on a segmental and distributional basis and have expressed the child's phonological system in terms of the adult's phonemic system; one may cite, for example, Cohen (1969); Grégoire (1937); Jakobson (1941); Jakobson and Halle (1961); Leopold (1939, 1947, 1961); Lewis (1936); Ohnesorg (1959); Velten (1943) and Weir (1962). Such studies, valuable though they be, cannot be said to have succeeded in explaining the relationship between the forms and structures of child and adult and have left many questions unanswered, such as:

1) What governs the choice of sound that the child will use as a 'substitute' for an adult sound?
2) Why does the child 'drop' certain sounds of the adult form or 'substitute' for them when he is already capable of making such sounds and is in fact using them in some other contexts?
3) Why does the child use homonyms for adult forms which appear to be quite unlike each other and which have been proved to be semantically clearly differentiated for the child?
4) What governs the form that reduplicated words take?

This paper offers an approach which provides new insights into the relationship between a child's phonetic forms and phonological structures and those of the adult system through the use of a non-segmental analysis which gives greater freedom to express various correlations between child's and adult's forms and structures. What is suggested is an articulatory feature analysis for the phonetic description and prosodic analysis for the phonology. The features used are those that arise from the material under investigation, i.e. those required to describe the particular forms of the child and adult at the time the child was approximately 18 months old. They are not the distinctive features of generative phonology and are not intended to be considered universal. Current phonetic terminology and systems of transcription are not geared to non-segmental description, so the terminology used in the phonetic account is sometimes clumsy and terms are not always used in a familiar way.

The aim of this paper is to show by means of a non-segmental type of analysis that a child's language has its own independent system which, though different from the adult system, is closely related to it even where the child's forms appear to be quite unlike the adult's. The analysis proposed here, by demonstrating the relationship between child's and adult's forms and structures, makes it possible to suggest solutions to the questions listed above. The paper does not deal with the sequence in which a child acquires the different sounds of a language. This aspect of language acquisition has already been widely discussed by Jakobson and others (Jakobson 1941; Jakobson and Halle 1961; Leopold 1939, 1947, 1961; Lewis 1936; Ohnesorg 1959; Velten 1943).

The study is based on the writer's first child, P. Daily records were kept but the material was not analysed until some years after the collection of data was complete. As a child's linguistic development is individual, being conditioned by his particular environment, the phonetic and phonological descriptions given here are applicable only to the speech of the child P. However, it is possible that the way he acquired his speech forms is similar to that of other children and thus the findings may have a more general application. A brief outline of P's environment is now given to put the individual aspect of his acquisition of speech into perspective.

P, when a baby, was spoken to a great deal and was given plenty of attention at times when he wanted it. He was not left to cry or to lie awake inactive for long periods in his cot or pram with nothing to see or do. In his waking hours he was often put on the floor indoors or the ground out-of-doors to look around and engage in exercising his limbs, and was given toys and other material to investigate. He started walking holding-on at 6 months, and unaided at 9 months. His interest in objects and activity around him was always encouraged. Nursery rhymes were often sung to him and this obviously had relevance to his language learning as he began to recite nursery rhymes at the early age of 1;8. He had an excellent memory from an early age and a very well-developed sense of humour. He showed a great interest in the household pets, i.e. 'Bob'/'Bobby' the dog, the two cats referred to as 'kitties' and the two goats, 'Rooney' and 'Anne'. His vocabulary can be seen to be that of names of humans, animals and objects in his close environment, names of objects in picture-books, and actions concerned with the daily life and activities of the family.

A child is constantly exposed to something of the phonological system of the adult. To begin with, the sort of language that is used to a baby is restricted mainly to that associated with the baby's routine. The routine is carried out several times in twenty-four hours and this means that the baby hears frequent repetitions of the same sort of vocabulary and therefore many of the same combinations of sound features, and of course the same sort of sentence structures in the same sort of contexts for several months: as Fry pointed out (1966: 188), a child needs to hear speech in context in order for it to be meaningful. Later when he attempts to speak, he gets encouragement, correction and reinforcement from those around him and this is usually in the form of a repetition of the whole utterance, i.e. non-segmental.

Deviances from the norm in the speech of adults, whether phonological or grammatical, generally do not occur frequently enough in the same form for a child to pick them up and remember them. One may expect that he would be far more likely to pick up the forms that keep coming up regularly and occur in the same sort of situation, and it therefore seems reasonable to consider that most forms used by a child are his own creations made on the basis of regular, non-deviant adult forms. From observation of the child P, it seems probable that when beginning to operate language as opposed to simple repetition or imitation, a child perceives only certain of the features of the adult utterances and produces only those that he is able to cope with. (A fuller discussion of this point may be found in Waterson 1970.) This results in his forms sometimes appearing to be quite unlike those of the adult. As his input increases and his experience grows, so he is able to perceive and produce more, and his phonological system develops closer and closer to the adult system.

It was found that some of P's early forms seemed so different from the corresponding adult forms as to appear to have no relationship to them at all, but they are known to be the same by their function in context (see overleaf). Examined segmentally, such child's forms show very little congruence with the adult forms; e.g., comparing some of P's words with initial [ɲ] and the corresponding adult forms which have been established as having the same meaning by their function in context, no meaningful correlation can be shown. The adult's forms with which the child's forms are compared throughout the paper are those of his mother unless stated otherwise.

	Child's forms	Adult's forms
finger	[ɲẽːɲẽ/ɲiːɲi] (i.e. two forms were in use)	[fĩŋgə]
window	[ɲeːɲeː]	[wĩndəu]
another	[ɲaɲa]	[ənʌðə]
Randall	[ɲaɲɵ]	[rændɫ]

'Randall' is the name of a friend and neighbour who helped to look after P and who was always addressed and referred to as 'Mrs. Randall' until P started to call her [ɲaɲɵ]; after this she sometimes referred to herself as [nænə] but not before, so that P's use of [ɲaɲɵ] arose from the form [rændɫ] and not [nænə]. In comparing child's and adult's forms in ʷ terms of segments, adult's initial [f, w, ə, r] appear to correspond to the child's intial [ɲ], and adult's medial [ŋ]ʷ or [ŋg], [n] or [nd], and [n] or [ð] appear to correspond to the child's medial [ɲ]. Analysed in terms of features, as in the pages that follow, it is possible to show a much clearer relationship between these forms.

For the purpose of this paper a selection had to be made from P's vocabulary, and examples were chosen mainly from the period 1;6 because at the time he was regularly using many forms of words which seemed quite unlike the corresponding adult forms. At this time, his vocabulary consisted of approximately 155 words; about 104 monosyllabic, 48 disyllabic and 3 or so trisyllabic. Of the 48 disyllabic forms, 36 were of the CVCV structure. The child was already using three-word to four-word sentences, e.g., [dada tiː ɔː gɔn] 'Daddy's tea's all gone'; [baː gɔn gaːtn] 'Bob's gone in the garden'; [mɵ geːk dada] 'more cake, Daddy'. It is not possible to give exact figures for the number of words, either monosyllabic or disyllabic, nor the length of sentences in number of words without entering into discussions of whether the child's forms such as 'do it', 'sit down', 'all gone', etc. are one word or two.

The aim was to see what correlations could be established at the phonetic and phonological levels and to try to determine how much of the adult form the child was producing. The child's words selected for study were therefore chosen for their phonetic form, the only relevance of their meaning is that through semantic correlation child's and adult's forms can be identified as being the same word. The semantic correlation was established by the function of the word in context, i.e., the words were regularly used by the child in the same contexts and with reference to the same objects or actions as the adult word so used, and the adult's reaction in response to the child's usage produced satisfaction for the child, i.e., it produced the desired result. The child made it quite plain in various ways if he was not understood in the way he intended. As a simple example one may take one of the child's forms for 'fly', viz., [βæ]. The child's father sometimes amused the child by pretending to hunt flies that came into the kitchen by pointing at them and trying to chase them out of the window, saying, 'Fly! fly! Daddy go bang! bang!'. Whenever P noticed a fly, he would say [βæ, βæ] and point at it, or say [βæ, βæ, dada gəu bæŋ bæŋ], thus clearly using [βæ] in the way 'fly' was used by the adults. P's forms were identified with their adult correlates in the way shown above and their semantic correlation is to be taken as established; only the non-semantic correlations are to be established here. The words selected for study are the child's forms for 'finger' [ɲẽːɲẽ/ɲiːɲi]; 'window' [ɲeːɲeː]; 'another' [ɲaɲa]; 'Randall' [ɲaɲø]; 'fish' [ɪʃ/ʊʃ]; 'fetch' [ɪʃ]; 'vest' [ʊʃ]; 'dish' [dɪʃ]; 'brush' [byʃ], all in use at 1;6, and forms for 'fly' at 1;5 [wæ/bβæ] and at 1;6 [væ/βæ/bβæ]; 'barrow' at 1;5 [wæwæ] and at 1;6 [bʌwʊ]; at 1;6 'flower' [væ/væwæ] and forms for 'Rooney' [ẽñẽ/hẽñẽ]; at 1;5 'hymn/angel' [ahɔ/æhə/añũ] (see p. 36); and at 1;8 'honey' [ahuː]. Also the following at 1;6: 'biscuit' [beːbeː]; 'bucket' [bæbuː]; 'pudding' [pupu]; 'Bobby' [bæbuː]; 'Kitty' [tɪtɪ]; and 'dirty' [dɔːtɪ]. A detailed phonetic account is given of these forms but only a brief account of the phonology. A detailed phonological analysis of these forms is the subject of a separate paper in which regular correspondences are shown between child's and adult's structures, and these correspondences are used to predict some child's forms and structures from the adult's (see Waterson 1971b).

It was found that correlations at the phonetic level could be stated between the child's and adult's forms by reference to the following:

1) Various features of articulation, such as nasality, sibilance, glottality, stop (complete closure), continuance, frontness, backness, voicing, voicelessness, labiality, rounding, non-rounding. (A distinction is made between 'labiality' and 'rounding'. Labiality is used to refer to the action of the lips as being concerned in the articulation of a consonant such as lip protrusion which is part of the articulation of initial [r], or the lip contact of the labiodental stricture of [f]. Rounding, which includes labiality, refers to lip action which extends over the syllable, e.g., in the second syllable of 'barrow' [bærəu].)
2) Degree of vowel opening.
3) The syllable structure of the words.
4) The prominence of syllables (cf. Jones 1962:55, who used the term 'prominence' in relation to sounds: 'the prominence of sounds may be due to inherent sonority..., to length or to stress or to special intonation, or to combinations of these').

In order to make a comparison between the child's and adult's forms, the child's forms are first examined and analysed into features and are then grouped into different types of structure according to the selection of features which goes into their composition, viz:

I) Labial structure
II) Continuant structure
III) Sibilant structure
IV) Stop structure
V) Nasal structure

It will be found that some features are common to all five types of structure, others to only three or two; but from the detailed descriptions given under each of the five headings, it will be seen that no one type of structure has the same selection of *basic* features as any other type. For what is meant by 'basic' features see below.

Type I: Labial structure
The child's forms for 'fly', 'barrow' and 'flower' at 1;5 and 1;6 belong to this type.

	fly	barrow	flower
1;5	[wæ/bβæ]	[wæwæ]	_¹
1;6	[βæ/væ/bβæ]	[bʌwu]	[væ/væwæ]

They have the following features in common: labiality at the onset of each syllable [w, b, bβ, v, β]; continuance [w, β, bβ, v]; voiced onset of every syllable, voiced ending of every syllable, broad degree of openness of vowel (as opposed to closeness); prominence of one syllable, and the syllable structure CV. These features account for the similarity of these forms and such features will be called the *basic* features. The structures may be symbolized as KV and KVKV at 1;5 and KV, KVKV and PVKV at 1;6.

Features which are not shared by all the forms but may be shared by some and which account for the differences between them are as follows: friction [bβ, β, v]; non-friction [w]; affrication [bβ]; bilabiality [w, β, bβ, b]; labiodentality [v]; stop [b]; centrality of the syllable [bʌ]; rounding of the syllable [wu]; backness of the syllable [wu]; the finer distinction of frontness of syllable as opposed to centrality, i.e. [wæ, bβæ, βæ, væ] as opposed to [bʌ] ([æ] in the speech of the child and his mother is fully front, [ʌ] is advanced from central but is not fully front); word structure CVCV and CV. Such features as account for differences of form will be called *differential* features.

It is seen that at 1;6 the form for 'barrow' has developed closer to the adult form and has the greatest number of differential features of all the child's forms belonging to this type of structure. The child's form [wæwæ] at 1;5 had more features in common with the other forms belonging to the labial structure than his form [bʌwu] at 1;6.

Type II: Continuant structure
The child's forms for 'Rooney', 'honey' and 'hymn/angel' belong to this type of structure (see overleaf).

---

1 The sign - stands for 'no recorded form'. The first recorded form for 'flower' was at 1;6.

	Rooney	honey		hymn/angel
1;6	[ẽñẽ/hẽñẽ]	-	1;5	[ahɔ/æhə/añũ]
		1;8 [ahuː]		

The basic features of these forms are as follows: glottality [h, ɦ]; continuance [h, ɦ];[2] prominence of the first syllable; voiced onset of syllable 1;[3] voiced ending of syllables 1 and 2; the disyllabic structure of the word. The structure may be symbolized as V^hV, h having prosodic function (see pp. 35-6).

The differential features of these forms are: voiceless onset in syllable 1 [hẽñẽ] and in syllable 2 [ahuː, ahɔ, æhə]; voiced onset of syllable 2 [ẽñẽ, hẽñẽ, añũ]; frontness in ʷ[ẽñẽ, hẽñẽ] and syllable 1 of [æhə]; backness in ʷ syllable 2 of [ahuː, ahɔ, añũ]; centrality in syllable 1 of [ahuː, ahɔ, añũ]; nasality ʷ in ʷ[ẽñẽ, hẽñẽ] and in syllable 2 of ʷ[añũ]ʷ (onlyʷ the strongest nasality was recorded when transcribing the ʷ child's forms); the degrees of vowel openness, i.e., same grade of vowel (mid) in both syllables, [ẽñẽ, hẽñẽ]; more open vowel in syllable 1 followed by more close in syllable 2 [ahuː, ahɔ, æhə, añũ]; and the structure $^hV^hV$.

If the ʷ basic features of this type of structure are compared with the basic features of the labial structure, it will be seen that the feature continuance is the only basic feature shared by them and that some features that are basic in the labial structure, e.g., labiality and non-rounding, are not basic but are differential in the continuant structure. Thus features that are basic in one type of structure are not necessarily basic in another type nor are the differential features identical in different types of structure. What should be noted is that the *selection of basic features* in the two types of structure is different and this accounts for the difference in the basic shape and structure of the child's words belonging to the two different types of structure. For what determines which particular features will be basic and thus which words will be grouped into the same type of structure, see pp. 40-3.

Type III: Sibilant structure

The child's forms for 'fish', 'fetch', 'vest', 'brush' and 'dish' belong to this type.

	fish	fetch	vest	brush	dish
1;6	[ɪʃ/ʊʃ]	[ɪʃ]	[ʊʃ]	[byʃ]	[dɪʃ]

The basic features of these forms are as follows: broad degree of

---

2 [h] and [ɦ] are analysed as glottal continuants, not as fricatives, because the stricture is at the vocal cords and there is no stricture in the supraglottal area in common with other sounds classed as continuants—sounds classed as fricatives have supraglottal stricture.

3 [hẽñẽ] was a rare form and is grouped together with the other forms under this type of structure because of its obvious similarity—it is the only one with voiceless onset.

Child phonology: a prosodic view 31

closeness (as opposed to openness) of vowel [ɪ, ʊ, y]; voiced onset of word [ɪ, ʊ, b, d]; syllable ending with the following features: voicelessness, sibilance, continuance, frontness, labiality, palato-alveolarity; monosyllabic word structure.

The differential features are: rounding of the word [ʊʃ, byʃ]; non-rounding of the word [ɪʃ, dɪʃ]; backness of onset [ʊʃ]; frontness of onset [ɪʃ, byʃ, dɪʃ]; ([b] and [d] followed by front vowels have a more front quality than when followed by back vowels); the finer distinction of close-mid vowel grade (i.e., [ʊ, ɪ] as opposed to close (i.e., [y]); bilabiality [b]; alveolarity [d]; word structures VC and CVC. They may be symbolized as VS and PVS.

The child has homonyms for 'fish' and 'fetch' and for 'fish' and 'vest'. This suggests that the corresponding adult forms have many features in common.

It may be noted that the basic features of this type of structure are different from those of the two types of structure already described.

Type IV: Stop structure
The child's forms for 'biscuit', 'Bobby', 'pudding', 'bucket', 'Kitty' and 'dirty' belong to this type of structure.

	biscuit	Bobby	pudding	bucket	Kitty	dirty
1;6	[be:be:]	[bæbu:]	[pupu]	[bæbu:]	[tɪtɪ]	[dəːtɪ]

The basic features are as follows: oral stop at syllable onset; voiced ending of syllables; prominence of syllable 1; disyllabic word structure.

The differential features are: syllable features of frontness [be:, bæ, tɪ]; backness [pu, bu:]; centrality [də:]; rounding [pu, bu:]; non-rounding [bæ, be:, tɪ]; voiced onset [be:, bæ, bu:, də:]; voiceless onset [pu, tɪ]; labial onset [b, p]; non-labial onset [t]; the degrees of vowel openness, i.e. same (mid) grade of vowel in both syllables [pupu, tɪtɪ, be:be:]; more open vowel in syllable 1 and more close in syllable 2 [bæbu:, dəːtɪ]; bilabiality [b, p]; alveolarity [d, t]. Some of the structures are fully reduplicated monosyllables, i.e. (CV)², e.g. [be:be:, pupu, tɪtɪ], some are partially reduplicated, having only the consonants reduplicated, i.e. (C-)², e.g. [bæbu:], and one is reduplicated only as far as two consonantal features are concerned, viz., stop and alveolarity, i.e. [dəːtɪ]. There is thus a relationship of types of onset of the two syllables within the word, i.e., both syllables have onset with voice or with voicelessness, and with labiality or with non-labiality. Only one form does not conform to this pattern, viz., [dəːtɪ].

The word 'dirty' was frequently used to the child from an early age, e.g., 'dirty mouth', 'dirty hand', said when washing the child after meals. He learnt it early (at 1;3). It was the only stop structure word to have the vowel [ə:] and the only one to have a contrast of voiced and voiceless syllable onsets. Final [ɪ] was little used in disyllabic forms at this time apart from the form [tɪtɪ] which is discussed later (p. 39). The form [dəːtɪ] thus has the character of a loanword. (cf. Velten (1943: 284): '...ʷ words which introduce a new sound have at first the character of loan-words'.)

The child has homonyms for 'Bobby' and 'bucket' and the features of his forms are identical. This leads one to suspect that the adult forms of 'Bobby' and 'bucket' have many features in common with each other, perhaps more than with the rest of the adult forms which correspond to the child's forms belonging to this type of structure.

Type V: Nasal structure
The child's forms for 'finger', 'window', 'another' and 'Randall' belong to this type of structure.

	finger	window	another	Randall
1;6	[ɲẽ: ɲẽ: / ɲi:ɲɪ]	[ɲe:ɲe:]	[ɲaɲa]	[ɲaɲø]

They have the following basic features: nasality [ɲ]; stop, i.e., the palatal closure of the nasal consonant; voiced onset of the syllable; voiced ending of the syllable; prominence of the first syllable; syllable structure of word CVCV.

Differential features are: frontness of syllable [ɲe:, ɲe, ɲi:, ɲø, ɲɪ]; centrality of syllable [ɲa]; length of syllable [ɲe:, ɲi:]; rounding ʷ of syllable [ɲø]; non-rounding of syllable [ɲe:, ɲe, ɲi:, ɲɪ, ɲa]; same grade of vowel in both syllables [ɲe:ɲe:, ɲẽ:ɲẽ, ɲaɲa]; more open vowel in syllable 1 and more close in syllable 2 [ɲaɲø]; more close vowel in syllable 1 and more open in syllable 2 [ɲi:ɲɪ]. Some of the structures are fully reduplicated monosyllables, i.e., (CV)², e.g., [ɲe:ɲe:, ɲaɲa]; some are partially reduplicated, i.e., (C-)², e.g., [ɲẽ:ɲẽ, ɲi:ɲɪ; ɲaɲø]. The structures may be symbolized as follows: fully reduplicated (NV)², partially reduplicated NVNV.

Each of the five types of structure has a different selection of basic features, i.e., the basic features account for the major structural differences between one type of structure and another, and the differential features account for the finer distinctions among the words within the one type of structure. Moreover, a feature that is basic in one type of structure may be differential and not basic in another and vice versa.

The fact that the child's words can be grouped into different types of structure according to their basic features suggests that the corresponding adult forms must also share some features among themselves and that features composing the adult forms must bear some relation to those of the child's. The adult forms corresponding to the child's are therefore examined to see what features they are composed of and what features they have in common among themselves and with the child's forms. In fact, it will be seen that the adult forms can be grouped under the same five headings.

I: Labial structure
All the adult forms corresponding to the child's belonging to the above structure, viz., [flaɪ] 'fly', [bærəu] 'barrow', [fla:/flawə] 'flower' share the following features: labiality ʷ ʷ [b, f, r, w]; the liquid feature, i.e., partially interrupted vowel-like sound [r, l];ʷ continuance [fl, r, w]; openness of vowel [æ, a, a:, aɪ]; broad degree ʷ of frontness (as opposed to backness) of the first or only syllable [flaɪ, bæ, fla:, fla]; centrality of one or more syllables [flaɪ, fla: fla, wə, rəu]; non-rounding and prominence of the first or only syllable; voiced ending of all syllables; syllable structure CV. For ease of comparison [fl] is analysed as one complex unit, labiodental fricative with lateral release. The above are therefore the basic features of the adult forms belonging to the labial structure.

Features not shared by all the forms, i.e. the differential features,

are as follows: bilabiality [b, w]; labiodentality [f]; friction [f]; lateral release [fl]; alveolarity [r]; stop [b]; voiceless onset of syllable [fl]; voiced onset of syllable ʷ[b, r, w]; the finer distinctions of syllable ending, i.e., front ending in [flaɪ]ʷ and [bæ]; back ending in [rəu]; close ending in [flaɪ, rəu]; length of vowel [flaɪ, flɑː, rəu], as opposedʷʷ to shortness of vowelʷʷ[bæ, fla, wə]; the relationship ʷof more open vowel in syllable 1 to more close vowel in syllable 2 in [flawə] and [bærəu]; word structures CV and CVCV.
ʷʷ

Each of the adult forms belonging to this type of structure has ten basic features and fewer differential features. The differential features may be shared with some forms or with none, e.g., [flaɪ] has front ending of the syllable shared with [bæ]; close ending shared with [rəu]; lateral release shared with [flɑː] and [flawə]; length of vowel sharedʷʷ with [flɑː] and the second syllable of [bærəu]; labiodentality shared with [flɑː] and [flawə]; friction shared withʷ ʷ[flɑː] and [flawə], and word structure CV shared with [flɑː], i.e., it has eight differential features compared with ten basic. [flɑː] has length of vowel shared with [flaɪ] and syllable 2 of [bærəu] and the following features shared with [flaɪ] and [flawə]: friction, labiodentality, lateral release and voiceless onset. It shares word structure CV with [flaɪ]. It has six differential features. [flawə] has labiodentality, lateral release, voiceless onset, and friction, all shared with [flaɪ] and [flɑː], and bilabiality, the relation of more open vowel in syllable 1 and more close in syllable 2, voiced onset of syllable 2 and word structure CVCV shared with [bærəu], i.e., eight differential features. [bærəu] has the differential featuresʷʷ stop, rounding of syllable, alveolarity andʷʷ frontness (i.e., the finer distinction of front as opposed to advanced from central); these are not shared with any of the other words belonging to this type of structure and are four in number. [bærəu] also has some shared differential features: bilabiality, voice at syllʷˡaʷble onset, the relation of more open vowel in syllable 1 and more close in syllable 2, and the word structure CVCV, these being shared with [flawə], and length of vowel, i.e., in [rəu], which is shared with [flaɪ] and [flɑː], i.e., a further five differentiaʷlʷ features, making a total of nine differential features in all. [bærəu] has the greatest number of differential features that are not sharedʷ ʷand it seems that the differences therefore stand out for the child as he makes a fairly quick adjustment to bring his form closer to the adult's, i.e., from [wæwæ] at 1;5 to [bʌwu] at 1;6.

As was expected, the adult forms corresponding to the child's share a large number of features among themselves, viz., ten. Furthermore, if the child's basic features and the adult's basic features are compared, it can be seen that a number of them are shared. These are: labiality at syllable onset, continuance, voiced syllable ending, broad degree of openness of vowel, and the following features of the first or only syllable: broad degree of frontness, non-rounding, prominence, and syllabic structure CV; i.e., eight features are shared by the child's and adult's forms. The child's forms do not have the adult's basic features of liquid and centrality, and the adult's forms do not have the child's basic feature of voiced onset of syllable.

If the differential features of the child's and adult's forms belonging to the labial structure are now compared, it is seen that there is some similarity here also, e.g., friction (which is differential for child and adult) is common to adult's [flaɪ] 'fly', [fla:] and [flawə] 'flower' in [fl]; it is also common to some of the child's forms for 'fly', viz., [β, v, bβ] and to both forms of 'flower', viz., [v]. Labiodentality is common to child's and adult's forms for 'flower', adult's [f], child's [v]; the relationship of more open vowel of syllable 1 to more close vowel of syllable 2 is common to child's and adult's forms for 'barrow' at 1;6; bilabiality is common to the onset of child's and adult's forms for 'barrow' at 1;5 and 1;6, child's [w] and [b], adult's [b]; labiality at the onset of syllable 2 is common to both, child's [w], adult's [r]; voiced onset of both syllables is also common to both. At 1;6 plosivẅ onset of syllable 1 and rounding of syllable 2 are shared by the child's and adult's forms.

The fact that the child's and adult's forms share a large number of basic features seems to offer an explanation why all the child's forms for these words are composed of those particular features and can be grouped into one type of structure. It seems that the child perceives these particular features in the adult forms and produces them. He also produces some of the differential features which make the individual differences between the various adult forms belonging to the one type of structure so that his forms too are different from each other except for [væ] which is used both for 'fly' [flaɪ] and 'flower' [fla:], which are very similar apart from the ending.

If one now examines how the features are combined in the child's and adult's forms, it is seen that they are not always combined in the same way, e.g., the onset of the adult's form for 'fly' has the combination of features labiality, labiodentality, friction, continuance, lateral release, voicelessness, viz., [fl]. The child's forms for 'fly' have onset of several different combinations of features, all of which have voice, continuance and labiality, and the additional features as follows: labiodentality and friction [v]; bilabiality and non-friction [w]; bilabiality and friction [β]; bilabiality and affrication [bβ], i.e., the main differences are in the type of stricture and in the vibration or non-vibration of the vocal cords.

In 'barrow', adult's [bærəu], child's [wæwæ], child's and adult's syllable 1 have onset with voiẅcẅe, labiality and bilabiality, but the adult has the stop feature [b], and the child has frictionless continuance, [w]. Child's and adult's syllable 1 also shares the features voice, frontness, and openness of vowel. Syllable 2 of child's and adult's forms has onset with voice, labiality and frictionless continuance, but where the adult has alveolarity, [r], the child has bilabiality, [w]. The child's form is a reduplicated ẅ monosyllable. From the whole of the adult form [bærəu], he abstracts the consonantal features of labiality, voice and laxnesẅsẅ, together with the open vowel grade and frontness of the prominent syllable, giving the form [wæ] which is reduplicated to give a disyllabic form. He does not produce the stop feature and it is possible that he does not perceive it here (see p. 39). At 1;6 the child has acquired the stop feature initially in the word in place of frictionless continuance, the relationship of more open vowel in syllable 1 to more close vowel in syllable 2, the feature centrality in syllable 1, and the features backness and rounding in syllable 2, i.e., [bʌwu]. In this, his form for 'barrow' is moving away from the general pattern of his labial structure words which had no stop feature and no backness and rounding, i.e., his form for 'barrow' has now acquired features which were not in the composition of his labial structure words before, so that now his labial structure has expanded to accommodate a wider range of forms. Thus at 1;6 the child seems to perceive and produce more features of the form of 'barrow' than he could before and now presumably the framework within which he observes adult forms has been extended so that he is able to perceive more and produce more than he was able to at 1;5. This then may be taken as an example of how the child's structures expand and change, thus changing the whole phonological system and bringing it closer to the adult system.

II: Continuant structure

The adult forms corresponding to the child's forms belonging to this structure, i.e., [rũːnĩ] 'Rooney', [hʌnɪ] 'honey', [hɪm] 'hymn', [eĩndʒəɫ] 'angel', all share^w the following features: continuance, which is combined either with labiality or with glottality (with labiality in [r] of [rũːnĩ], [ɫ] and the fricative release of [dʒ] of [eĩndʒəɫ],^{w} and glottality in [h] of [hʌnɪ] and [hɪm]); nasality in the stops ^{w} [n] and [m] and a certain amount in the vowels. Where the word has voiced onset there is fairly strong nasality over the word, e.g., [rũːnĩ] and [eĩndʒəɫ]; where the onset is voiceless, the nasality is weak, e.g., [hʌnɪ] and [hɪm]. Also common to all the forms are voiced syllable ending, frontness of a syllable, vowel with broad degree of closeness, and prominence of the first or only syllable. The above features are therefore basic for the adult forms belonging to this structure. Differential features are as follows: glottality, labiality, alveolarity, bilabiality, affrication, sibilance, the liquid feature, long vowel [uː, eɪ], broad degree of openness of vowel (as opposed to closeness) [ʌ, ə]; the relation of vowel of syllable 1 to syllable 2 as more open to more close, and more close to more open, and the following syllable features: centrality, backness, voiced onset, voiceless onset, syllabic structures CV, CVC, VC, and word structures monosyllabic and disyllabic.

It is seen that the adult forms share several basic features. Some of these basic features are also common to the child's forms, viz., continuance, voiced syllable ending, prominence of the first syllable. The child's forms also have several differential features in common with the adult's, e.g., glottality, labiality, more open vowel in syllable 1 followed by more close vowel in syllable 2, the syllable features of rounding, non-rounding, backness, centrality, nasality, and CV syllable structure and disyllabic word structure.

In the case of the adult forms belonging to this type of structure, the articulation of the nasal stops is weak, as they are found in weakly stressed positions in the word, i.e., at the onset of unstressed syllables in [rũːnĩ] and [hʌnɪ] and in syllable final position in [hɪm] and [eĩndʒəɫ]. Also,^{w} in the latter case, the nasal stop is followed by sibilance and this is a context in which the nasal stop is very weakly articulated in the speech of the child's mother. The child does not produce the nasal stops, so it is possible that he does not perceive them clearly in these contexts, but he does produce the syllable feature of nasality, cf. adult's [rũːnĩ] and child's [ẽñẽ]. In fact, there are no strongly articulated consonantal features in the adult's forms belonging to this type of structure nor are there any in the child's. It is possible that the child does not perceive the consonantal articulations clearly enough to attempt to produce them at this stage, but he is presumably aware of the disyllabicity (as the majority of his forms have the same number of syllables as their adult counterparts), and produces it with separation of the syllables by glottal continuance. The glottal continuants are thus not part of his consonantal system but act as a link between the two syllables and are therefore prosodic. As far as the syllabic structure of the words is concerned, there is a difference: the child's forms all have the structure V^{h}V (apart from the rare form [hẽñẽ]), whereas the adult forms have the structures CVC, CVCV and VCCVC.

P's forms [ahɔ/æhə/añũ] were used with reference to 'angel' and 'hymn'. He had a hymn-book with angels on the cover so that the words 'angel' and 'hymn' were both often used in connection with it. On the same day P used the form [ahəm] once for 'hymn-book' and [ahɔ] and [æhə] for 'angel'. Four days later, he used [añũ] for 'angel', pointing at the angels on the cover one at a time and naming them. On the same day he used [bu añũ] for 'hymn-book', i.e., 'hymn/angel-book'. It seems that the words 'hymn' and 'angel' were not clearly differentiated for him and so the forms were confused and features common to both the adult forms were therefore used in his forms. The disyllabic form of the child's words probably shows their relationship to the disyllabic adult form [eĩndʒət] as the majority of monosyllabic adult words had monosyllabic correlates in the child's forms. Adult's [hɪm] (with initial glottal continuant and final labial nasal stop) and [eĩndʒət] (with nasality and stop and sibilant continuance and with labiality in the second syllable) are produced by the child with the following forms: [ahɔ/æhə/añũ], i.e., all having a medial glottal continuant, and with the labiality feature in the form of rounding of the second syllable in two cases as well. The adult form [hʌnɪ] with initial glottal continuant and no labiality is produced by the child as [ahu:] with medial glottal continuant and with labiality in the form of rounding of the second syllable. There is some correlation of the features nasality and non-nasality. There is nasality in the child's forms of 'Rooney' [ẽñẽ/hẽñẽ], in common with the adult form [rũ:nĩ], and in one of the child's forms of 'hymn/angel', viz., [añũ] in common with the adult form [eĩndʒət]. That is to say, where the adult has voiced onset and heavy nasality, the child has nasality in the word, but where the adult has voiceless onset and weak or no nasality over the word, the child has no nasality, e.g., adult [hʌnɪ], child's [ahu:]. It has already been shown that the words 'hymn' and 'angel' are apparently not clearly differentiated semantically for the child and it seems that they are therefore not phonetically differentiated. It is possible to link the two forms without nasality [ahɔ] and [æhə] more closely with the adult form [hɪm] (which has voiceless onset and little nasality over the word) and the one form with nasality [añũ] more closely with the adult form [eĩndʒət] (with voiced onset and stronger nasality). A correlation of vowel grade can be stated. In the adult forms [hʌnɪ] and [eĩndʒət], the vowel of the first syllable is more open than the vowel of the second, and this difference of vowel grade is maintained by the child, i.e., in [ahu:] and [ahɔ/æhə/añũ], the first vowel is more open than the second. In the adult form [rũ:nĩ] the vowels are close, [u:], and close-mid, [ɪ], and in the child's forms they are in the mid range, [e].

In words belonging to this type of structure it is seen that features common to the child's and adult's forms are not always in the same combinations, nor are they always in the same sequence.

III: Sibilant structure

The adult forms corresponding to the child's belonging to this type of structure, viz., [fıʃ] 'fish', [fetʃ] 'fetch', [vest] 'vest', [brʌʃ] 'brush' and [dıʃ] 'dish', all share the following basic features: broad degree of frontness of vowel; non-rounding; labiality in [br, ʃ, f, v, tʃ]; friction in [f, v, ʃ], in the release of [tʃ] and in the onset of [st]; continuance in [f, v, ʃ] and in the release of [tʃ] and [br] and in the onset of [st]; sibilance in [st, tʃ, ʃ]; and the syllable structure CVC. [st] of [vest] is analysed as one unit, a checked sibilant, and [br] of [brʌʃ] is similarly treated as one unit, stop with liquid continuant release. The differential features are voiced onset [vest, brʌʃ, dıʃ]; voiceless onset [fetʃ, fıʃ]; labiodentality; bilabiality; alveolarity; palato-alveolarity; stop and the liquid feature.

As expected, the adult forms have a large number of features in common and here again is a reason why the child's forms belong to one type of structure. The basic features shared by child's and adult's forms are labiality and voiceless ending, together with sibilance and frontness, and monosyllabic word structure. Differential features that are shared are: frontness and non-rounding of the syllable, viz., child's [ıʃ] and adult's [fetʃ], child's [ıʃ] and adult's [fıʃ]; mid vowel grade except in the case of 'brush', where the adult has open-mid [ʌ] and the child has the close vowel [y]; labial onset; some of the child's forms which correspond to adult forms with labial onset and labial or non-labial ending have rounding throughout, viz., child's [uʃ] and adult's [fıʃ], child's [uʃ] and adult's [vest] and child's [byʃ] and adult's [brʌʃ]; the stop feature in the forms for 'brush' and 'dish', and the syllable structure CVC in the same two examples. The child has a simple unit where the adult has a complex unit, e.g., child's [ʃ], adult's [st], child's [b], adult's [br].

Where the adult form has onset with the stop feature, the child's form also has onset with the stop feature; where the adult form has onset with labial continuance, the child has vocalic onset, which in some cases is labialized. It appears that when non-sibilant continuance (simple, not complex) occurs in the same syllable as sibilant continuance, the child produces only the more forcefully articulated sibilant continuance. This results in his forms having vocalic onset where the corresponding adult forms have non-sibilant continuance at the onset. As the initial stop features of adult's 'brush' and 'dish' are produced by the child, one may conclude that they are easily perceived by the child in spite of competition from the sibilant continuance. Stops are already well established in the child's system but labiodental fricative continuants are not; cf. labial structure words, where the child used a variety of labial continuants with different kinds of friction, or with no friction at all. In the adult forms of 'fish', 'fetch' and 'vest', the initial fricative continuants are simple and relatively weak articulations, viz., [f] and [v], and are not produced by the child, so that his forms have vocalic onset; but in labial structure words the initial fricative continuants of the adult forms are complex, viz., [fl], and are more forcefully articulated, and the child's corresponding forms have a consonantal onset.

IV: Stop structure

The adult forms corresponding to the child's belonging to this structure, i.e., [bıskıt] 'biscuit', [bɔbi] 'Bobby', [pudıŋ] 'pudding', [bʌkıt] 'bucket', [kıtı] 'Kitty', [daːtı] 'dirty', have the following basic features: stop at syllable onset, syllable with mid-vowel, front syllable, non-rounded syllable, and disyllabic word structure. Several differential features are shared by the various forms, e.g., bilabial onset of syllable 1 in [bɔbɪ, pudɪŋ, bʌkɪt]; non-bilabial onset of both syllables in [kɪtɪ] and [dəːtɪ]; voiceless onset of syllable: syllable 1 of [pudɪŋ], syllables 1 and 2 of [kɪtɪ] and syllable 2 of [bʌkɪt] and [dəːtɪ]; voiced onset of syllable 1 in all cases except [kɪtɪ] and [pudɪŋ]; mid vowel in both syllables [bɪskɪt, pudɪŋ] and [kɪtɪ]; more open vowel in syllable 1 and more close in syllable 2 in [bɔbɪ], [bʌkɪt] and [dəːtɪ]; rounding in syllable 1 of [bɔbɪ], [pudɪŋ] and [dəːtɪ]; centrality of syllable 1 of [bʌkɪt] and [dəːtɪ]; syllable structure CV in five forms and CVC in three forms.

In the stop structure, bilabiality and non-bilabiality at word onset seem to have an important role for the child. Where the adult form has bilabial onset in syllable 1, the child has bilabial onset of both syllables; where the adult form has non-bilabial onset in syllable 1, the child has non-bilabial onset in both syllables. This is because the child's forms are mostly reduplications of the first syllable of the adult forms. Some are reduplications of the whole of syllable 1 of the adult form (i.e. full reduplication) where the vowel grade of the adult form is the same in both syllables, e.g., child's [pupu] from adult's [pudɪŋ] (where the features of the child's reduplicated syllable are identical with syllable 1 of the adult form) and [beːbeː] (which has the features of syllable 1 of adult's [bɪskɪt] apart from the sibilant ending and the finer distinction of vowel grade), i.e., child's and adult's forms have mid vowels but the child's is open-mid and the adult's is close-mid. Some of the child's forms are partial reduplications of the adult's forms, e.g., the child's forms for 'bucket' and 'Bobby', viz., [bæbuː], where the consonantal onset of the first syllable of the adult form is reduplicated and the different vowel grades of adult's syllable 1 and syllable 2 are maintained by the child. The child's and adult's forms for 'dirty' are identical so here the child's form is not a reduplication of part of the adult's form but it does have something of a reduplicative nature in that both syllables have onset with alveolar stops. This may be the reason why the child was able to produce it successfully.

If the adult forms for which the child has homonyms, viz., [bʌkɪt] and [bɔbɪ], are compared, they can be shown to share a large number of features, e.g., disyllabic word structure; syllable structure of syllable 1, viz., CV; bilabial and voiced onset of syllable 1; stop at onset of syllables 1 and 2; voiced ending of syllable 1; non-frontness of syllable 1; frontness of syllable 2; more open vowel in syllable 1 and more close vowel in syllable 2; non-rounding of syllable 2. The main differences are in the syllable structure of syllable 2, i.e., CVC and CV, in the rounding and non-rounding of syllable 1, and in the backness of syllable 1 of [bɔbɪ] as opposed to centrality of syllable 1 of [bʌkɪt]. The child's form [bæbuː] has all the features that are shared by the forms [bʌkɪt] and [bɔbɪ] except that the frontness and non-frontness of the syllables are reversed, i.e., the child has frontness of syllable 1 and non-frontness of syllable 2. He also has non-rounding of syllable 1 and rounding of syllable 2, which is the reverse of [bɔbɪ]. In view of the fact that [bʌkɪt] and [bɔbɪ] have so many features in common, it seems reasonable that the child should use the same form for them both. The analysis shows that the child uses the same form for them because he perceives the same features in them and not because of any similarity in the objects to which the words refer or any lack of semantic differentiation.

P's form [tɪtɪ] is now considered in relation to the adult form [kɪtɪ]. From what has been said earlier, it appears that he is able to perceive the difference between onsets with bilabial and non-bilabial stops but it is not clear whether he is yet able to perceive the difference between velar stop and alveolar stop at syllable onset. At 1;5 he already had [g] at the onset of monosyllabic and disyllabic words but [k] only at the ending of monosyllabic words. He had a wider range of combinations of features in monosyllabic words than in disyllabic words. This suggests that perception and production are easier in shorter stretches than in long stretches. It is likely that this is linked with syllable prominence, i.e., that the child perceived prominent syllables more easily than the non-prominent. It is probable that of the consonantal features of the disyllabic adult form [kɪtɪ], it is the features of stop and voicelessness at the onset of both syllables that the child perceives most clearly, i.e., features that are reinforced by virtue of occurring in two places in the word. As he has the combination of the features voicelessness and stop only either with bilabiality or with non-bilabiality (alveolarity) in disyllabic forms, he has to make a choice between bilabiality and alveolarity. The fact that the difference between bilabial closure and non-bilabial closure is visible, and that the second stop of the adult form is combined with alveolarity (a combination already familiar to the child), no doubt helps him to perceive the non-bilabial nature of the stops of the adult form and he therefore produces the combination of features without bilabiality, viz., voicelessness, stop and alveolarity for the consonantal element, together with the vowel grade and syllable features of the adult form, which resulted in the reduplicated form [tɪtɪ].

The second stop in the child's reduplicated forms bears some relation to the second stop of the adult forms because the child only has reduplicated stop forms as a reflex of adult disyllabic forms with a stop at the beginning of each syllable. (cf. 'barrow' (which, in the adult form, has a voiced bilabial stop at the onset of syllable 1 and a labial continuant at the onset of syllable 2, and in the child's form at 1;5 does not have stops but labial continuants at the onset of both syllables, viz., [wæwæ]). It seems as if the stop feature has to occur in two places in the disyllabic adult forms—that is to say, it has to be reinforced—for the child to produce it and reduplicate it.)

V: Nasal structure

The adult forms corresponding to the child's forms belonging to this structure, i.e., [fĩŋgə] 'finger', [wĩndəu] 'window', [rændɫ] 'Randall', and [ənʌðə] 'another', have the following basic features: ʷcontinuance [f, w, r, ɫ, ð]; nasality combined with the stop feature in [n, ŋ] and in varying degrees over the word; non-rounded syllable; voiced ending of all syllables; voiced onset of syllable 2; prominence of penultimate syllable.

There are very many differential features and only those of special interest are listed here to save repetition; they are as follows: nasal homorganic with the following oral stop [ŋg, nd]; labiality [f, w, d, r]; more close vowel in syllable 1 followed by more open vowel in syllable 2 in [fĩŋgə] and [wĩndəu]; more open vowel in prominent syllable and more close in the following syllable in [rændɫ] and [ənʌðə], i.e., [æ] followed by a lateralized mid labio-velar ʷqualityʷ [ɫ] in [rændɫ], and [ʌ] followed by [ə] in [ənʌðə]; non-rounding is shared by [fĩʷŋgə] ʷand

[ənʌðə]; rounding in the second syllable is shared by [wĩndəu] and [ræn̪d̪ʉ].
   It can be seen that the basic features nasality and stop are common to all the child's and adult's forms. Prominence of the penultimate syllable is also basic to child and adult, as are the following: non-rounded syllable, voiced ending of all syllables, voiced onset of syllable 2. The adult's basic feature continuance is not produced by the child.
   The nasals of the adult forms, apart from [ənʌðə], are homorganic with the following oral stops and are thus complex articulations and strongly articulated. In [ənʌðə] the nasal stop is at the onset of a stressed syllable and is also strongly articulated. These strongly articulated nasal stops are produced and reduplicated by the child (cf. the weakly articulated nasal stops of continuant structure words which are not produced by the child). In nasal structure words the nasal stops are more forcefully articulated than the continuants and it may be that they are therefore more clearly perceived by the child and hence are produced by him.
   As the differential features are many, a more detailed comparison is needed to show the close relationship of the child's and adult's forms. Prominence in the first syllable of the adult's forms of 'finger' and 'window', which have strong nasality in addition to the other qualities which go to make a syllable prominent (Jones 1962: 55), is matched in the child's forms by length of syllable, i.e., the first syllables of [ɲẽːɲẽ/ɲiːɲi] 'finger' and [ɲeːɲeː] 'window'. The second syllable of 'window' in the child's and adult's forms, although less prominent than the first syllable, has more prominence than the final unstressed syllable of their forms for 'finger'; i.e., [ɲe] and [ɲi] in the child's forms for 'finger' are less prominent than [ɲeː] in syllable 2 of his form for 'window', and [gə] in the adult's form for 'finger' is less prominent than [dəu] of 'window'.
   A correlation of degree of openness of vowel can be shown. Four degrees of openness of vowel are needed to describe vowels of the child's and adult's forms being discussed here: close [iː], close-mid [ɪ], open-mid [ə, e, ø] and open [æ, a, ʌ]. [u] is a labial glide.
   The child's forms belonging to this structure may be described as reduplicated structures. Some are fully reduplicated, i.e., [ɲaɲa] and [ɲeːɲeː], and others are partially reduplicated, i.e., [ɲẽːɲẽ], [ɲiːɲi] and [ɲaɲø]. In the case of [ɲaɲa], it is the prominent syllable of the adult form that is reduplicated; in the case of the rest, the strongly articulated nasal plus stop of the adult form is produced by the child as a simple nasal stop and this is reduplicated to provide the consonantal elements for the disyllabic forms. The degrees of openness of vowel of the first and second syllables of the adult forms are maintained by the child in the main, as was described above, but the syllable features are only partially maintained, e.g., in 'finger' the child has frontness in syllables 1 and 2 where the adult has frontness in syllable 1 and centrality in syllable 2, but both have non-rounding in both syllables; in 'window' the child has frontness and non-rounding in both syllables but the adult has frontness and non-rounding in syllable 1 and centrality and rounding in syllable 2. (See tabulation of adult's forms and child's forms on opposite page.)

   The relationship between the child's forms selected for study and the corresponding adult forms has now been demonstrated phonetically (by

Adult's forms		Child's forms	
[fĩŋgə]	First vowel close-mid, second open-mid, i.e., both broadly mid and second more open than first.	[ɲẽːɲẽ] [ɲiːɲi]	Both vowels mid. First vowel close, second close-mid, i.e., both broadly mid and second more open than first.
[wĩndəu]	First vowel close-mid, second open-mid, i.e., both broadly mid.	[ɲeːɲeː]	Both vowels mid.
[ənʌðə]	Penultimate vowel open, final vowel open-mid, i.e., both broadly open.	[ɲaɲa]	Both vowels open.
[ræ̰nd̯ɫ̩]	First vowel open, second syllable a labio-velar lateralized open-mid quality, second syllable has labial quality.	[ɲaɲø]	First vowel open, second open-mid, second syllable rounded, i.e., has labial quality.

the shared basic and differential features) and phonologically (by the child's and adult's forms being assigned to the same types of structure). In establishing this relationship it was possible to observe which features of the adult forms the child produces and to draw some tentative conclusions about what the child is best able to perceive when at the start of language learning. It has been found that the child's linguistic perception at this early stage appears to be more limited than his perception in imitation and repetition and he is best able to perceive the generally broader distinctions and the most forceful articulations. He appears to perceive an utterance as a whole unit and perceives certain features of the utterance but seems not to be always aware of the combinations and sequence in which these features occur; cf. Ladefoged (1967: 149):

> Listening to speech often requires the identification of differences in order which are smaller than a syllable. Normal adults have no difficulty in hearing the difference between 'waist' and 'waits' or 'fits' and 'fist'. But children and foreigners often make mistakes of this kind;...If we use unfamiliar sounds it is easy to show that listeners can differentiate between complex stimuli which differ in the order of their components, but may not be aware of the differences in order. They differentiate between the stimuli as wholes, and have to learn to interpret as order those cues which the ear transmits about the relative times of arrival of the different parts.

To summarize, one may say that it seems that the child produces the features of the adult form that he perceives most clearly, and what he perceives most clearly is (1) features that are already established in his repertoire and (2) the most strongly articulated features and features that are reinforced in the utterance, i.e., those that occur in more than one place in the utterance, and also the broad distinctions rather than the fine.

The features that the child acquires the earliest in his phonological system are presumably those that he perceives most clearly when he is listening linguistically. Stop consonants which many children have been observed to acquire earliest of the consonants can be assumed to be among the most clearly perceived as they are the complete cutting off of the airstream, an extreme articulation in comparison with the clear passage which is obtained with an open vowel which is observed to be the vowel commonly acquired earliest. This links up with the views of Jakobson and others on the sequence in which sounds are acquired, but it is not just a simple matter of acquiring sounds in a certain sequence because if this were so, once a child had acquired a particular sound, he would use it in all the places in which the adult used it; but this is not the case and hence we have the problems of child language referred to earlier (p. 25), e.g., why a particular sound is used in some words but not in others, why a child 'substitutes' a sound for one he is already able to make, why he 'drops' sounds that he is able to make. The answer to these questions may be as suggested earlier—i.e., that out of the selection of features of which the utterance is composed, the child perceives some more clearly than others and therefore produces those and not the others. The features he perceives most clearly and those that he is able to produce therefore form the basis for his phonological structures and the differences between the child's and adult's forms can thus be explained in terms of the child's limited perception of the adult forms and the operation of his own phonological system which results from his limited perception and limited ability to produce certain features and combinations of features.

The hypothesis of the child's perception of the more strongly articulated features and the broader distinctions generally as suggested by the analysis presented in this paper is in line with what was proposed by Leopold (1961: 352) when dealing with phonemic contrasts:

> It is safe to assume that the small child's perceptive faculties develop gradually. When the child's attention turns to language, it will first distinguish in what it hears only the coarser contrasts, and will need time to appreciate the finer sub-contrasts between the sounds which reach its ear. The same applies to the efforts to reproduce the sounds in its own articulation.

Furthermore, it seems reasonable to suppose that when a child is acquiring his first language, his perception of utterances is not conditioned to as great an extent as that of the adult. The adult's perception is conditioned by the context of situation and by his linguistic competence, i.e., by the grammatical probabilities (e.g., morphology and syntax), by lexical probabilities (e.g., his lexicon and collocations) and by phonological probabilities (e.g., probabilities of combinations of sounds in his system, the rhythmic shape of words) (cf. Ladefoged 1967: 144, and Gimson 1964: 3-4)—i.e., the adult has a high expectancy of what is to follow. For a child, the relationship between the utterance and the context is in the process of getting established through the function of utterances in context. He has only the rudiments of linguistic competence or none at all. He is therefore listening with very little expectancy, i.e., at something like a phonetic 'nonsense' level, and thus very likely produces those features that strike him most clearly and those that he is best able to produce at the time. To illustrate this point one may take P's production of the adult's strongly articulated nasal stops and the non-production of the adult's weak continuants in his nasal structure words, and the non-production of the adult's weakly articulated continuants and nasal stops in his continuant structure words. Also the production of labial continuance in his labial structure words, where the adult forms have complex, strongly articulated continuants, but the non-production of labial continuance in his nasal structure words, which, in the adult forms, have strongly articulated nasal stops but weak labial continuants.

The concepts of substitution, elision and metathesis have been used a great deal in order to try and explain differences between child's and adult's forms. Many linguists agree that there is some system and regularity about these phenomena but find it difficult to state the underlying rules for the regularity except in terms of the debatable principle of the child using sounds involving the least amount of effort and the principle of the use of the earliest acquired sounds being substituted for those acquired later. Lewis (1936: 180-5) notes certain limitations in the range of articulations within which substitutions can be made. Leopold discusses the various theories of substitution very fully (Leopold 1947: 257-74) and tries to explain the irregularities he finds in terms of assimilations, dissimilations and metathesis, which he considers upset the regularity of substitutions. He is thus able to account for several of his child's forms but is still left with some that he cannot explain. However, the irregularities arise from the nature of the analysis, i.e., because an independent phonological system is not set up for the child and all the child's forms are interpreted in terms of the adult's phonological system. Another interpretation of some of the irregular forms which shows them to be quite regular is given on pp. 46-8.

A few examples of the sort of problems usually dealt with by the concepts referred to above are now taken from forms used by P in order to show how they can more satisfactorily be explained by reference to the child's perception of sounds and his phonological system. The forms have already been analysed, so now only the restriction on the use of certain sounds, viz., [v, w, ɲ, b], to specific contexts is summarized and explained.

The sound [v]

It was seen that the child uses [v] in his labial structure words, e.g., initially in one of his forms for 'fly', [væ], and for 'flower', [væwæ]. He does not, however, use [v] in his form for 'vest', i.e., he appears to substitute [v] for [f] in his form for 'fly' and 'flower' but does not use it in 'vest' where the adult does. As he has no [f] in his system, it seems reasonable that he should have no initial consonant for his forms of 'fish', [ɪʃ/uʃ], and 'fetch', [ɪʃ], but the question that is usually asked is why, when he is able to articulate a particular consonant (e.g., [v]), does he not use it wherever the adult does (e.g., in 'vest'). The reason for this is probably that as sibilant fricative continuance (here [s] in [st]) is more strongly articulated than non-sibilant fricative continuance (here [v]) he perceives the former more easily than the latter, and when both types of continuant occur in the same syllable, as in 'vest', the child produces the type that he perceives more clearly, i.e., the sibilant fricative continuant and not the labial fricative continuant. This also accounts for sibilant continuance being a basic feature for the structural type under which the words 'fish', 'fetch' and 'vest' are grouped. The adult forms with stop initial and sibilant fricative continuant final, e.g., [brʌʃ] and [dɪʃ], are produced by the child with initial stops and final sibilants, i.e., [byʃ] and [dɪʃ]. The stop feature was established early in the child's system and the child appears to have had no difficulty in perceiving and producing it in competition with sibilant continuance within the same syllable.

In adult forms belonging to the labial structure there are only non-sibilant continuants. These are complex articulations, e.g., [fl] in [flaɪ] and [flaː] and are fairly strongly articulated, and there is no competition from any more strongly articulated consonants, so the child produces the labial continuance; but he has not as yet acquired the adult combination of the features labiality, friction and continuance in his system and therefore produces the labial continuance variously with friction [v, β], or affrication [bβ], or without friction [w].

In view of the above, the sound [v] cannot be expected in the child's form for 'vest' but can be expected in his forms for words such as 'fly' and 'flower'.

The sound [w]

P uses the sound [w] initially in some of his labial structure words, e.g., one of his forms for 'fly' [wæ] and 'barrow' [wæwæ], but he does not use [w] in his form for 'window'. As has already been shown, he appears to perceive the most clearly and strongly articulated features and those that are already established in his system from among the selection of features of which his model is composed. In labial structure words, the adult combination of the features labiality, friction with lateral release and continuance is produced by the child as labiality and continuance accompanied by friction [v, β], or affrication [bβ], or non-friction [w]; here there are no other more strongly articulated features in competition with the labial continuance so the child appears to perceive the labial continuance and produces it. [bærəu] has the stop feature which may be considered to be more strongly articulated than the non-sibilant continuant [r]. For an explanation of why [b] is not produced by the child, see opposite page. In the adult form [wĩndəu], the articulation of the complex [nd], i.e., homorganic nasal and stop, is more forceful than the articulation of the non-complex [w], i.e., bilabial frictionless continuant. The child appears to perceive the stop feature and the nasality more clearly than the weakly articulated continuant, and produces the nasal stop,[4] and uses reduplicated nasal stops for the consonantal elements of his disyllabic form. He does the same in 'finger' and 'Randall', where the initial non-complex continuant articulation is less forceful than the complex nasal and stop articulation, and thus the reduplicated nasal stops are basic for a particular type of structure in his system, viz., the nasal structure.

This explains why the child uses [w] in 'fly' but not in 'window'.

The sound [ɲ]

The child uses a nasal in some words where the adult has a nasal, e.g., 'window' and 'another', but not in others, e.g., 'Rooney' and 'honey'. As has been shown earlier, the nasal stops in [wĩndəu] and [ənʌðə] are strongly articulated and are therefore produced by the child in reduplicated form to give a disyllabic structure, i.e., [ɲeːɲeː] and [ɲaɲa], but the more weakly articulated continuants [w] and [ð] are not produced.

---

4 Phonetically the homorganic nasal and stop may be considered as one unit, a stop in which the soft palate is lowered at the onset and raised before the release.

In [rũ:nĩ] and [hʌnɪ] the nasal stops are at the onset of unstressed syllables and are thus weakly articulated. The continuants [r] and [h] are also weakly articulated so it seems that no consonant features stand out clearly for the child; but, as pointed out earlier, he does seem to perceive the difference between monosyllables and disyllables, and perceives these forms as disyllabic and produces them as such, the syllables being linked by glottal continuance in the form of breath in 'honey', i.e., [ahu:], and breath and voice in 'Rooney', i.e., [ẽh̃ẽ]. The nasality of [rũ:nĩ], which is spread over the whole word in addition to the nasal stop, is produced by the child as a feature of the whole word, i.e., [ẽh̃ẽ], but the very weak nasality of [hʌnɪ] is not produced. This accounts for the establishment of the child's continuant structure for words in which the adult forms have no strongly articulated consonants.

The use and non-use of nasal stops in the child's forms corresponding to adult forms with nasal stops is thus explained by reference to the child's perception of the features nasality and stop in relation to the rest of the features of which the adult form is composed.

The sound [b]

There are several examples of the use of the sound [b] initially and medially in P's speech. The use of medial [b] has been explained as resulting from the reduplication of the first syllable of adult disyllabic forms which have more than one stop consonant, e.g., child's [be:be:], adult's [bɪskɪt], child's [bæbu:], adult's [bʌkɪt], so that there is no case for saying that the child substitutes [b] for adult [k] in these examples.

Although the child uses initial [b] where the adult form has initial [b] (cf. examples of stop structure words), an example has been given where he does not do so, viz., in his form for 'barrow' [wæwæ] at 1;5. In view of the arguments that the child perceives and produces the most strongly articulated consonantal features out of the selection of features of which the adult form is composed and also the features that are already established in his system, it would seem that the child should have produced the [b] of [bærəu], as a stop is more strongly articulated than a frictionless continuant (here [r]), but the child's form is [wæwæ], i.e., with continuants, not stops. This can be explained as follows: the child has oral stops in disyllabic words only when the adult form contains two or more stops (cf. the stop structure words). It seems therefore that the stop feature has to be reinforced (i.e., has to occur in more than one place) for the child to produce it in a disyllabic form. There is only one stop in [bærəu] (i.e., [b]) and the articulation of this stop is lax and is combined with the feature labiality. The onset of the second syllable is also lax and labial and is combined with continuance (i.e., [r]). The features of laxness, voice and labiality seem to be reinforced in the word and thus are apparently more clearly perceived by the child than the stop feature, which, although well established in the child's system, is not reinforced and is thus not produced. The labiality, voice and laxness together with continuance are produced as [w]. Thus it seems that the child perceived the same features in 'barrow' as in 'fly' and 'flower'. Hence his form for 'barrow' belongs to the same type of structure as his forms for 'fly' and 'flower', viz., the labial structure, and did not have the stop feature until his system had developed further.

It is possible to give rules that govern reduplication in the speech of the child P. These are related to the different types of structure. In stop structure words there is 'forward'[5] reduplication of the prominent syllable of the adult form when the initial consonant of the adult form already functions as an initial consonant in the child's system (e.g., bilabial stops). (cf. full reduplication: e.g., child's [pupu], adult's [pudɪŋ]; child's [be:be:], adult's [bɪskɪt]; and partial reduplication in child's [bæbu:], adult's [bɔbɪ] and [bʌkɪt].) When the initial consonant of the adult form does not function as an initial consonant in the child's system, the child's form may be described as a 'reverse' reduplication of the initial consonant of the second syllable of the adult form, and of the grade of vowel and the syllable features of the prominent syllable of the adult form (cf. child's [tɪtɪ], adult's [kɪtɪ]). Similarly, in the labial structure, stops do not function as initials in the child's system at 1;5, so there is reverse reduplication, giving child's [wæwæ] for adult's [bær�085u]. In the nasal structure where the initial consonant of the adult form͏ʷʷ does not function as an initial in the child's system, the child's form is a reverse reduplication of the ending of the prominent syllable of the adult form, e.g., the child has no [f] and therefore has [ɲe:ɲe/ɲi:ɲɪ] for adult's [fĩŋgə]. Where the initial consonant of the adult form functions as an initial in the child's system belonging to a different structure, the child's form is also a reverse reduplication (either full or partial). For example, in the child's system initial [w] and [r] are used only in labial structure words (one of his forms for 'rabbit', ʷadult [ræbɪt], was [ræwæ]); therefore the consonantal elements of the child's formʷs for 'window'ʷ and 'Randall' (which are nasal structure words) are a reverse reduplication of the ending of the first syllable of the adult form (i.e., [ɲe:ɲe:] and [ɲaɲø]), with the vowel grades and syllable features of the adult forms partially maintained.

Quite a large number of 'substitutions' in the examples of reduplications in children's speech given in the Appendices in Lewis (1936) can be explained in terms of reverse reduplication as described above. This sort of reduplication has been observed before, but was interpreted in terms of assimilation (e.g., by Leopold 1947).

By way of illustration of how the approach used in this paper can be applied to another child's speech in order to explain phenomena that cannot be accounted for by substitution, assimilation, etc., a few examples are taken from Leopold's material (1947: 257-74) which his theory could not explain, to show how easily the 'irregularities' can be explained by the type of analysis suggested here. For instance, Leopold found it difficult to account for his daughter's [deʃ] for 'steht' (stands), [dɔɪʃ] for 'stone' and [lɔ·ɪʃ] for 'story', all these being used by his child at 1;11. His daughter Hildegard was bilingual English and German. He suggests [deʃ] is 'steht' with metathesis of initial [ʃ] or 'steh-' plus English -z. He compared [dɔɪʃ] with [deʃ] and at first considered that it had an incorrectly placed plural [z] (the word was used to refer to one stone), but then decided it might be due to metathesis of initial [s]. However, from his excellent phonetic records it is plain that at 1;10 and 1;11 his child had a type of structure with sibilant final which had three different kinds of initial: (1) stop, (2) continuant, and (3) nasal (cf. P's sibilant structure at 1;6). The following is a representative selection of the forms

---

5 When reduplication is described as being 'forward' or 'reverse', the terms are used as convenient labels to describe patterning in the child's phonological structure in relation to the adult structure rather than any process.

the child had, taken from Leopold (1939: 53-137):

1) **Stop initial and sibilant final**
[biʃ] piece; [beʃ] bathe; [baɪʃ] beiss(en) (bite); [daʃ] crash, dress, Katz (cat), kratzen (scratch), Glas (glass); [dɪʃ] kiss; [duʃ] juice, Kuss (kiss). cf. the adult forms, which in both English and German, have the basic features onset with oral stop, and fricative (generally sibilant) in final position. Child's and adult's forms share the basic features of voiceless and fricative ending; voiced onset is basic for the child but not for the adult; sibilant ending is basic for the child but not for the adult although most of the adult forms do have sibilance.

2) **Continuant initial and sibilant final**
[haɪʃ] heiss (hot); [hauʃ] Hause, house; [wɑʃ], [waʃ] waschen, wash; [wɪʃ] abwischen (to wipe up); [juʃ] lutsch(t) (sucks). cf. the adult forms, which have the basic features continuant onset and fricative ending. Sibilant ending is common to most adult forms but is non-basic; it is basic for the child. The onset is voiced for child and adult except where there is glottal continuance, e.g., [haɪʃ], heiss; voiceless ending is basic for both in the first or only syllable.

3) **Nasal initial and sibilant final**
[mauʃ] mouse; [naɪʃ] nice, knife; [naʃ] nass (wet); [maɪʃ] much; [mauʃ] mouth; [nɔʃ] nose. cf. the adult forms, which all have nasal stop initial (basic) and fricative (basic), generally sibilant ending. Voiced onset is basic for both child's and adult's forms. Voiceless ending is basic for the child but not for the adult although it is common to most of the adult forms.

One may note that Hildegard maintains the distinction of labial and non-labial onset in all the examples quoted under (1), (2) and (3). cf. P's stop structure forms, where he kept this distinction.

Hildegard's system appears to be based on adult forms having sibilant fricative final and initials with oral stop, continuant, and nasal stop. The following 'irregular' forms given by Leopold are now examined in relation to the three types of structure set up for the child's phonological system: [deʃ] 'steht'; [dɔɪʃ] 'stone', and [lɔ·ɪʃ] 'story'.

The adult form 'steht' has the features (checked) sibilance and friction [ʃt], mid vowel [e], stop [t] and there is frontness over the whole word. The child's form [deʃ] has the features sibilance and friction [ʃ], mid vowel [e], stop [d] and frontness over the whole word—i.e., it has features almost identical with those of the adult form. In structures of the child's system with such a selection of features, the stop feature comes first and the sibilant feature last (cf. (1) above), and the onset is always voiced whether the onset in the adult form is voiced or voiceless—i.e., voiced onset is basic for the child. The sequence of sounds as in the child's form [deʃ] is therefore the only possible one to fit her system and is thus perfectly regular. If one examines the features composing the child's and adult's forms for 'stone', they are also found to be similar to each other. Adult's [stəun] has the features (checked) sibilance and friction ([st]), stop (nasal) ([n]), more open vowel followed by more close ([əu]), and rounding of the whole word. There is voiceless onset and voiced ending. The child's form [dɔɪʃ] has the features sibilance and friction ([ʃ]), stop (oral) ([d]) (nasality is not a basic feature of the child's stop initial and sibilant final structures, so it is not relevant here; it is only relevant when onset with nasality plus stop is basic in the adult form), more open vowel followed by more close ([ɔɪ]), and rounding and voicing at the onset of the word, and non-rounding and voicelessness in the ending. As noted above, the child's system requires the stop to be initial and the sibilance to be final, with voiced onset and voiceless ending. The vowel grades are the same as in the adult form (viz., more open followed by more close), but the rounding feature does not extend as far over the child's form. The form [dɔɪʃ] is thus just as regular as the form [deʃ] and the other forms listed under (1) above.

The form [lɔˑɪʃ] for 'story' puzzled Leopold so much that he doubted the interpretation of the word as 'story' although the context in which it was used seemed to suggest it: it was given as the answer to the question 'Was hat Mama dir erzählt?' (What did Mummy tell you?), the answer being [ʔə lɔˑɪʃ], which Leopold interpreted as 'a story' but said that if it was 'story', it was quite irregular as none of his patterns of assimilation, etc., could explain it. However, it is possible to show that it shares many features with [stɔːrɪ] and as far as the child's own system is concerned, is quite regular. The adult form [stɔːrɪ] has the features (checked) sibilance and friction ([st]), liquid and continuance ([r]), more open vowel followed by more close ([ɔː] and [ɪ]), and rounding and backness in the first syllable and non-rounding and frontness in the second, with voiceless onset and voiced ending of the word—i.e., it has the same features as the adult forms grouped under (2) (continuant initial and sibilant final), but in a different sequence. The child's form [lɔˑɪʃ] has sibilance and friction ([ʃ]), liquid and continuance ([l]), more open vowel followed by more close ([ɔˑ] and [ɪ]), rounding and backness in the first syllable, and non-rounding and frontness in the second; all these features are shared with the adult form, but the child's form has voiced continuant onset and voiceless sibilant ending, which is a different sequence from the adult's but is required by the child's system, as seen in (2) above. The child's form thus shares most of the features of the adult's while conforming to her own system referred above, viz., continuant initial and sibilant final structure. This form is thus considered to be completely regular. In none of these cases is it necessary to bring in the concepts of substitution or metathesis to explain the differences between the child's and adult's forms. The child's forms conform to the patterns of her own phonological system and, as noted in the case of P, the sequence and combinations of features in the child's and adult's forms are not always the same.

It is possible that the perception of phonetic features that have been described in articulatory terms is, in fact, some kind of perception of acoustic cues similar to what Fry suggests for the development of the phonemic system (1966: 197):

> It is clear that a very important part of this development of the phonemic system is bound up with the use of acoustic cues, both for the monitoring of the child's own speech and for the reception of other people's. We now have a considerable body of information about the operation of these cues in adult speech, although we are still far from understanding fully how they function, but have no knowledge of the ways in which the use of the cues develops as speech is acquired.

It is possible, also, that there may be some parallel in the perception of phonetic features (whatever their nature) with what Piaget calls 'verbal syncretism' (1959: 131-2). He writes:

> Recent research on the nature of perception particularly in connecxion with tachistoscopic reading, and with the perception of forms, has led to the view that objects are recognised and perceived by us, not because we have analysed them and seen them in detail, but because of 'general forms' which are as much constructed by ourselves as given by the elements of the perceived object, and which may be called the schema or the *gestaltqualität* of these objects. For example, a word passes through the tachistoscope far too rapidly for the letters to be distinguished separately. But one or two of these letters and the general dimensions of the word are perceived, and that is sufficient to ensure a correct reading. Each word, therefore, has its own 'schema'.

Piaget considers that such schemata are far more important for the child than for the adult, as they develop long before the perception of detail, the natural course of development being from syncretism to a combination of analysis and synthesis, and not from analysis to syncretism. It thus seems reasonable to consider that a child perceives some sort of schema in words or utterances through the recognition of a particular selection of phonetic features (the basic features) which go into the composition of the forms of the words or groups of words, and this recognition of a schema results in his producing words of the same type of structure for such adult forms, e.g., words with consonantal features continuance and strongly articulated nasal followed by stop have in the forms of the child P a reduplicated nasal stop pattern, i.e., the nasal structure. A child also recognizes differences in form within the particular type of structure (the differential features) and this results in his having different forms within the structure, and as his skill in perception and articulation increases, so he perceives and produces more and more of the features of the adult forms. Such a hypothesis seems to link up with what appears to be currently a widely accepted view of the cognitive development of the child, i.e., starting with a comparative lack of differentiation and progressing by way of increasing differentiation. This view may be briefly illustrated by the words of Brown:

> ...the primitive stage in cognition is one of a comparative lack of differentiation. Probably certain distinctions are inescapable; the difference between a loud noise and near silence, between a bright contour and a dark ground, etc. These inevitable discriminations divide the perceived world into a small number of very large (abstract) categories. Cognitive development is increasing differentiation. The more distinctions we make, the more categories we have and the smaller (more concrete) these are. I think the latter view is favored in psychology today. (1958: 89)

> Psychologists who believe that mental development is from the abstract to the concrete, from a lack of differentiation to increased differentiation, have been embarrassed by the fact that vocabulary often builds in the opposite direction. This fact need not trouble them, since the sequence in which words are acquired is not determined by the cognitive preferences of children so much as by the naming practices of adults. (1958: 91)

In the analysis presented in this paper, the adult forms, like the child's, were grouped into five types of structure on the basis of the particular selection of features which they have in common and these were suggested as the schemata of the words which the child perceives.

Perhaps the first reaction to such a classification will be to ask whether it is not always possible to find enough common features among words to group them into any type one may wish. This may be so when one is dealing with the adult's whole lexicon, but the child is building up his phonological system from nothing—i.e., one may consider his competence to be nil at the start (that is to say, at the time when he first begins to *understand* what is said to him, not when he first begins to talk), and it seems that the basis on which he builds is the input he receives, i.e., utterances which are meaningful to him by their function in context, and these at the start are few in number. He therefore has little or no expectancy and no conditioning to influence his perception of sounds until he gets some system built in—i.e., when he gets some competence. Thus it seems that it is the selection of features composing the utterances which are the input for the child that determines the patterns he will acquire, and the input is decided more by the adults than by the child (cf. Brown, above). This means that the sequence in which he 'registers' various utterances will determine which features he will learn to perceive and produce first and will thus determine the different types of structures he will have in his phonological system. One may take as an example the words 'Randall', 'window' and 'finger', which were all used frequently to P. He sees them operating in context. They thus become meaningful for him and therefore claim his attention. He appears to perceive certain features common to them, i.e., nasal stop, which is forcefully articulated, broad degrees of vowel openness in syllables, certain syllable features, and produces these features in a particular way (e.g., reduplicated nasal stops), and thus he has a new type of structure.

Every child has a different input, as different children have different environments and different things are said to them. This means that it is possible for every child to register a different set of words and perceive some similarity in the selection of features of different groups of words, thus perceiving and producing different sets of features. This will result in different kinds of structures in their phonological systems so that children learning the same language will have different forms. This does not of course mean that there cannot be similarity (cf. P's and Hildegard's sibilant structures). Although it has been noticed that there is a tendency for children to acquire certain sounds earlier than others (see references to Jakobson and others on p. 26)—i.e., those of which the articulation does not require great skill in timing and co-ordination (e.g., stops and nasals and an open unrounded vowel), this does not mean that their phonological patterns will be the same; in fact they are usually different, and that is why when children first begin to speak, they are often not understood by speakers of the same language outside the family.

It is not possible on the evidence of the analysis given in this paper to suggest whether in the very early stages a child first observes similarity in the feature selection of several words before he attempts to produce them in speech or if he perceives particular features in each word independently and produces them. Whatever way it happens, the child produces similar forms (i.e., with the same basic features), and thus a type of structure with a particular selection of features in a particular sequence becomes established in the child's phonological system. Once such a structure is established, he has a framework within which he perceives other utterances which have the same selection of features, i.e., he has some competence which gives him a certain expectancy. This may be illustrated from the structures of Leopold's child with final sibilant fricative quoted on p. 47, which were obviously based on adult forms with final sibilant friction. Other words with the same basic features but in a different sequence (i.e., with sibilant onset instead of ending, e.g., 'story' and 'stone') were produced by her with features in the same sequence as the rest of her words belonging to that particular structure (i.e., with sibilant ending), and not in the sequence found in the adult forms; thus her competence conditioned her performance. Presumably, when a child's perception sharpens and the input includes more adult forms with the same selection of features but in a sequence different from the one on which the child's structure is based, the child's structure expands to include the new sequence.

The writer has not yet made a thorough study of P's acquisition of grammar but has reason to believe that it is possible to show that the grammar of the language was acquired in a similar way, i.e., a child observes an utterance as a whole and perceives certain basic features of grammatical structure in the utterance which are linked with stress and prominence. It is mostly the stressed and prominent words of a sentence that a child produces, so that many unstressed words are left out—hence the 'telegraphic' effect, to borrow a term from Fraser, Bellugi and Brown (1963, reprinted 1968: 50). These then are the basic features or units on which his sentence structures are built. Such basic units of grammar are established on the basis of regularly recurring structures which can easily be related to the context by the child, i.e., such as are functional for him (e.g., in the case of P, such sentences as 'Bob's a good boy', said to the dog when he does as he is told, and 'Anne's a good girl', said to the goat at milking time). Ungrammatical or anomalous sentences are unlikely to play a part because they do not recur often enough for a child to register them. It is possible, therefore, that a child perceives certain basic patterns of regularly used sentence types, i.e., the schemata of the sentences. These are produced by him and he uses such patterning as a model for his own sentences; cf. P's reciting of sentence patterns which are obviously his own creations: e.g., at 1;6, he said [æn guɡəː, dada guɡəː, baː guɡəː] (Anne's a good girl; Daddy's a good girl; Bob's a good girl). These are apparently modelled on 'Anne's a good girl'. As a child gains more experience and as his phonological system develops and he is able to perceive more, he appears to grow more aware of finer grammatical distinctions, many of which occur mainly in unstressed positions in the utterance, such as prepositions, conjunctions, inflections, auxiliaries, etc., which in the early stages are not produced and probably are not so clearly perceived; they get gradually incorporated into his sentence structures and so his grammatical system grows. The basic units of sentences can be expected to vary to some extent from one child to another, as what would be basic for each child would depend on the type of sentence structures which were the input for him; but it seems that more similarity can be expected in the basic units of grammatical structures than in phonological structures of English children because English-speaking adults seem to use the same sort of sentence structures to children in the main, so that they have mostly the same sort of structures as input (e.g., simplified grammatical structures such as 'Mummy do it', 'Where's pencil?', 'Baby want Teddy?').

The study of the pattern of the acquisition of the grammar requires a separate paper and the brief comment on the subject is only put forward here as the obvious corollary of the pattern of the acquisition of the phonological system of the child P, thus showing that the pattern of the acquisition of grammar and phonology seems to be a coherent whole. It is somewhat rash to put forward speculations about the acquisition of grammar before the grammatical study is complete, but they are made in the hope that those concerned with problems of language acquisition will be provoked either to support the views expressed here or to offer reasoned arguments to disprove them.

At the present time there is much speculation about what constitutes a child's capacity for language acquisition, e.g., Chomsky (1965: 3-62, 1966: 111-13, 1967: 397-442); Katz (1966: 240-82); McNeill (1966: 65-85); Lenneberg (1965, 1966a, 1966b, 1967). The evidence given in this paper suggests that P perceived some sort of schema through the recognition of a particular set of features out of the selection of features of which groups of adult forms were composed, and this resulted in his producing his own related forms with one structural pattern. If this proves to be the general pattern of how a child acquires the phonological system of his mother tongue, it may be that part of a child's capacity for the acquisition of the phonological system is the ability to perceive schemata in the sound patterns of utterances.

4
PERCEPTION AND PRODUCTION
IN THE ACQUISITION OF PHONOLOGY

First published in: von Raffler Engel, W., and Lebrun, Y.(eds.) (1976). *Baby Talk and Infant Speech*. Amsterdam: Swets & Zeitlinger. 294-322.

Language acquisition has been described as a process of socialization (von Raffler Engel 1970a). The child learns to speak in the context of everyday life and in a way that is appropriate to the community in which he lives while at the same time absorbing the culture of that society. This being so, it seems that a study of the data of a child's learning to speak in the home, in the course of life, is more likely to produce insights into the processes involved than a study of data collected under experimental conditions. The validity of any hypotheses based on studies made under such naturalistic conditions can then be tested experimentally and either proved or disproved. It is with this in mind that the writer's views on perception and production in relation to the acquisition of phonology are put forward. An attempt is also made to infer some of the processes involved from the evidence presented. It may seem presumptuous for a linguist and phonetician to do this but the justification is that there is still a great deal that is unknown about the processing of speech and it has been said that in order to learn how the brain controls speech, one must look at speech itself (Laver 1970).

It seems therefore that before a child develops a need to speak, he must have some understanding of his environment. His understanding begins with what is salient for him, i.e., with what is important for him because he is directly involved. For the way he learns to perceive the world about him, one may take the account given by Vernon (1971: 13-31). A child begins to recognize samenesses and differences in his environment, aided by the fact that certain of its aspects are repetitive; for instance, there is the picking up, feeding, bathing, changing, having things pointed out and named, and so forth. Mothers generally talk to their babies while attending to them and it has been noted that babies seem to respond at a very early age to pitch patterns, rhythm and other related features, as for example, caressing tones or those of disapproval, no doubt aided by the facial expressions which accompany them.[1] Mothers tend to say the same sort of things in the same sort of contexts. The stretch of time between some of these repetitions is not very long as the child is attended to at fairly frequent intervals so that in spite of a limited memory span, at some stage he appears to recognize a sameness in parts of utterances, in a similar manner perhaps to the way in which he recognizes samenesses in his environment, and he associates the sameness of the acoustic signal with the sameness in the environment. Thus, at some point, it appears to dawn on the child that speech has reference to objects and events and has magical properties—i.e., it can produce results more efficiently than any other means that he has available to him, such as crying or gesture. This may well cause him to become interested and pay more attention to speech and perhaps begin to look

---

[1] For some discussion of this point see Crystal (1970), Lewis (1936: 38-52), and Menyuk (1971: 56-64).

out for parts of utterances which can be associated with something that is meaningful for him.

Utterances addressed to the child have words that are prominent by stress·and pitch as well as certain other features which will be considered in the course of this paper. Such words usually refer to something that the child gets to understand because he is constantly involved, e.g., 'Time for your *bath*'; 'Let's get your *coat*'; 'Come to *Mummy*'; 'Here comes *Daddy*'; 'Where's your *shoe*?'; 'Here's your *milk*'; 'Pudding's *all gone*'. Words and expressions of this sort are easily associated by the child with objects, states and actions, but the background noise of home, street, shop, etc., provides some masking of the less prominent parts of the utterances. There is also the difficulty of making sense of words that do not have a clear relation to something in the environment, such as 'function' (as opposed to 'content') words. In addition, it seems that there is a limitation on the length and complexity of utterance that a child can manage.[2] All this means that he cannot cope with the whole of any but the shortest, simplest utterance. Thus in the very early stages, he is only able to make use of certain portions of the acoustic signal (phonetics); he associates these with something he understands, so gets a meaning for them (semantics); and he builds up a system of his own of specific sound patterns (phonology) but he gets by for quite a time without morphology and syntax. The importance of the role of phonology in language acquisition has been emphasized by Fry (1966). The view that semantics precedes syntax in language acquisition is being recognized by a growing number of workers in this field (Slobin 1966; von Raffler Engel 1970b; Bloom 1970; Francis 1971), and a study of hearing errors under natural conditions suggests that syntax does not play such a vital role in the interpretation of speech in adults and older children (Waterson 1971a).

Vernon has said that from childhood upwards, people habitually overlook what they do not understand unless it is forced on their attention (Vernon 1971: 38); the writer's evidence suggests that in the very early stages, what the child does not understand in his environment, and stretches of speech that are not easily perceivable and that cannot be related to something that is meaningful, are not relevant for him and are therefore not taken into account. Evidence that children learn from speech that is functional for them comes from the fact that in the data of the speech of young children, the early vocabulary consists of names of objects, states and actions of their restricted environment, such as names of people with whom they are closely connected, e.g., Mama, Dada; words for food and drink: milk, egg, bread, butter, meat, apple, banana; everyday things: pram, chair, bath, bed, cup, spoon, jug; everyday actions and events: dinner, tea, lift up, put down, go away, all gone; parts of the body: hand, finger, foot, eyes, nose, mouth; toys: car, dolly, Teddy; greetings: hello, bye-bye; household pets: Kitty, doggie, and of course 'no'. The meaning of a word is generally not the same for a child as for an adult, e.g., 'bath' may be the specific one in the home (i.e., white and of a particular shape and size) and [hoʃ] may mean a dog as well as a horse, as in the case of Lewis' child (Lewis 1936: 352)).[3]

---

2 See Brown and Fraser (1964) for constraints in relation to syntax.
3 For more on how a child's meaning for a word differs from that of adults, see Brown (1970) and Lewis (1936: 189-99).

As a large part of the phonological system seems in general to be acquired before the syntax and its acquisition is closely related to the learning of meaning, it seems proper to start with a study of the acquisition of phonology and semantics if one wishes to arrive at an understanding of how a child starts learning to speak. Having briefly indicated something of how he learns the meaning side of language (viz., by noting the relation of the utterance to what he understands of his environment), this aspect of learning, which deserves a separate study, is set aside so that the rest of the paper may be devoted to phonology.

The evidence for this paper is taken mostly from the data of the acquisition of English of the writer's first child, P, and examples given are mainly from his speech. An examination of the data of some other children, not only English but also French and German, shows that the basic principles which will shortly be expounded seem to apply in the main to them also although the strategies used may vary from child to child. However, before one can claim that these principles have a universal application, a great deal of work needs to be done on the acquisition of non-European languages to see how far confirmation can be found.

A child generally starts off with short simple forms, mostly monosyllables and reduplicated monosyllables; there is a great deal of articulatory harmony and there are simple consonantal onsets where the adult has clusters, all of which makes the production of the child's words simple in comparison with the adult model. For example, at around the age of 1;5, P had monosyllables of the PVN and PVP types, both having onset and ending with stop consonants—oral onset and oral or nasal ending. These usually had the same place of articulation at the onset and ending of the word; they were either both labial, C_pVC_p, both apical, C_tVC_t, or both dorsal, C_kVC_k, whereas the adult models have the additional possibility of a contrast of labial: apical, C_pVC_t; apical: dorsal, C_tVC_k; apical: labial, C_tVC_p; dorsal: labial, C_kVC_p and dorsal: apical C_kVC_t. (For examples, see tabulation of adult's and child's forms overleaf.)

At the start, P's strategy for dealing with a disyllabic or trisyllabic model was generally to reduplicate the whole or part of the stressed syllable (e.g., [bæbæ] or [pæpæ] for 'Patrick' [pætrɪk]), and this is a common feature of children's early speech. This, and the harmonic form of children's monosyllables suggests that at the start a child's capacity for the planning, production and perception of speech is very limited, i.e., there is a constraint on what can be coped with in terms of complexity within a limited stretch of time. One may compare the rapid colloquial of adults where there also appears to be a constraint on complexity in production probably because of the shortness of time available for processing and where a great deal of harmonizing also takes place, e.g., [aɪ mʌsə̃steɪ] 'I mustn't stay', in place of the slower style [aɪ mʌsnt steɪ], and [dəumbɪ lɔŋ] 'Don't be long', for [dəunt bɪ lɔŋ].[4]

If indeed a child can only cope with a limited stretch of utterance both in the perception and the production of speech, it means that he can only use a small part of the incoming speech signal. Some clue as to how the selection from the signal is made may be gained from a comparison of the forms the child produces with those of the adult models.

---

[4] For further discussion of this point see Waterson (1971a).

PVN	Adult's forms		Child's forms	Harmony	
plane	[pleɪn]	$\widehat{PL}_p VN_t$	[beɪm]		
stamp	[stæmp]	$\widehat{SP}_t VNP_p$	[bem]		
pram	[præm]	$\widehat{PL}_p VN_p$	[bæ̃/bæm]	$P_p VN$	labial
plum	[plʌm]	$\widehat{PL}_p VN_p$	[bʌm]		
down	[daun]	$P_t VN_t$	[daun]	$P_t VN$	apical
chin	[tʃɪn]	$\widehat{PS}_t VN_t$	[dɪn]		

PVP					
bib	[bɪb]	$P_p VP_p$	[bɪp]		
pip	[pɪp]	$P_p VP_p$	[bɪp]		
cup	[kʌp]	$P_k VP_p$	[bæp/bʌp]	$P_p VP$	labial
plate	[pleɪt]	$\widehat{PL}_p VP_t$	[beɪp]		
grape(s)	[greɪp(s)]	$\widehat{PL}_k VP_p$	[beɪp]		
truck	[trʌk]	$\widehat{PL}_t VP_p$	[gʌk]		
jug	[dʒʌg]	$\widehat{PS}_t VP_k$	[gʌk]		
stick	[stɪk]	$\widehat{SP}_t VP_k$	[gʌk]		
crab	[kræb]	$\widehat{PL}_k VP_p$	[gʌk]	$P_k VP$	dorsal
duck	[dʌk]	$P_t VP_k$	[gʌk]		
cart	[kɑ:t]	$P_k VP_t$	[gʌk]		
cake	[keɪk]	$P_k VP_k$	[gʌk]		

This shows what bits of the model he is trying to reproduce and therefore in all probability what he perceives, but of course, not necessarily all that he perceives. However, he is unlikely to regularly produce meaningful forms that are not related to the model (i.e., that are not based on what he perceives) at as early an age as when a child starts to speak (viz., generally somewhere between 9 months and 1½ years); he is not likely to invent a whole host of names 'out of the blue'. It has been said that a child has to select from the speech signal but this is not to imply that his hearing is poor. The fact that a young child can often imitate an adult form more accurately than the form he produces in his spontaneous speech shows that he can hear quite a lot of detail, but a distinction has to be made between the hearing and imitation of a stretch of utterance in a repetition situation, and the perception and identification of what is functional in a stretch of utterance in a learning situation, when a child is trying to find the label for some item by associating something of the utterance with something in the situation. This is a far more complex situation requiring a bigger spread of attention from the child—i.e., too much is going on for him to be able to give his full attention to the whole of the acoustic signal. Added to this, as has already been mentioned, a child is not provided with a quiet background to enable him to listen to speech; he learns in the course of life, which means that there is generally noise of varying degrees of loudness, and other distractions, with resultant masking of such speech sounds as are articulated with less energy or are weak for other reasons, and this makes it harder for him to pay attention to them,[5] and at first he has no means other than acoustic salience (i.e., what is easiest heard) and relation to context for sorting out what is or is not relevant. This situation in relation to speech perception may be likened to Vernon's 'figure from ground' differentiation which she has said is fundamental to perception, i.e., something needs to stand out clearly from its environment in order to be easily perceivable (Vernon 1971: 41-5).

A comparison of some of P's forms with the adult models in terms of phonetic features showed that he was producing certain features but not others (Paper 3). The features found useful for such analysis are:

Syllable features: associated with the whole or part of a syllable but not with place within a syllable, e.g., frontness, backness, centrality, lip-rounding, lip-spreading, nasality, voicing, voicelessness.

Segmental features: associated with places within the syllable, i.e.,
  a) manner of interrupting the airstream, e.g., plosion, continuance, friction, sibilance, nasality, raising or lowering of the tongue (open, mid, close vowel grade);
  b) place at which the airstream is constricted, e.g., labial (bilabial, labiodental), apical (dental, alveolar, postalveolar), dorsal (palatal, velar).

It will be noted that these syllable and segmental features are not the distinctive features of generative phonology, where the features are tied to the segment, each segment having a set of features which makes it distinctive from the rest.

In monosyllables P was found to respond fairly accurately to the syllable features and to certain segmental features, including vowel grade, but disyllables were in general less accurately produced, the stressed syllable often being a closer match than the unstressed, the latter having the correct vowel grade but not the syllable features. On the whole, P seemed to get the manner of articulation better than the place, and manner has been found experimentally to be the dimension that carries the greatest functional load (Peters 1963; Denes 1963), whereas place is the most susceptible to distortion (Denes 1963; Peters 1963; Gray 1970; Miller and Nicely 1955). The features of vowel grade are associated with the first formant. Ilse Lehiste found that the first formant contained the greatest amount of energy relative to the other formants (Lehiste 1964: 157) and this makes F1 (and hence features of vowel grade) prominent. The features of frontness, backness, lip-rounding and lip-spreading are associated with F2 and F3, which have less intensity, and this would account for such features being less accurately produced. The manner of articulation is associated mostly with F1 transitions (which again have relatively high intensity) and place of articulation with F2 and F3 (which are generally of lower intensity); this has been shown in the experimental work of the Haskins Laboratory (cf. the report by Liberman (1961)). That the child should respond to some features and not to others is not surprising in view of experimental findings

---

[5] Some features of speech are intelligible at a lower sound pressure level than others (cf. Denes and Pinson 1972: 137-8).

that consonants and vowels are coded in short-term memory in terms of features rather than as whole segments and that such features can be forgotten and recalled independently as well as perceived independently. One may cite the work of Wickelgren (1965, 1966) and Miller and Nicely (1955) in this connection with reference to adults. The testing of errors in child language (von Raffler Engel 1967) has also led to the view that a consonant is coded as a set of features, each of which may be 'emphasized individually or connectedly, and induce the total or partial oblivion of the others'.

A few examples of P's forms in relation to the adult models are now examined to try and demonstrate some of the acoustic correlates of the 'strong' features which he produced in the early stages, and the 'weak' that he did not, which are described in articulatory terms in Paper 3. The description is given with the aid of spectrograms and mingograms of a selected number of examples of models spoken by P's mother.[6] The pitch traces and oscillograms, which were made simultaneously with the intensity and nasal traces, are given on the mingograms to help identify the different parts of the utterance. Mingograms in figs. 1-6, 11 and 12 were made with a pitchmeter and are used to demonstrate relative intensity and duration of different stretches within the utterance as well as the overall intensity pattern. Mingograms in figs. 7-10 were made with the aid of an Electro-Aerometer to provide in addition a nasal trace to demonstrate the extent of nasality. In these latter mingograms a laryngeal microphone was used so the intensity traces and oscillograms are not comparable with those in the rest of the mingograms, which were made with a 'mouth' microphone. It is interesting that the child seemed to respond to the intensity pattern as shown by the 'mouth' microphone, not the larynx. The spectrograms are used to show relative intensity and duration as well as voicing, the formants, the plosive bursts, and the stretches corresponding to continuant articulations. Unfortunately, the large number of harmonics makes identification of some second and third formants and formant transitions rather difficult.

While recording the examples, an attempt was made to keep the tempo, loudness and pitch the same so that the results would be comparable, and the aim was to get a natural effect of addressing a child. All the spectrograms, and the mingograms in figs. 7-10 were made on a rising-falling intonation, as is often used when pointing out and naming objects. Mingograms in figs. 3-6 were made with a high fall, which is another type of pointing-out intonation. Mingograms of 'dog' and 'doll' are also shown with a high rising pitch (figs. 1 and 2) to show that the intensity pattern of a word is not fixed (i.e., it varies with the different pitch pattern on which it is said), but it will be seen in the examples given that whether the pitch falls or rises, the greatest intensity is as-

---

[6] The spectrograms and mingograms were made with the assistance of Mr. A. W. Stone, technician in the Department of Phonetics and Linguistics at the School of Oriental and African Studies. The spectrograms (wideband), were made on a Kay Sono-Graph. The settings used were AGC 3, Mark Level 2.5 FL 1. Logarithmic and linear displays were made of each example. The mingograms were made with a Frøkjaer Jensen (Denmark) Pitchmeter and an Electro-Aerometer, both in conjunction with a mingograph. The settings were log. scale, 10 ms. Paper speed for the mingograms was 100 mm. per sec. The spectrograms and mingograms are shown in the reproductions on pp. 74-86.

sociated with the same stretch and the ending has the relatively lowest intensity. It is of course possible to say the examples with emphasis on the final consonant and thus to increase its intensity, but this would be a particular rather than general usage. Transcriptions are provided under the mingograms and spectrograms as an aid to identification and are not intended to mark an exact correspondence with the different articulations. The examples considered are:

	dog	doll	fish	vest	woman	honey	window	another
Mother's forms	[dɔg]	[dɔl]	[fɪʃ]	[vest]	[wumən]	[hʌnɪ]	[wɪndəu]	[ənʌðə]
Child's forms	[dɔ]	[dɔ]	[ɪʃ/uʃ]	[uʃ]	[ẽɦẽ]	[ahu:]	[ɲe:ɲe:]	[ɲaɲa]

'Dog' and 'doll': child's [dɔ] and [dɔ]. Figs. 3, 4, 13 and 14:
In the spectrograms, the plosive burst at the onset of 'dog' and 'doll' is followed immediately by voicing (seen on the voice bar) and a sudden increase in intensity, seen as deep blackness in the lower frequency range. In the mingograms, the increase in intensity is shown as a steep upward movement from the baseline, and this initial plosion was produced by the child. The plosive burst at the end of 'dog' has a very low intensity release (see figs. 3, 13) which is of short duration and there is no voicing, and this is not produced. Similarly, the low intensity, relatively short duration lateral continuant at the ending of 'doll' is not produced (see figs. 4, 14). In both examples the voice bar extends over the stretch associated with the vocalic articulation and has high intensity and long duration, as also has the first formant (which is said to reflect the vowel grade), and the child produced the voicing and the vowel grade, viz., open. In these monosyllabic examples the child also produced the syllable features of backness and rounding which are associated with the lower intensity F2 and F3. The place of articulation of the plosive, viz., alveolar, is also produced, place being generally associated with second formant transitions. However, as mentioned above, it is difficult to identify transitions in these spectrograms and it is possible that there are also other cues for place that the child used. Because the features that the child apparently perceived as functional were the same for both words, he produced homonyms for them both, viz., [dɔ].

'Fish' and 'vest': child's [ɪʃ/uʃ] and [uʃ]. Figs. 5, 6, 15, 16:
In the above two examples, the stretch at the onset is associated with relatively low intensity noise of relatively short duration, and is not produced by the child, but the high frequency aperiodic noise of the ending has relatively greater intensity and longer duration and is produced in the form of sibilance. The plosive burst which follows the sibilant in 'vest' is of short duration and low intensity, as in the case of the final plosive of 'dog' above, and is not produced. The F1 of both examples has relatively high intensity and long duration, and the acoustic effect of a mid grade vowel is produced, i.e., there is a mid type vowel in P's [ɪʃ] and [uʃ]. The features of frontness and non-rounding (reflected in F2 and F3) are produced in one form of 'fish', viz., [ɪʃ], but not in the other, viz., [uʃ], nor in 'vest', which is also [uʃ], the last two forms having backness and rounding. P may have recognized the feature of labiality at the onset of 'fish' and 'vest' and possibly at the

ending of 'fish', and produced it as a feature of the whole word (cf. the parallel production of nasality as a feature of the whole word in his form of 'woman' below). Voicing is produced for the stretch where the voice bar shows high intensity and long duration, viz., in the vocalic stretches.

'Woman' and 'honey': child's [ẽɦẽ] and [ahu:]. Figs. 7, 8, 17, 18:
In the spectrogram of 'woman' there is relatively low intensity and short duration in the stretch associated with the frictionless continuant onset, the medial bilabial closure and the final alveolar closure (fig. 17), and these were not produced by P. Nasality extends over nearly the whole of the word (fig. 7) and is produced as such by the child, viz., [ẽɦẽ]. The voice bar and F1 in both the stretches associated with the vocalic elements have high intensity and the first stretch has relatively long duration, and the child produced the mid grade of the vowels but not the features of backness and rounding of the first syllable, which are generally associated with F2 and F3 and which have relatively less intensity than F1. It is interesting to compare 'honey', for which the child had [ahu:]. Here again the medial closure is of relatively short duration and is not produced, but in this case there is little nasality in the whole word (cf. fig. 8) and the child has no nasality in his form. The relatively low intensity stretch at the onset of 'honey' is not produced either although it is of relatively long duration (fig. 18). The F1s relating to the vocalic stretches have relatively long duration, and high intensity for at least some part of the stretch and the vowel grade of both syllables was produced, viz., more open in the first syllable and more close in the second. The syllable features (associated with F2 and F3) of the first syllable are produced but not those of the second syllable.

'Window' and 'another': child's [ɲe:ɲe:] and [ɲaɲa]. Figs. 9, 10, 19, 20:
In contrast with 'woman' and 'honey', the stretch associated with the nasal closure in 'window' has long duration and there is high intensity along the voice bar (fig. 19). The nasality can be seen clearly on the mingogram (fig. 9), and the nasal closure was produced in the child's [ɲe:ɲe:]. The stretch associated with the frictionless continuant at the onset is of relatively short duration (cf. 'woman' above) and is not produced. The closure of the plosive seems to be of very short duration (figs. 19 and 9) and is not produced. The stretch associated with the vocalic element of the first syllable, although of relatively short duration, has a high intensity F1 and the vowel grade is produced fairly accurately as a type of mid. The syllable features of frontness and non-rounding are also produced. In the second syllable the first formant has the greatest intensity and a mid grade vowel is produced; the second and third formants are of lower intensity and the syllable features of central to back and rounded are not produced. In 'another' the place of closure of the nasal again has relatively long duration and is produced, as also are the vowel grades. The stretch related to the first syllable has relatively short duration and low intensity (figs. 20 and 10) and is not produced, P having a disyllabic form in response. The stretch associated with the medial fricative is of very low intensity and of relatively short duration with no voice, and is not produced. It may be noted that unstressed syllables appear to have a generally lower intensity than the stressed.

From the evidence given above, it seems that at this early stage in the acquisition of phonology, viz., around 1;5-1;7, relatively high intensity and relatively long duration were important cues for P, and features associated with them were produced; voicing too seemed to play an important part, whereas features associated with relatively low intensity and short duration (and sometimes voicelessness) were generally not produced. It is interesting to note here that Reddy, in his work on the computer recognition of connected speech, came to the conclusion that duration and intensity are at least as important as any spectrum dependent parameters and that more attention should be paid to them in research (Reddy 1967). From the writer's study of hearing errors (Waterson 1971a), it seems that relative intensity and duration are also important for adults who were found to use basically the same cues as those described above for the child but in addition took certain less salient ones into account, such as the low intensity aperiodic noise of friction, for instance, in the confusion of 'knife' and 'mouth' in the utterance 'I just rinsed my knife', which was interpreted as 'I just rinsed my mouth'. Words and utterances that were confused were in general found to have the same intensity pattern (see figs. 11 and 12) and the same 'schema'. The schema for the parts confused, viz., 'knife' [naɪf] and 'mouth [mauθ] may be described as follows: nasal onset, N; vowel grade, open (long), $\tilde{a}$, and friction at ending, F, i.e., N$\tilde{a}$F, with syllable features at onset being front and non-breathy, i.e., ^{y}$_{-}$NVF, and with a breathy ending, NVF^{h}. It seems that what happened was that the labial place of the ending of [naɪf], viz., NVF$_{p}$, was not recognized as such and the labiality was interpreted instead as a syllable feature, viz., NVF^{w}, the syllable feature of frontness at the ending being missed. This schema, viz., ^{y}$_{-}$N$\tilde{a}$F^{wh}, formed a kind of 'skeleton' for which the 'flesh' was supplied from the adult's knowledge of his language and the constraints of the context in which the utterance was made. This resulted in the interpretation as 'mouth' [mauθ] ^{y}$_{-}$N$_{p}$$\tilde{a}F_{t}$^{wh} instead of 'knife' [naɪf] ^{y}$_{-}$N$_{t}$$\tilde{a}F_{p}$^{yh}.[7] Whereas the adult takes the weak friction into account in his perception of what is said because he knows that such friction is functional, the child in the early stages does not, but with the passage of time and greater experience of language, he learns to do so. It thus seems that it is the whole pattern with the sequence of relatively greater and lesser intensity and duration that is relevant, but that it is the features associated with high intensity and long duration which make the schema that the child perceives and recognizes in the early stages of learning—i.e., the 'strong' features stand out from the whole utterance and hence his seeing a sameness in several words and producing the same kind of pattern for them, which often results in homonyms. This may be considered an example of 'syncretistic' perception, which Piaget has shown to be typical of young children (Piaget 1959: 131-4).

It is plain that what is suggested above is an oversimplification of the cues used by the child, and it is not claimed that they are the only ones. Some of the cues have had to be inferred (e.g., those for the place at the onset of 'dog' and 'doll' which the child produced correctly),

[7] For further discussion and examples see Waterson (1971a).

and are not evident in the form of second formant transitions in the spectrograms, and it is likely that other cues are involved. It is obvious that a great deal more instrumental work needs to be done but it is hoped that this attempt, which is only a beginning, will encourage others to do more on the acoustic side of the acquisition of phonology. Here mention must be made to the work of Olmsted who postulated that the 'most discriminable phones' are learned first, and tested children in relation to nasality, voicing, friction and place. He found, as expected from the findings of Miller and Nicely (1955), that voicing and nasality contribute more to discriminability than friction and place (Olmsted 1971: 242).

It has been suggested that in the early stages a child responds more to the F1s and F1 transitions than to the second and third. An examination of logarithmic scale spectrograms suggests further grounds why this should be so. Spectrograms of speech are usually displayed on a linear scale, as in figs. 13-20, but the ear is said to hear in terms of a logarithmic scale, and a logarithmic scale spectrogram shows that the first formants and transitions occupy a relatively large part of the frequency range, as in figs. 21-8. Although one cannot claim a direct correspondence between a logarithmic scale spectrogram and what the ear hears, it is nevertheless more likely that the logarithmic scale display gives a truer picture than a linear one, and if this is so, this provides another reason why F1s and transitions are responded to and therefore probably more easily perceived by the child and indeed by adults. It is interesting that Labov (1972), when considering the merger of certain diphthongs in an English dialect, found that 'speakers are quite sensitive to first formant position (roughly, vowel height) but not at all sensitive to second formant position (fronting and backing)'.

The study of what parts of the adult model the child produces, both in articulatory terms (as in Paper 3 and Waterson 1970) and in acoustic terms (as outlined in this paper), provides strong evidence that the forms the child acquires in the very early stages result from his perception of mainly the acoustically and auditorily most salient features of the model, and it is thus possible to predict which part of the model he is most likely to reproduce in the creation of his own forms. This has been demonstrated in Waterson (1971b).

One of the major problems in the study of the acquisition of phonology is the question of how far the child is constrained by limitations in perception and how far by production. The child P, in the early stages of his production of monosyllables, often got the manner of articulation (e.g., plosive or nasal) correct, but harmonized place, as in the case of [gʌk] and [beɪp] and the other examples given on p. 56. This resulted in production (and of course planning) being simple as fewer operations are required where there are fewer contrasts. One cannot know what a child perceives, and one cannot ask him, but it is possible to draw conclusions from the linguistic behaviour which results from his perception. One cannot tell whether P perceived the place differences in, for example, 'plate' [pleɪt] (i.e., bilabial onset versus alveolar ending), but produced [beɪp] (i.e., bilabial onset and ending), because it was easier, or whether he did not notice the difference; but as it has been found that the adult makes errors more often of place than manner, and this has been shown experimentally (e.g., Miller and Nicely 1955; Gray 1970), as well as under natural conditions (e.g., Waterson 1971a), it seems probable that a child does not pay attention to place at every point in the utterance, and this is what one would expect, as he seems quite unable to cope with everything at the same time at any level in the early stages. If indeed he cannot cope auditorily and articulatorily with complex changes within the stretch of speech under conditions of language use, it may well be that he would not pay much attention to them. If he did at first perceive a place difference but was not able to make it, he would then quite likely ignore it and no longer pay attention to it until such time as he was able to cope with more in his perception and production. It seems that the production of a place contrast was difficult for P as he had so many forms without one, so it may well have been both a perception and a production problem—an overlooking of something that could not be coped with, in the manner suggested by Vernon (cf. p. 54 above).

When a child says something, many operations must be involved. Various neural messages have presumably to be sent to enable him to get out of his memory store at the right moment what is appropriate for the situation and his needs, and to operate the articulatory organs with rapid changes in a very short space of time. These processes must in themselves be quite complex, and as the linguistic evidence is that a child cannot deal with too much complexity at any one time, it seems that his linguistic perception and production must be on a fairly simple level at the start.

It has been noted that a child is often able to produce a form closer to the model in direct imitation than in spontaneous speech. This was certainly true of P. The explanation for this may be that a child's spontaneous production is created from a remembered form of the model which has been constructed on the basis of his perception of its most salient features, and which has been categorized and stored in perhaps a mid or long term memory, but in the case of direct imitation, the model is before the child as he attempts to produce it and only needs to be held in the memory for a very short time and can presumably be retrieved more quickly, so in all likelihood he is able to cope with greater complexity in such a situation. In addition, in an imitation situation, the child is generally free to concentrate on perception and production without various pressures, such as having to make a selection from the longer term memory store of what is appropriate for the situation, or needing to express his wishes at the right moment.

The difficulties and limitations of production, and therefore of course of planning, also seem to be indicated by the evidence of the child's developing forms, where only a few features are seen to change at a time. This may also be taken as evidence for gradually increasing discrimination in perception. It has been observed that when a new feature is being acquired, some other part of the form is simplified articulatorily by, for instance, some features harmonizing instead of the child making use of recently acquired contrasting features. This has been illustrated in some detail in an account of the longitudinal development of P's forms for 'pudding' and 'fly' (Waterson 1970; also Paper 6). The same is seen in his acquisition of 'Patrick' [pætrɪk]; P started with a reduplicated form and progressed through various forms to [bætɪk] alternating with [pætɪt] at 2;1 and 2;2 (see appendix on p. 87). Thus when place of articulation in the *second* syllable contrasted, i.e., [tɪk] (alveolar versus velar), the syllable onset and ending harmonized, both being breathy but the *first* syllable had a lax, non-breathy onset, [bæ], which was the regular type of onset; but when place in the *second* syllable was not differentiated, viz., alveolar onset and ending, [tɪt], the onset of the *first* syllable, [pæ], harmonized with the breathy onset and ending of the *second*, [tɪt]—i.e., he used the new type of onset for the first syllable. There thus appeared to be a limit to the number of operations that could be carried out at any one time. The next form (at 2;3) was [pætɪk], combining breathy onsets and ending with a three-place contrast, viz., bilabial, alveolar and velar. So with experience, P was able to combine the different contrasts that he had apparently had to learn separately. At 2;4, when he began to attempt affrication at the onset of the second syllable (i.e., in the form [pætsɪt]), he again harmonized place at the onset and ending of the second syllable, making both alveolar instead of a final velar. It thus seems that it is not a matter of difficulty in the articulation of individual sounds but rather a case of difficulty in the planning and production of rapid changes of articulation in a short space of time, and of combining features in a specific way—i.e., a limitation on the complexity with which a child can cope in the planning and production of the whole utterance. If one measures progress by the number of changes that take place over time (cf. the dates of changes in the forms of 'Patrick' in the appendix on p. 87), it becomes plain that contrary to the popular belief that language acquisition is an astonishingly rapid process, it is remarkably slow.

The fact that the child acquired a contrast of different features at different times also suggests that he did not become aware of them all at the same time, and as he did not use recently acquired contrasts when trying a new one but used a combination of features for which the habits were well established, it seems that the same sort of learning is continued in the acquisition of new contrasts and combinations of features that Fry suggested to be the case with babbling as a preparation for language—viz., auditory feedback and kinaesthetic memory are used to establish articulatory habits (Fry 1966). A similar going back to simpler forms and limitations in complexity in relation to syntax have been shown by Slobin (1970: 183-4). This going back to what looks like an earlier form has been termed 'regression' in the literature instead of being seen for what it is—a necessary concomitant of progress. That the child responded mainly to the salient features of utterances and coped with only a few feature changes at a time may therefore be taken as a pointer to his limited capacity for perception, planning and production. This may help to explain the constraint on the length of utterance that a child can process. At the age of 1;4 to 1;6, P produced monosyllables and disyllables. The disyllables were very simple and were mostly completely or partially reduplicated. Apart from imitated forms, he did not produce a sequence of two highly differentiated syllables which would involve complex changes in articulation over a short stretch of time. Some experimental work on a sample of forms used to children has shown that given similar conditions, disyllables are not equal in length to two monosyllables but tend to be of the same length as one (Waterson 1970). There is therefore more to perceive and perform in a disyllable than in a monosyllable in the same length of time, so this will in part account for children's less accurate production of words of two or more syllables as compared with words of one.

All P's spontaneous forms were simple in structure. If, as has been suggested earlier, they were produced on the basis of a remembered form which he had constructed from his perception of the model, it seems that he was not able to perceive, store or retrieve anything complex; all the linguistic evidence points to the child only being able to cope with the simplest operations auditorily, neurally and cognitively, and this is just what one would expect to be the case with a very young child.

Homonyms are frequent in early child speech and present further convincing argument for the perception of the salient and overlooking of the less salient features because the child produces the same form for different words. These homonyms appear to result from the perception and recognition of the same set of salient features in the models—i.e., the child perceives the same schema based on the same acoustic cues in the words. This must mean that he is paying attention to the prominent features, the 'basic' features which the words have in common, but is overlooking the 'differential' features which differentiate the words (as explained in Paper 3) in a similar way, in fact, to what has been suggested for the perception of words for which P produced the same pattern but which are not homonyms (e.g., the pattern $(NV)^2$ to which belonged his [ɲe:ɲe:] 'window', [ɲaɲa] 'another' and [ɲi:ɲi] 'finger'). The fact that adults accept and appear to understand the child's forms must confirm to him that he has succeeded in producing the functional part of the models. As the child grows and develops and his experience increases, he begins to pay more attention to the less salient parts of utterances and his homonyms diverge and develop independently. Among those used by P at 1;6 were the forms [bæbu:] for 'birdie' and 'Patrick'. At this age, it is quite possible that he heard that the two words were not identical but he may have had difficulty in identifying what the difference was, and in all probability the difference was not significant for him at first; it was perhaps just part of the surrounding undifferentiated sounds which formed the background from which the acoustically prominent part stood out, but it is probable that at a later stage, the noise of the weak plosion at the end of 'Patrick' helped to differentiate the two words, and once he was able to identify what the difference was, he tried to produce it.[8] At the time when P had homonyms for 'birdie' and 'Patrick', the salient parts of the two utterances must have seemed the same to him, at least for a while, as he produced the same acoustic effect in response to them both, viz., [bæbu:]. He appeared to recognize the plosion at the onset of both syllables, PVPV, and the labiality of the first one, P_pVPV; the more open vowel grade, A, in the first syllable contrasting with the more close, I, of the second, i.e., PAPI. He was not so successful, however, with the syllable features. It will be noted that the similarity is not in the referents (i.e., the objects to which the names refer), but in the sound schemata of the words. This kind of homonymity is found synchronically, as in the examples just considered, and also longitudinally; for instance, from the examples in the appendix, p. 87, it will be seen that at 1;4-1;5, P had [bæbæ] for 'Patrick' and at 1;6 he had [bæbæ] for 'butter'. At 1;5,

---

8 Ingram (1971) has also taken the view that a child may be aware of the non-identity of words for which he uses homonyms and that what makes the difference is at first just 'noise' for him.

'birdie' was [bæbu:] at the time when 'Patrick' was [bæbæ] and 'bucket' was [bʌbu] and [bʌbu:]; at 1;6 [bæbu:] was used as one of the forms of 'Patrick', and for 'birdie' and 'bucket'. At this time too he acquired 'Bobby' and 'button', also as [bæbu:]. All these adult models can be described as having the same schema—viz., P_pAPI, plosive onset of both syllables, with labial place of the first, and a more open vowel grade of the first syllable followed by a more close grade in the second; the final nasal of 'button' and the final stop of 'bucket' are 'weak' and thus do not form part of the schema. It could be argued that P was aware of the [t] of 'bucket' right from the start and this is what helped him to distinguish it from 'birdie', for example, but it seems that the main reason for the non-ambiguity of homonyms for the child is the context because they were used in the presence of the referent. As he regularly did not produce sounds which are acoustically weak (cf. the initial fricative of 'fish', the final lateral continuant of 'doll', the final plosive of 'dog', etc., discussed earlier), the conclusion that he was not paying attention to them and was treating them as non-functional seems inescapable.

The presence of so many [bæbu:] homonyms may be accounted for by the fact that having got a pattern of reduplicated stop + vowel, with a more open vowel grade in the first syllable and a more close one in the second, when the child recognized the same schema in a new model, he had a ready response from his past experience and was therefore able to process it rapidly and did not need to give it detailed attention. This would be 'assimilation' in Piaget's terms, i.e., the incorporation of new objects and experiences into existing schemata (Piaget 1971: 63).

Another point of interest in the acquisition of phonology is the way in which a child's vocabulary expands and the phonological system grows and becomes more complex. At the very beginning, all the utterances the child hears are new and unfamiliar and therefore need a great deal of attention. At 1;5 and 1;6 P had very simple patterns, viz.:

PV	(PV)^2	NVP
NV	(NV)^2	NVN
KV	(KV)^2	
VP	VPV	PVP
V	(V)^2	
VN		PVN

There was a great deal of harmony and reduplication, and stops, nasals and labial continuants were the only consonantal articulations used.[9] This provides further evidence that in the very early stages the child's capacity for planning, production, storage, etc., is very limited. At 1;6-1;7 more patterns were added, viz.:

PVS	VNV	PVPVN
VS	VLV	

---

9 Note, however, that the continuants sometimes had a lax stop element preceding, as in one of the alternative versions of 'fly', viz., [bβæ], which varied with [wæ] and [βæ], but this was probably an articulatory 'accident'.

That is to say, with the passage of time and with experience, P's system was increased by the addition of liquids and sibilants, and he was able to produce non-reduplicated disyllabic patterns: there was thus an increase in complexity.

At the start, each word appeared to be learnt as an individual item and the first of any particular pattern seemed to be learnt on a phonetic basis, as described earlier—i.e., the child perceived the salient features of the model and created a form which went into his memory store. At first there were only one or two examples of a particular pattern and then there would be quite a sudden increase. In the case of P, the pattern PV was one of the earliest to increase, and examples are shown in the appendix (p. 87). At 1;2 P had [dɔ] for 'dog' and [du:] for 'cockadoodle*doo*. Then at some time during 1;4 he acquired another PV pattern, viz., [du:] for 'two'. He then appeared to make the discovery that there was more than one word having this PV pattern and hence must have had the expectation that more would follow, because eleven more words of this pattern were acquired in quick succession, i.e., within the 18 days that followed. Thus, when the PV patterns turned up, P appeared to recognize the schema (as in the case of the [bæbu:] homonyms), and this made processing quicker because part of the utterance was familiar. In the majority of cases, the type of onset in the model was lax and non-breathy, i.e., h̲PV, and this was generalized by P to all the PV patterns. He first acquired a two-term contrast, viz., labial versus apical, P_pV and P_tV, and later added the dorsal, i.e., P_kV. There was a two-term contrast in the grade of vowel in the models, viz., open α, and close ι, and this he produced accurately. The syllable features of backness, frontness, rounding and non-rounding were produced less accurately. There is evidence of what looks like a second discovery, that of $(PV)^2$ at around 1;4 (see appendix, p. 87), which is followed by six more $(PV)^2$ patterns in 12 days, and then by the discovery of PVP around 1;5, which is followed by other examples of the same kind. Menn (1971: 226) also has an example of a discovery in her child's system which enabled him to acquire words more rapidly—viz., that disyllabic words could be broken down into monosyllable + ər(z), which was followed by a rapid increase in the acquisition of words ending in -er(s).

It is possible that rather than being a fresh discovery in the case of $(PV)^2$, P was generalizing his first—viz., that there is more than one exemplar of a particular pattern. A child who generalized in this way would be a fast learner; others may have to make the discovery for two or three patterns before generalizing to the rest, and some may not generalize across patterns at all—these would be slower learners.

There is an interesting example of a form that was first learnt as an individual item and then adapted to fit a specific pattern. This was P's form for 'stick'. His first form, at 1;4.27, was [dɪk], which changed to [gʌk] after he had acquired several [gʌk] forms, as shown overleaf. It thus seems that the child's [dɪk] was re-categorized to fit the more general $əP_kVP_k$ pattern. This suggests that in the early stages, what the child first constructs has to fit into a limited number of patterns in order to avoid complexity and consequent overloading in the memory store, and a re-categorizing of this nature results in fewer patterns and hence makes storage and other operations simpler.[10] P's [gʌk] homonyms

---

10 This may explain the sequence NV rather than VN in P's reduplicated nasal

		Child's form		Adult's form	
1;4.27	stick	[dɪk]	$^{y}PV_tVP_k$	[stɪk]	$^{y}\hat{SP}_tVP_k$
1;5	truck	[gʌk]	$^{ə}P_kVP$	[tʳʌk]	$^{ə}\hat{PL}_tVP_k$
	jug	[gʌk]	$^{ə}P_kVP$	[dʒʌg]	$^{ə}\hat{PS}VP_k$
1;5.1	cake	[gʌk]	$^{ə}P_kVP$	[keɪk]	$^{y}P_kVP_k$
1;5.2	stick	[gʌk]	$^{ə}P_kVP$	[stɪk]	$^{y}\hat{SP}_tVP_k$
1;5.14	stick	[gɪk]	$^{y}P_kVP$	[stɪk]	$^{y}\hat{SP}_tVP_k$
	clock	[gɔk]	$^{w}P_kVP$	[klɔk]	$^{w}\hat{PL}_kVP_k$
1;5.19	cake	[gek]	$^{y}P_kVP$	[keik]	$^{y}P_kVP_k$

diverged fairly quickly (i.e., as seen above); at 1;5.14 'stick' was [gɪk], and he used [gɔk] for 'clock' the same day, and at 1;5.19 his 'cake' was [gek].

As a child grows and his experience widens, he is able to cope with more. In this connection one may quote Slobin, who said that advances in language development

> seem to be tied to such variables as increasing ability to perform a number of operations in a short time, increasing short term memory span, and increasing cognition of the categories and processes of human experience. (Slobin 1970: 184)

Thus, in the course of time, the child acquires more patterns and the 'filter' by which he processes speech signals grows. What he now perceives is either one of the known patterns or an unknown one; if it is known, it can be categorized quickly; if not, it has to have more attention.

It has been shown how the child starts off with a vocabulary of limited patterns which are related to models. At some point after he starts making his first efforts, the adults around him recognize that he is using his forms meaningfully; they show their pleasure and act in a way that tells him that they understand what he is saying, and when he asks for [bu], he gets a book. But although the adults understand him, and his forms function adequately enough for his needs, instead of sticking to his infantile forms, he keeps adjusting them closer to the models. Why should he do this? In these very early days, a child does not often need to communicate with anyone outside the family circle where he might not be understood, so this cannot be the incentive to change, although it may well play a part in the later stages. There does not seem to be any convincing evidence that the encouragement he gets from his parents is enough to make him put extra effort into getting a better match. The teaching of parents does not seem to help much either: both P's parents tried to teach him to say 'please' and 'thank you' and it took several months before he learnt to say them in the adult way. From 1;6 onwards he was regularly taught to use the word 'please' but it was two months before he managed to say [pliːz]; i.e., at 1;6: [piːs],

---

patterns referred to on p. 65. (cf. the discussion of a similar categorizing in the case of Leopold's child in Paper 3).

1;7: [piːʃ/piːs/biːs/piːz/pliːs], 1;8: [piːs/pliːs/pliːz]), and another 3 months before he used it consistently (i.e., at 1;9: [pliːz/pliːs], 1;10: [pliːs], 1;11 onwards: [pliːz]). Similarly, with 'thank you' (i.e., at 1;6: [ækə], 1;7: [aːkuː/aːkju/ækju/ˀæŋku], 1;9: [ˀæŋkju]), and at 2;0 he had only got to [fæŋkju]. Menn shows how difficult it was to change her son's 'mispronunciation' of 'tub', for which he used the harmonized form [bʌb] (Menn 1971). Studies in the acquisition of syntax have also shown that a child cannot be taught something for which he is not ready (e.g., Braine 1971).

If one takes experience and maturation into account, it seems reasonable to expect that the child's capacity to perceive more from the acoustic signal will increase, as well as his ability to cope with greater complexity in planning and production, storage and retrieval. As he begins to discriminate more, so he must perceive the adult model differently from the way in which he first perceived it—i.e., he takes more note of the less salient features. As mentioned earlier, the fact that a child's forms develop over a period of time and change mostly by a few features at a time can be taken as evidence not only for increasing ability for production but also for increasing discrimination in perception. The stimulus (i.e., the acoustic signal) remains the same but the child's response changes. Something must trigger off these changes. It is unlikely to be only an increased ability for production because the child in any case does not always produce sounds that he is articulatorily capable of producing, as for instance, in the case of the apical nasal in P's learning. As explained earlier, he produced one in contexts where it was acoustically prominent in the model, e.g., in 'another' [əˈnʌðə] (his [ɲaɲa]), but not in 'honey' [ˈhʌnɪ], where it is in an unstressed syllable and is weak, and for which he had [ahuː]. But as time went on, he began to produce the weak apical nasals, and 'honey' became [ʌnɪ]. If it is true that a child's linguistic perception improves with time and experience, one may still ask why he should bother to change his forms when they are already efficient from the functional point of view. Why, after kinaesthetic habits have become established to produce a particular acoustic effect, should he take the trouble to change? There is not enough evidence to prove that the reasons usually advanced (such as being rewarded by parents' pleasure, or his own delight at sounding more like mother, or even correction by parents) are strong enough to spur a child to such great effort. The answer may well be that *he does this because he cannot help it*. Evidence has been given in the course of this paper that a child 'latches on' to the most salient features of the model and it has been suggested that he constructs a form on the basis of what he perceives, and this goes into his memory store. Thus when he needs to use a word, he presumably tries to reproduce what he remembers of his construction of the model—i.e., he has to match the form in his memory store. This production on the basis of a speaker's constructed form in the memory can be illustrated from the regular mispronunciations of some words by adults; for instance, one speaker used the form [stræˈdʒetɪk] for 'strategic' [stræˈtiːdʒɪk]. This possibly resulted from an error in visual perception in the first place—i.e., the word was misread as 'strategetic'. The adult remembered the word as [stræˈdʒetɪk] and kept producing it on the basis of this remembered form until his attention was drawn to the error. The child probably produces either (1) the same as he perceives (i.e., when the memory of his constructed form can be produced in an articulatorily simple way that is within his capacity) or (2) both more and less than he perceives (i.e., when he is constrained by what he can handle in his production). Thus his production may include features which he did not perceive in the model but which he uses because he is only able to produce what is non-complex, as in harmonic and reduplicated forms; and he may produce less than he perceives if the acoustic effect cannot be produced simply; and he continues to produce less until such time as experience enables him to cope with more complex articulatory operations.

A child must constantly be making (unconscious) judgments as to how far he is matching what is in his memory store and building up the kinaesthetic habits to produce the desired acoustic effect at will, and auditory feedback tells him how far he has succeeded (cf. Fry 1966). As long as the child perceives the model the same as before, his perception matches what is in his memory and so the stored form is rehearsed, and he continues to produce his form from the same memory, so it remains unchanged. As with maturation and experience he begins to discriminate more, and as kinaesthetic habits for his current form become established, he is able to give more attention to the less salient features that were previously overlooked; he thus perceives more in the model and perceives it differently. Every time he now hears the model, it no longer matches the stored form so that this form is no longer rehearsed. He constructs a new form, closer to the model which is based on his improved discriminatory powers, and it is on the basis of this new stored memory that he now creates his forms, which are therefore more complex than before, and this in turn brings about changes in his phonological system. One may thus say that new responses bring about changes in organization, which is what Piaget has termed 'accommodation' (Piaget 1971: 63). Sometimes a child uses old and new forms side by side for a time (e.g., P's [bætɪk] and [pætɪt] at 2;1 and 2;2). This seemed to happen when he was in process of learning a new combination of features and before the old form had faded from the memory and the new one had become established. With continuing maturation and experience, a child's discrimination keeps improving and his forms keep changing until the forms in the memory store match the models and no further differences are perceived, and he produces acoustic effects which match the forms in his memory store. The forms then get stabilized and the phonological system matches that of the adult. The child thus gradually becomes more proficient in the interpretation of the speech signal and gets less heavily dependent on context than he was at the start. The creative view of how a child acquires the phonological system outlined above has much in common with Neisser's account of visual and auditory cognition as constructive processes (Neisser 1967).

As an example of how a child's form changes in relation to his changing perception of the model, one may consider P's acquisition of 'Patrick' (see appendix on p. 87). He started using [pæpæ] and [bæbæ] at 1;4 and progressed through various forms to [bʌbuː] at 1;6-1;7. When he began to use [bʌtɪk] and [pʌtɪk] at 1;8 at the same time as his other forms were beginning to get closer to the models (cf. some examples in the appendix on p. 87), his parents were sorry to see the baby form [bʌbuː] go out of use as they thought it rather appealing, so they started calling the child [bʌbuː] instead of 'Patrick' [pætrɪk]. The model for the child was thus changed and his [bʌbuː] form now matched the model whereas [bʌtɪk] and [pʌtɪk] were further from it. As may be seen from the records, P went back to using [bʌbu:] and continued to use it for as long as his parents kept calling him [bʌbu:], which was for 3 months, up to the age of two.[11] By this age P was speaking very clearly and using quite complex sentences (e.g., [mʌmɪ du: velɪ bɪg kju: laɪk ʔæt] 'Mummy do a very big Q like that'; [bʌbu: ɔnt si: bɔksɪŋ] 'Patrick wants to see the boxing', and [wɔt ə naɪs wumən; ʃəu ɪt tə dædɪ] 'What a nice woman; show it to Daddy' (about a picture of a woman)). His parents decided that the use of [bʌbu:] for his name was now quite out of place and started to call him 'Patrick' again. After approximately four weeks, his form began to change. He may have noticed a difference immediately but may not have been able to identify it sufficiently to be able to construct a form incorporating the new features until some time had elapsed and he had heard the new model several times. He already had the production ability, as his other forms were well developed, so it was more likely to be a perception rather than a production problem, especially bearing in mind that he had got as far as [bʌtɪk] and [pʌtɪk] at 1;8. Vernon has said that visual perception is gradual and needs a series of viewings (1971: 32), and the same may well be true of auditory perception—i.e., speech perception needs a series of 'hearings'.

In the case of P, as also with other children (e.g., Burling 1959), newly acquired words were generally found to be more complex in form and a closer match to the model than those acquired earlier. This may be taken as additional evidence for an increasing ability to cope with greater complexity in both perception and production in the course of time. As the child's understanding of the world around him widens, his need for new terms increases. This means that he has to pay attention to new words a great deal of the time. The new words are acquired on the basis of his improved discriminatory powers and his greater experience in production, and this would explain why they are usually closer in form to the model than earlier words, which have to be re-perceived before they change. As the child gets a wider vocabulary, the intervals between each hearing of a word must lengthen, so some time may elapse before the child finds a mismatch between the model and the older stored form, and it seems (bearing in mind the development of [bʌbu:] considered above) that time is needed for the child to sort out what the differences are before he is able to create a new version of the form in the light of re-perception. This would account for the lagging of some earlier forms behind the new. A child's system thus constantly changes and develops, but an examination of P's data shows that not everything changes at the same time. A large number of forms seem to 'consolidate' (i.e., to be used unchanged over a period), so there is always some stability as well as change; some forms change, others stay unchanged, and those that were unchanged, change, and so on. It is possible that this is so because the child is not able to pay attention to everything at once and because he has to hear a model several times to discriminate more of the less salient features before he can attempt to produce the appropriate acoustic effect. A child would in any case probably not be able to operate his language if all his forms were in a state of flux at

---

11 cf. a parallel case in the use of 'bap' for 'lamb' by Velten's daughter at 1;4.
Bap became the family name for 'lamb' and the child continued to use it until 2;3 (Velten 1943).

the same time.

The views that have been expressed in the course of this paper are put forward for discussion and criticism in the hope that a useful basis for future research may emerge and it is in the same spirit that a tentative hypothesis is now proposed of how a child acquires the phonological system of his mother tongue. The points are numbered for convenience of reference and do not necessarily represent the sequence in which the processes take place. They are *not* intended to represent stages.

1) The child begins to learn through his interaction with his environment. He associates the acoustically most salient parts of the utterance with an object, state or action that is meaningful for him after hearing the same acoustic signal several times in a repetitive context. Experience thus plays a vital role. He discovers that language has a useful function, and therefore pays attention to it.

2) He constructs a form based on his perception of the acoustically salient parts of the utterance which are the functional parts for him, and it goes into his memory store. Having learnt the relationship between various articulatory movements and the acoustic effect during the babbling period, he is able, within limits, to produce what he aims at with the help of auditory feedback, so when the need arises, he produces his own simple form on the basis of the stored form. This may be the same as what he perceives or it may be different, depending on how far he is able to achieve the desired acoustic effects. Articulatory harmony lightens the load on planning and production.

3) At first, every word is new and unfamiliar and requires a good deal of attention, so progress is slow. He learns each word as a separate item and gradually acquires several simple forms of different patterns in the manner indicated in (1) and (2).

4) At the start, every time a particular word he knows is uttered, he pays most attention to and recognizes the schema based on the salient features, and therefore what he perceives matches what is in his memory store, and there is thus constant rehearsal.

5) At some point he recognizes the same schema (based on the same set of salient features) in a new utterance. He already has a response established for that schema in the shape of his own simple related pattern, so does not need to give much attention to it and is thus able to acquire such new words quickly and easily. His vocabulary increases a little faster.

6) Sooner or later he makes the discovery that there is more than one of some or each of the different schemata that he knows. He therefore has an expectancy that he may meet more of them and this furnishes a kind of grid by which to filter the speech signal. He can expect either one of the familiar, known, schemata or an unknown one. The known are easily processed but the new are given more careful attention. Perception, recognition, planning, production, storage and retrieval thus become more efficient and the rate of acquisition increases sharply.

7) With maturation and experience and greater understanding of the world about him, the child is able to cope with greater complexity and can discriminate more as well as developing greater skill in planning, production, etc. He is able to pay more attention to the less salient features of the models that he was not able to deal with before. He therefore perceives schemata which are different from the ones perceived

previously and hence constructs new forms, more differentiated and complex, and closer to the adult models, which go into his memory. There is thus no more rehearsal of the earlier forms, which in time fade from the memory, and the child produces more differentiated forms on the basis of the new ones now in the memory store.
8) Old and new forms may be stored in the memory at the same time for a period, and the child may therefore use more than one form for the one word, one based on the old form and the other on the new, until the new one gets firmly entrenched and the old one fades.
9) Greater discrimination and experience thus cause the child to produce new forms closer and closer to the adult model until what is perceived matches what is in the memory store and increasing discrimination does not reveal anything new. When this stage is reached, the phonological system becomes stable.

The kinds of processes hypothesized here for the acquisition of the phonological system have much in common with those described by some psychologists for the development of cognition: e.g., Piaget's 'assimilation' and 'accommodation' and the syncretic, non-analytic perception of children; Neisser's constructive processes in visual and auditory cognition, and Vernon's figure from ground differentiation. The model proposed also has something in common with the 'Discovery-Procedures' model of Braine which he proposed for the acquisition of grammar (Braine 1971). The evidence presented in this paper thus suggests that the same processes are used for the learning of phonology as for cognitive development, so the question of an innate phonological system need not arise.

The above hypothesis requires only such processes as are well within the capacity of a very young child. No complexity is demanded and only a short memory span is needed. The child has to have the ability to make some sense of his environment and to recognize simple auditory patterns; he has to make the discovery that language is meaningful; he has to be spoken to repetitively and frequently so that he can relate what he hears to something in his environment, and he has to have some ability to produce acoustic effects fairly similar to what he hears. He must also have a wish to communicate. None of the above demands much intelligence. In fact, viewed in this way, language learning is so simple that a child can do it!

Figures 1, 2, 3

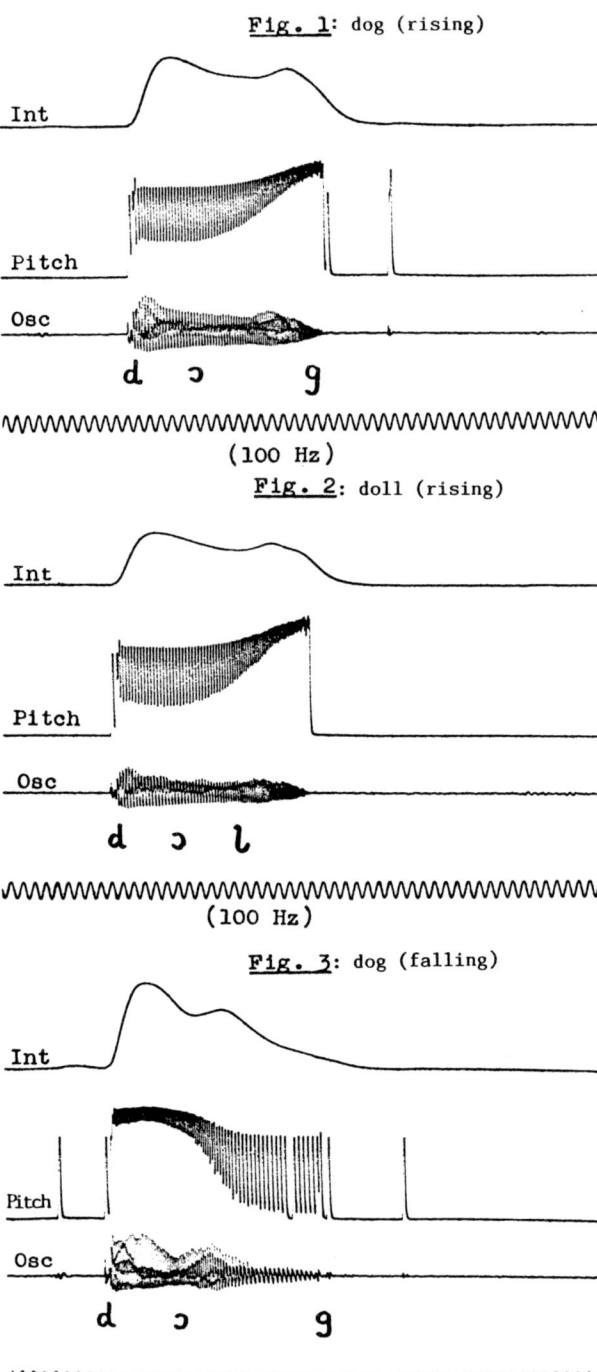

Perception and production in the acquisition of phonology 75

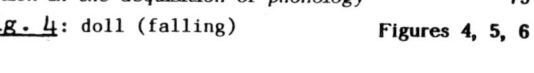

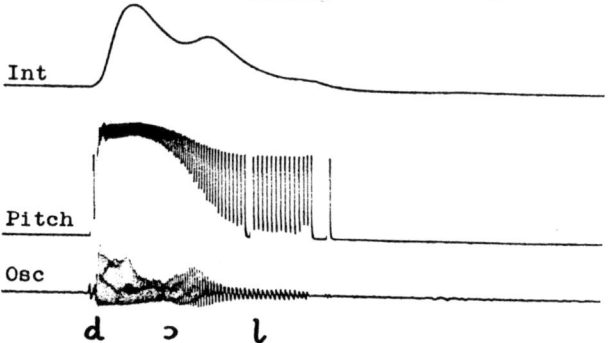

Fig. 4: doll (falling)

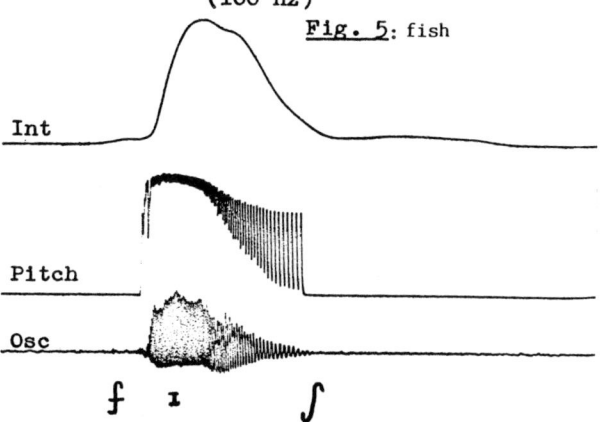

Fig. 5: fish

Fig. 6: vest

76
Figures 7, 8

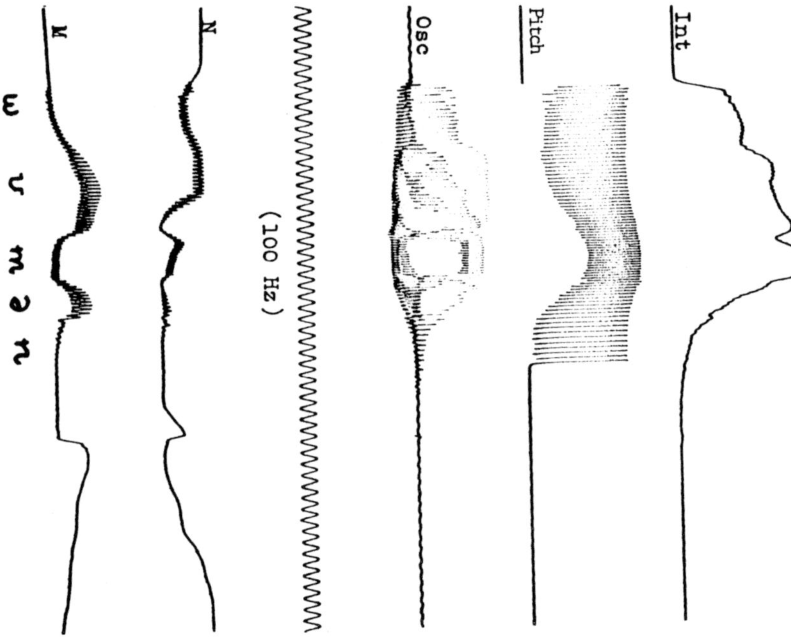

Fig. 7: woman

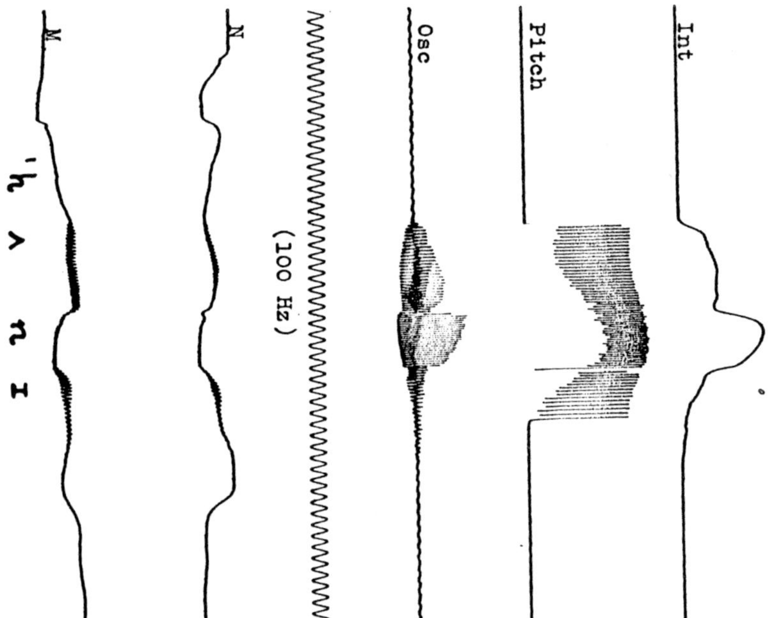

Fig. 8: honey

Perception and production in the acquisition of phonology

Figures 9, 10

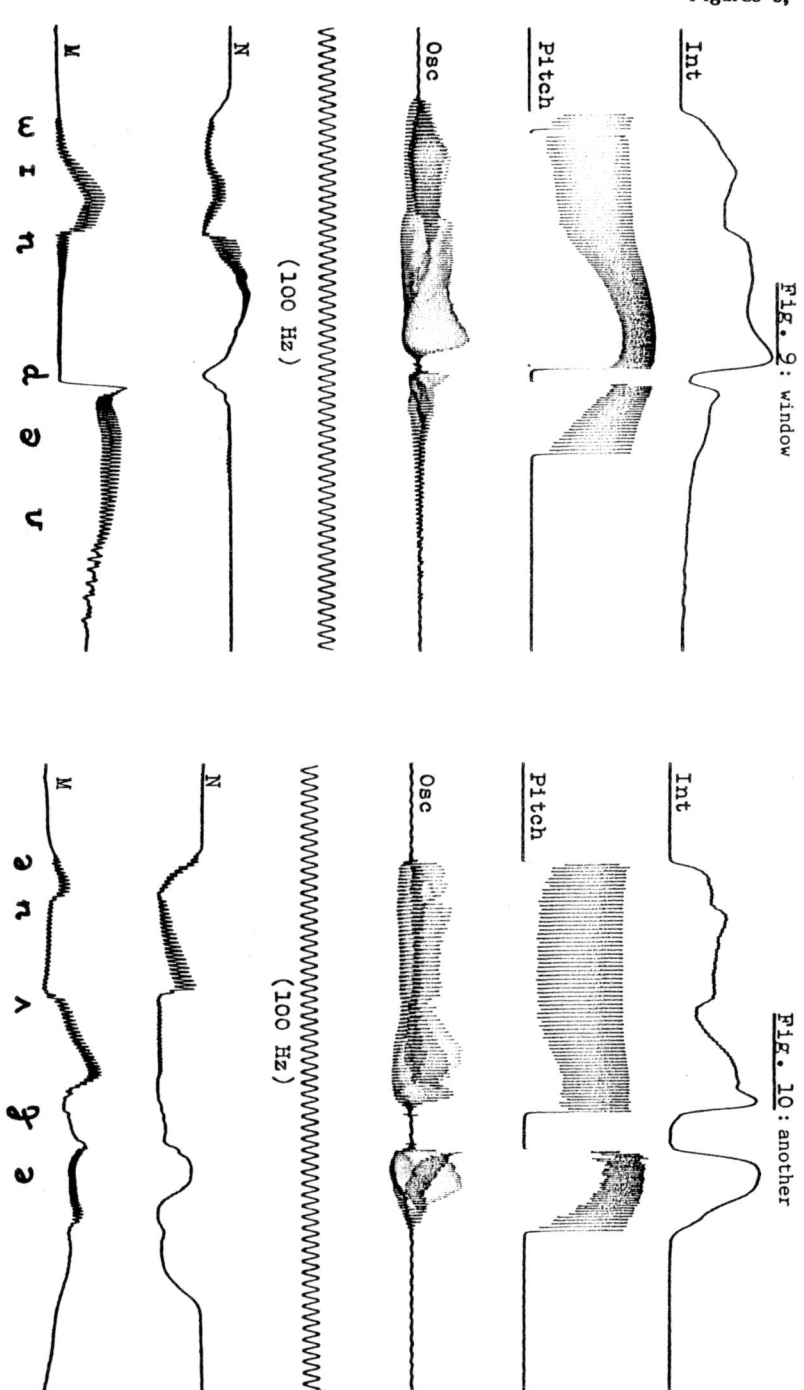

Fig. 9: window

Fig. 10: another

Figures 11, 12

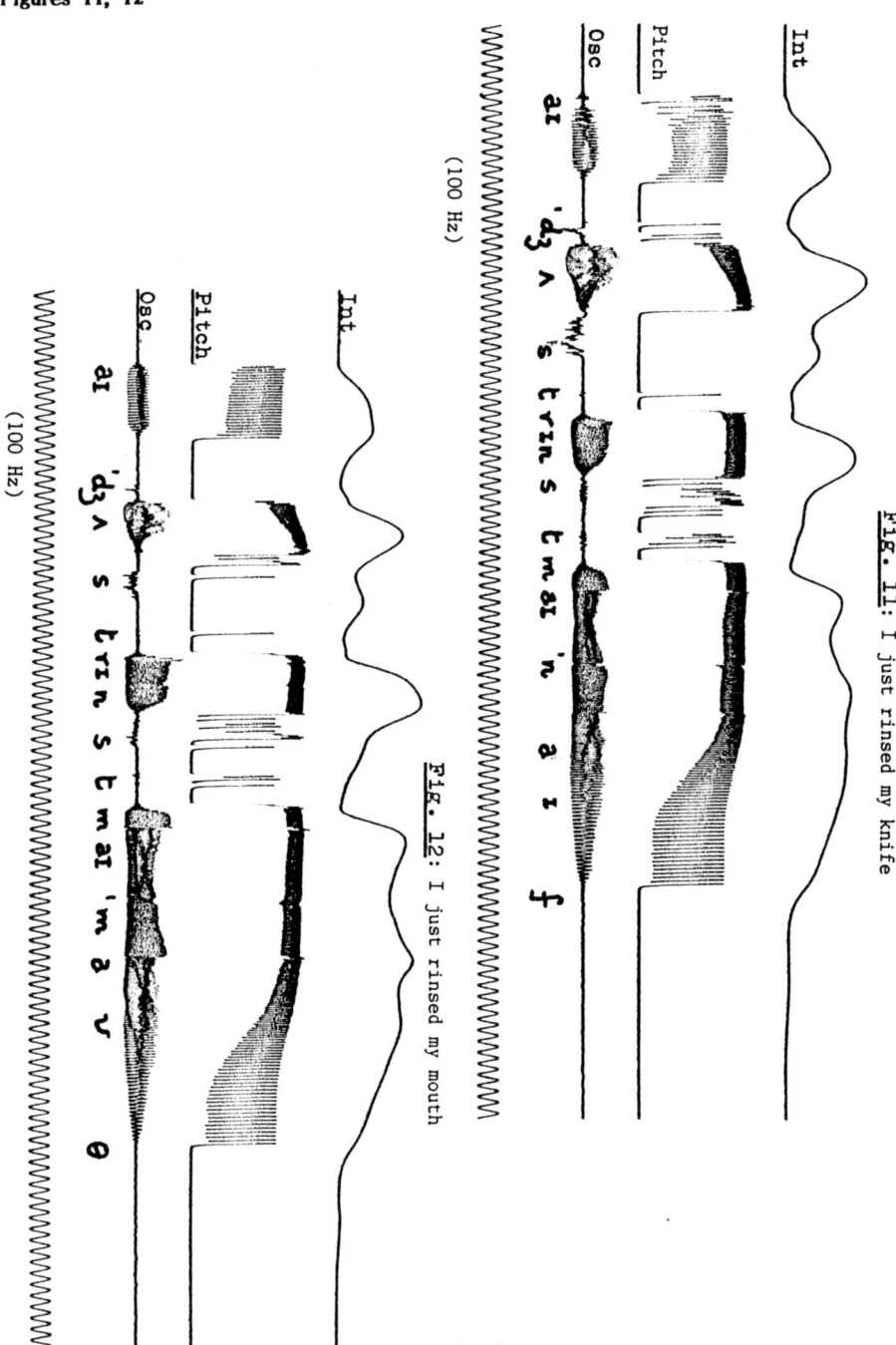

Fig. 11: I just rinsed my knife

Fig. 12: I just rinsed my mouth

Figures 13, 14

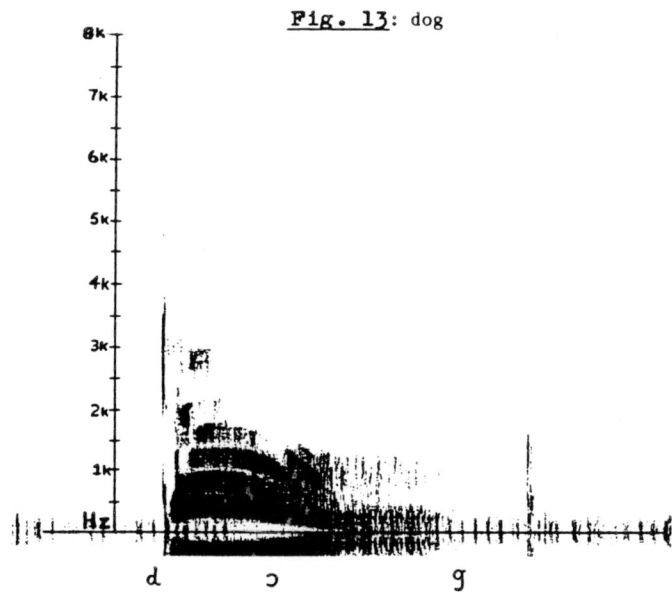

Fig. 13: dog

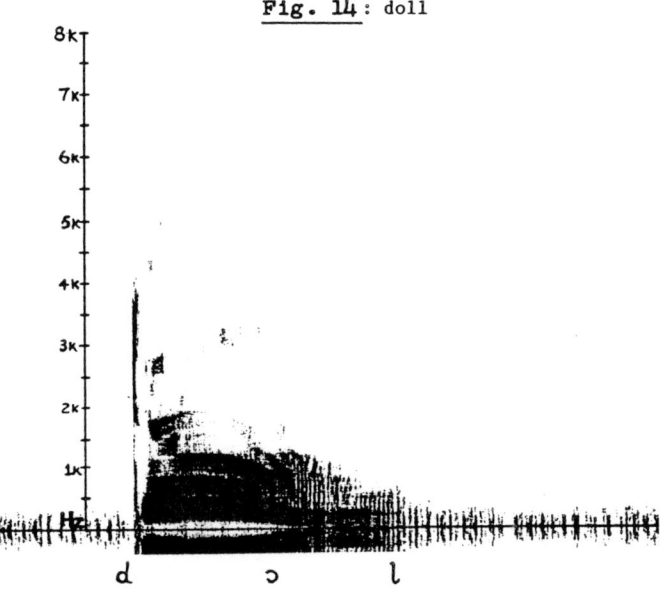

Fig. 14: doll

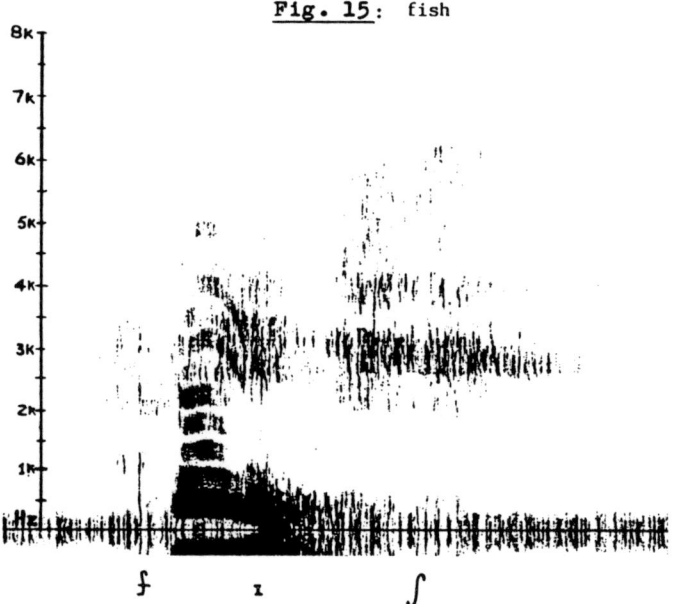

Fig. 15: fish

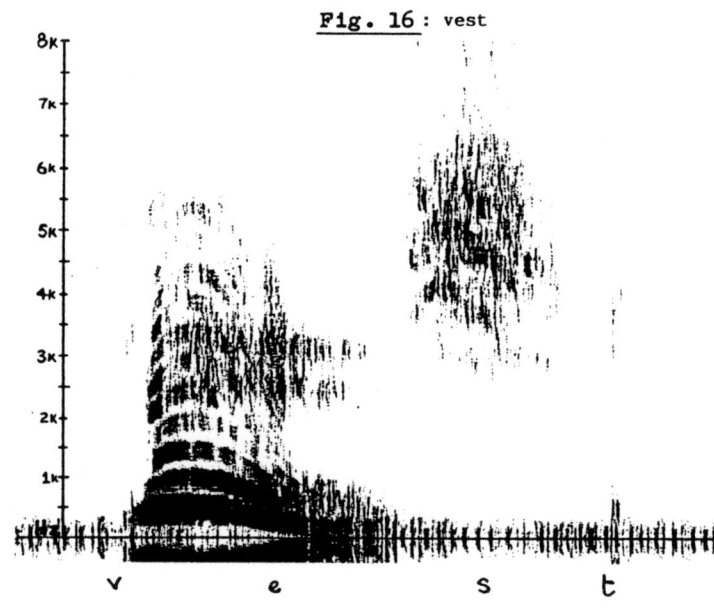

Fig. 16: vest

Figures 17, 18

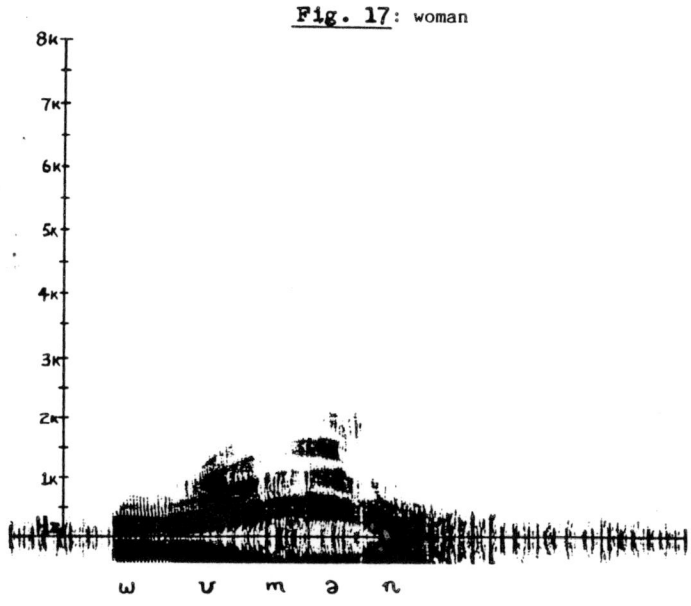

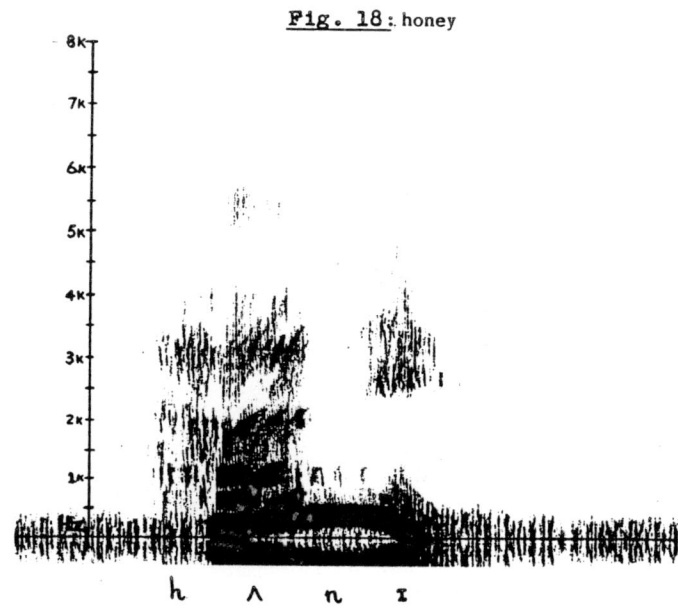

Figures 19, 20

Fig. 19: window

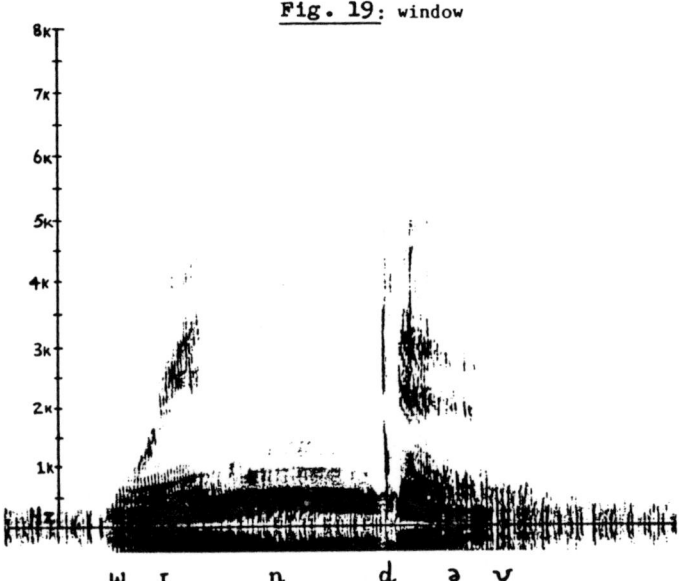

Fig. 20: another

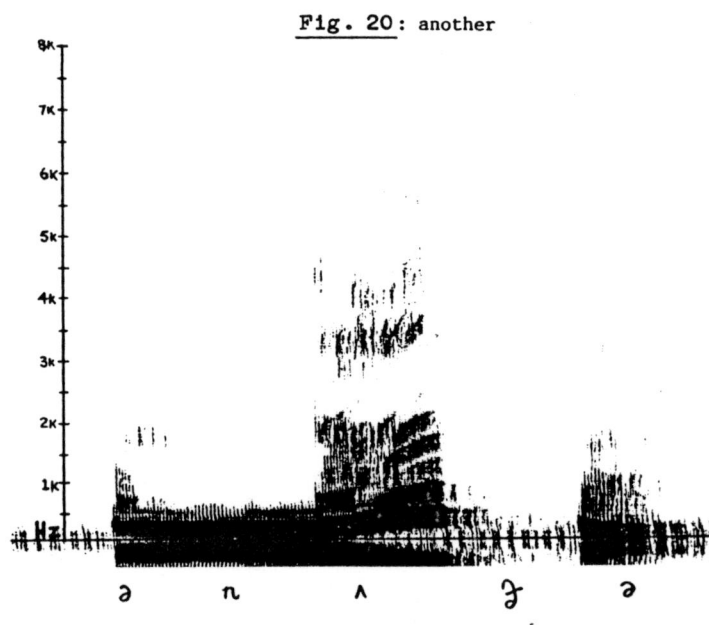

Fig. 21: dog

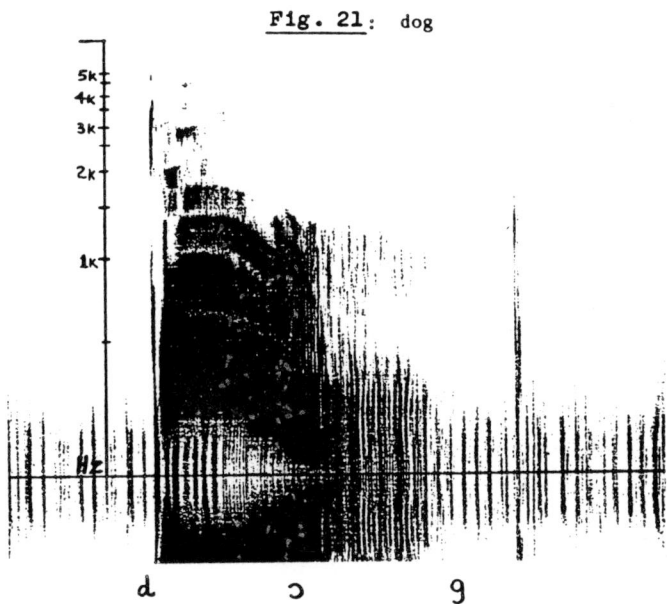

Fig. 22: doll

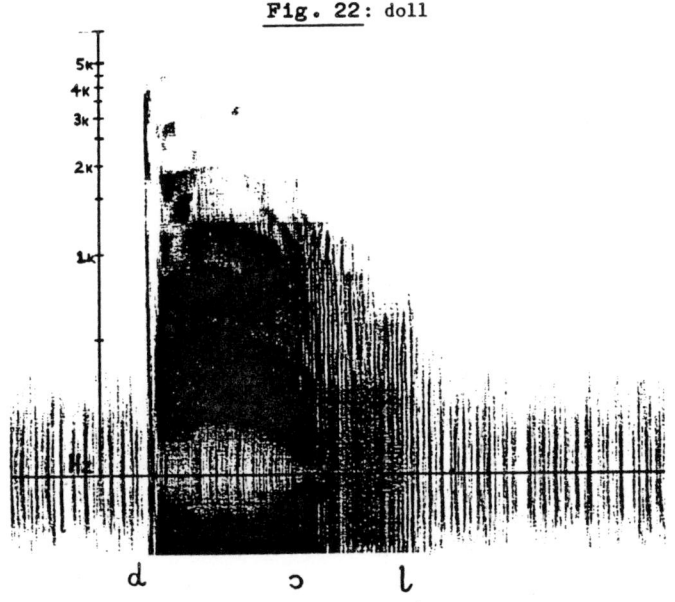

Figures 23, 24

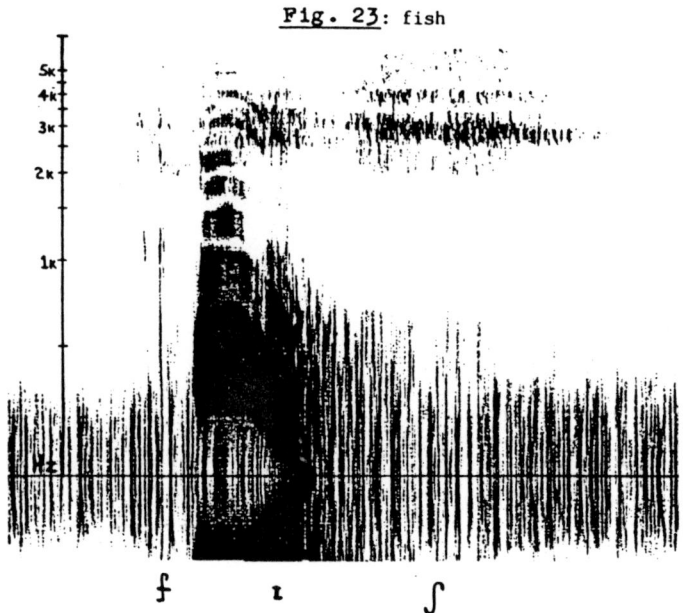

Fig. 23: fish

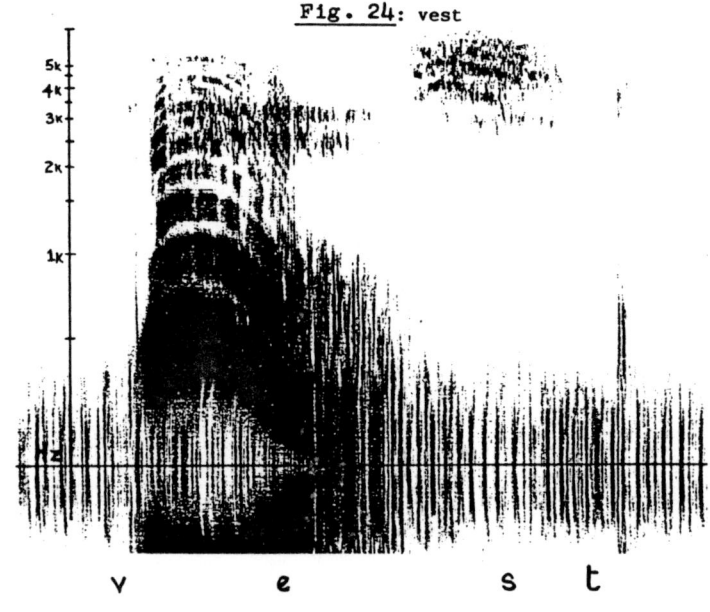

Fig. 24: vest

Fig. 25: woman

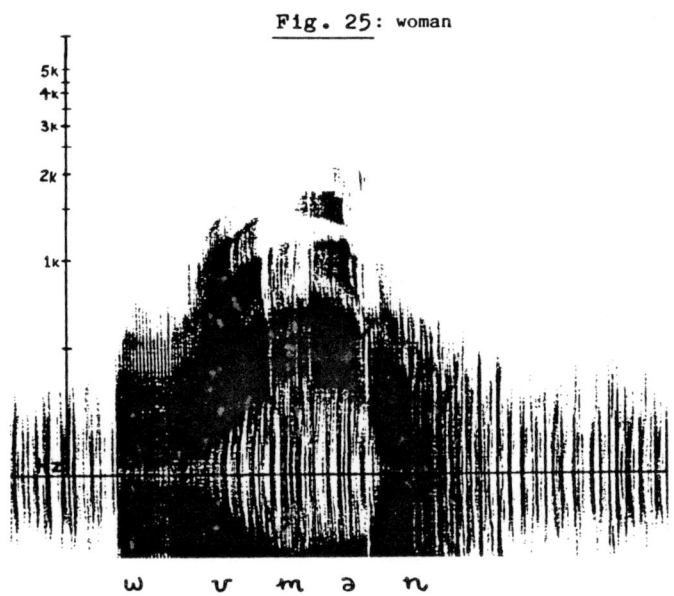

Fig. 26: honey

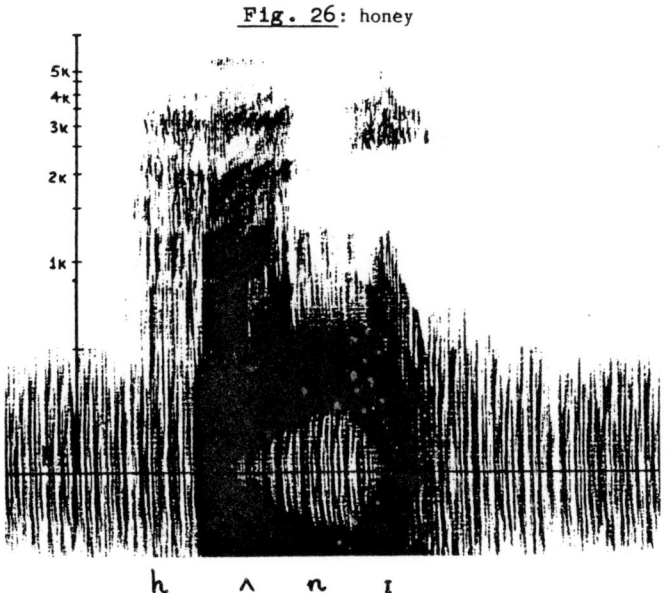

Figures 27, 28

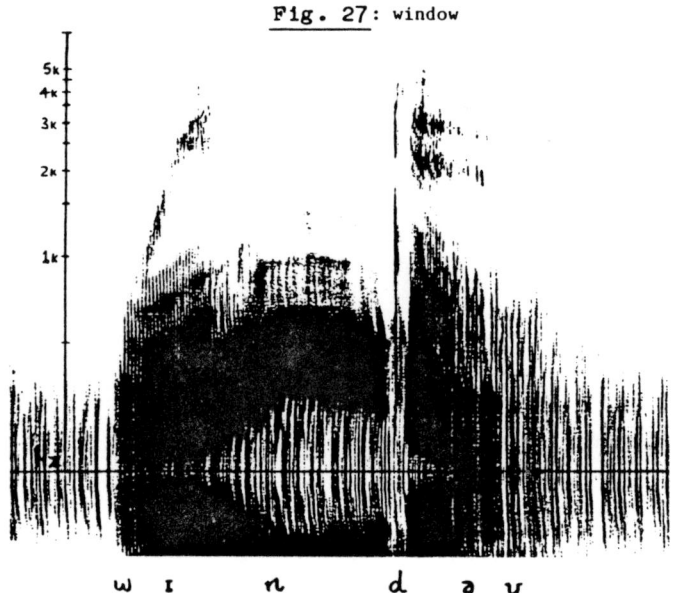

Fig. 27: window

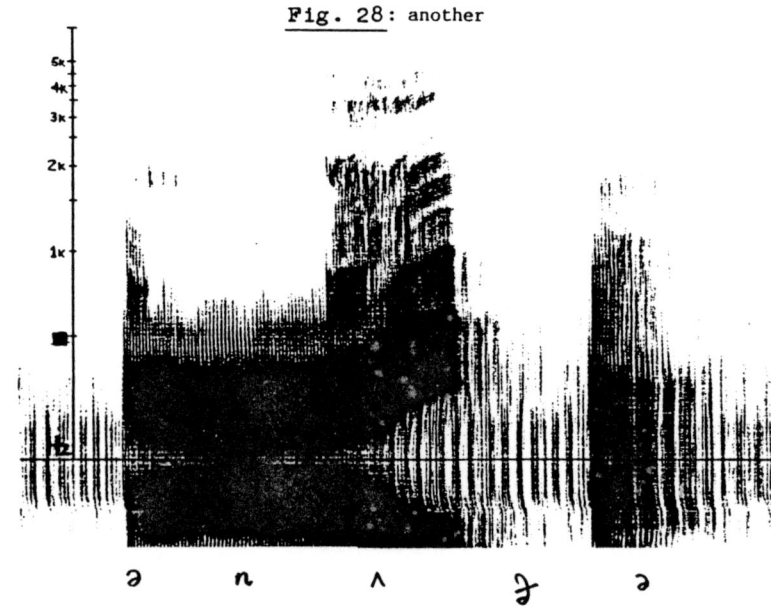

Fig. 28: another

Appendix

	Patrick	Bobby	butter	birdie	bucket	button
1;4	[pæpæ] [bæbæ]					
1;5	[bæbæ]			[bæbu:]	[bʌbu] [bʌbu:]	
1;6	[pæpu] [bʌbu] [bæbu:] [pæbu:] [bʌbu:]	[bæbu:]	[bæbæ] [bʌʔə]	[bæbu:]	[bæbu:]	[bæbu:] [bʌʔn]
1;7	[bʌbu:]	[bæbɪ] [babɪ]	[bʌtə]	[bə:dɪ]	[bʌtɪ] [bʌʔɪ]	
1;8	[pæʔtɪk] [bʌbu:] [bʌtɪk] [pʌtɪk]	[bæbɪ] [babɪ]				
1;9	[bʌbu:]					
1;10	[bʌbu:]					
1;11	[bʌbu:]					
2;0	[bʌbu:]					
2;1	[bætɪk] [pætɪt]					
2;2	[pætɪt] [bætɪk]					
2;3	[pætɪk]					
2;4	[pætsɪt]					
2;5	[pætsɪt] [pætɪk]					

PV pattern

1;2.22	[dɔ] dog
1;2.24	[du:] cockadoodle*doo*
1;4.3	[du:] two
	[bəu] boat
1;4.4	[bʌ] the letter *b*
1;4.6	[bæ] bag
1;4.7	[dau/daun] down
1;4.12	[ba:] Bob
1;4.14	[bɔ:] paw
1;4.16	[di:] cheese
1;4.17	[gu:] goose
	[bɑ:] boy
1;4.18	[pɔ:] paw
	[dɔ:] door
1;4.22	[bu:] bull
	[ba] banana
1;5	[gɑ:] car
	[bəu] bow
	[dʌ:] doll
1;5.1	[bə:] bird
	[dɛə] chair

(PV)² pattern

1;2.22	[dada] Daddy
1;3.7	[də:tɪ] dirty
1;4	[popo] potty
1;4.17	[beɪbɪ] baby
1;4.18	[bu:bəu] peep-bo
1;4.21	[be:bɔ:] bread-board
1;4.23	[pæpæ/bæbæ] Patrick
	[ʈuʈu] two kitties
1;4.29	[baba] bye-bye
1;5	[baɪbaɪ] bye-bye
1;5.1	[tɪtɪ/ʈuʈu] Kitty
	[bæbu:] birdie
	[bʌbu:] bucket

PVP pattern

1;2.8	[kəut] coat
1;2.13	[də:t] dirt
1;4.24	[gud] good
1;4.27	[dɪk] stick
1;5	[gʌk] truck
	[gʌk] jug
1;5.1	[gʌk] cake

GROWTH OF COMPLEXITY IN PHONOLOGICAL DEVELOPMENT

First published in: Waterson, N. and Snow, C. E. (eds.) (1978). *The Development of Communication.* Chichester & New York: John Wiley & Sons Ltd. 415-42.

A widely recognized principle is exemplified in this paper: that of progress from a simple beginning to greater complexity. The findings presented should therefore have a wider application than to the one case study on which most of the evidence is based, more particularly because the language development of the child in question showed the typical features of other children's acquisition of language (cf. Ingram 1978).

A longitudinal study of the child's phonetic and phonological development, made in the context of his language development in general, has convinced the writer that to get a fuller understanding of the processes involved, growth of complexity should be studied at the several levels of language: semantic, phonetic, phonological, lexical, and syntactic, taking into account their interrelations, together with the increase in amount of language used. However, the data available are not adequate for this and as work on child language has not yet reached the point when such complete studies are being made, reports covering only some of the aspects will continue to make a contribution, and here only limited interrelations are considered.

It has often been said that children learn the coarse, gross contrasts of language first, and in this paper an attempt is made to illustrate this at the phonetic and phonological levels, showing at the same time how such development is related to increases in vocabulary size, syntactic complexity, and amount of language use. In a short paper of this nature it is not possible to give a full longitudinal description of the phonetics and phonology, so a restricted aspect has been selected for consideration. What will be demonstrated is increase in syntagmatic differentiation and length of utterance.

Increase in syntagmatic differentiation is illustrated in relation to syllable, word, and sentence. Particular reference will be made to syllable structure, consonantal contrasts within syllables and words, contrasts of syllables within words, and word contrasts within sentences. A differentiated vowel system was acquired very early, as is often the case, so vowels are not included in the discussion. That syntactic patterns are learnt in a similar way to the phonological is implicit but a great deal more is involved in the learning of syntax (cf. for instance, Clark 1978; Miller 1978; Bruner 1975; Dore 1975).

It will be shown that increase in length, in degree of differentiation, and in amount of use at the levels of syllable, word, and sentence was achieved in a manner that was similar in many respects. Progress was from short, simple utterances, in which there were few articulatory contrasts and only simple syllable patterns, to quite long ones containing a large number of contrasts. The phonetic and phonological development of the child who is the subject of this study proved to be remarkably systematic, and this suggests that something of the same strategies and hence possibly the same neural processes were involved in the creation of the phonological structures of syllable, word, and sentence.

The evidence put forward in this paper shows that there are interrelations between the different levels of language dealt with (i.e., the phonetic, phonological, lexical, and syntactic) and amount of language use, and that in the early stages increase in complexity did not take place at the same time and at the same rate in them all. The picture that emerged is rather that if there was progress at one level, there was often little or no progress at another. This suggests that the child's overall organization for language was such that it was not possible for him to cope with growth at all the levels at the same time. Then at around 1;6 to 1;7 there was progress at a faster rate and at several levels at once; it was as if he had developed an organization which enabled him to process language material in a more efficient way and this speeded up his learning and use of language.

The main concern of this paper will be with the child's production. The important role played by perception and auditory salience in the acquisition of the phonological system has been described in detail elsewhere (Waterson 1970, 1971a, 1971b, Papers 3, 5). Briefly, at the start the child was found to produce his forms of words mainly on the basis of those parts of the adult models which had the greatest auditory salience and were at the same time semantically salient for him. Auditory salience, to put it over-simply, involves mostly stretches of relatively low frequency (F1 and F1 transitions), relatively high intensity, and relatively long duration (see Paper 4). The child was paying a great deal of attention to F1 and F1 transitions when beginning to speak and these have been found to be important in the auditory perception of babies in the pre-speech period (Fourcin 1978). He thus scanned the speech signal but made use of only a small part of it. To begin with, he operated with a very limited set of articulations, producing a limited number of sounds which he used in restricted contexts in short utterances of one or two syllables. These sounds were then used in a wider range of contexts so that the number of syntagmatic contrasts within his utterances increased, as also did his word patterns. As time went on and as he gained more experience, his perceptual discrimination, and the amount of attention he was able to give to the speech signal, appeared to improve because he began to take less salient features of the models into account and gradually produced more and more new sounds. These again first appeared in restricted contexts and later in a wider range. The syntagmatic differentiation in his utterances and hence also in his phonological system thus increased. Increase in length of utterance was first achieved by the use of what was familiar—either by repetition of an item or by the combination of familiar items, as shown by Clark for syntax (Clark 1974, 1978).

The aspect of language development dealt with in this paper is a small part of a longitudinal study of the phonetic and phonological development of the writer's first child. The period covered by the study starts at the beginning of the one-word utterance stage, at $10\frac{1}{2}$ months, and ends at around 2 years when the child was using relatively complex two-part multi-word utterances. Data of the child's linguistic and general development were collected daily and some notes were made of the context of use. When the data were analysed, it was found that the type and number of articulatory contrasts within a syllable, contrasts of syllables within a word, and contrasts of words within a multi-word utterance were important factors in relation to what the child was able to produce at different stages of language learning. This indicates that syntagmatic differentiation (i.e., contrast within the sequence of an utterance) is very important for child language studies and indeed for studies of speech processing in general. It seems probable that increasing differentiation in a child's phonetic and phonological systems reflects his growing ability to perceive and recognize more in the speech signal, as well as his increasing ability for planning, production, storage and retrieval. There is some discussion of this point in Paper 4.

Examples of syntagmatic differentiation in a one-word utterance and a two-word utterance are given below to clarify what is meant by the term. The degree of differentiation within the four-syllable one-word utterance [helikɔptə] 'helicopter', first used at 2;2, is compared with that of the four-syllable two-word utterance [mama, popo] 'Mama, potty', first used at 1;4. The same type of phonetic feature description is used here as in the writer's other studies of child phonology (see Waterson in References).

In [helıkɔptə] the syllable structure is CVCVCVCC: three open, CV, syllables and one closed, CVC. Each syllable is different: [he-lı-kɔp-tə]. In the CVC syllable a difference in place of articulation has to be made (velar [k] to bilabial [p]) which must involve greater difficulty in production than a CV syllable, where no such contrast needs to be made.[1] The word begins with a breathy onset [h] and there is a contrast of manner of articulation within the sequence: lateral [l] and plosive [k, p, t]. There are four changes in place of articulation: alveolar [l] to velar [k], to bilabial [p], to alveolar [t]; there are changes in lip position: from spread in [helı], to rounded in [kɔp], to neutral in [tə], and there are also changes in tongue position in the dimension of height and also in relation to front, back, and central positions in the mouth. Tongue height changes from half-close [e], to close [ı], to half-open [ɔ], to half-close [ə], and the start is with front tongue position in [helı], moving to back in [kɔp], and central in [tə]. There are also several changes involving voicing and voicelessness: the voiced stretches are [elı], [ɔ] and [ə] and the voiceless are [h], [k], and [pt].

In the two-word utterance [mama, popo] 'Mama, potty', there are only open, CV, syllables, so there are no place and manner contrasts within any of the syllables, and there is a minimum of contrasts in the whole utterance as both words have repeated syllables, i.e., (CV)^2. Only one place of articulation, bilabial [m, p], is involved and there is only one manner of articulation contrast: nasal [m] and oral [p]. Only one change in lip position is made: from relatively spread in [mama], to rounded in [popo], and there is one change in tongue position and tongue height: from relatively front and open in [mama] to back and half-close in [popo]. There is voicing throughout the first word [mama] and there are changes from voicelessness, [p], to voice, [o], in the two syllables of the second word.

When the two utterances, ['helı,kɔptə] and ['mama, 'popo], are compared in terms of the syntagmatic contrasts involved (bearing in mind also the accents and pitch changes which are of a different nature), it becomes clear that a one-word utterance like [helıkɔptə], in which a

---

[1] Difference of place of articulation within a syllable must involve some difficulty in production because the majority of children's early words have open syllables and do not have such contrasts.

large number of articulatory changes is involved, needs much more skill in planning and production than a two-word utterance with very few contrasts like [mama, popo], and may therefore be described as having a higher degree of complexity. Its production would seem to be more complex, even allowing for the fact that a two-word utterance involves the selection of two appropriate items from the memory store and their organization into a sequence, whereas in the case of a one-word utterance only one selection is made and no arrangement in a sequence is required. The high degree of complexity of 'helicopter' may well be one of the reasons why the child did not attempt it until 2;2 despite the fact that helicopters were phenomena almost as frequently commented upon in his environment as planes. 'Plane' [pleɪn] is much simpler and was first attempted at 1;6, as [beɪm]. Structural complexity thus appears to be one of the reasons for the late production of this word. (cf. Ferguson and Farwell (1973), who drew attention to phonologically determined selectivity in children's acquisition of words.)

The concept of syntagmatic differentiation as used in this paper has now been demonstrated, and it is plain that the more syntagmatic differentiation there is, the greater is the degree of complexity. Growth of complexity in phonetics and phonology will now be illustrated and related to growth in vocabulary, syntactic development, and to amount of language used. As mentioned earlier, only the briefest indication can be given here because of limitations of space. In the illustration that follows, selected examples are given which are representative of the increases in syntagmatic differentiation.

Growth in complexity

In the detailed longitudinal study, the phonetic and phonological development of the child is divided into seven stages on the basis of linguistic changes that took place, and the same divisions are used here. The stages and ages are given below. It will be seen that they vary in length, stages 1 and 7 being the longest and stage 4 the shortest.

stage 1   0;10.14 to 1;2.21
stage 2   1;2.21 to 1;4.10
stage 3   1;4.11 to 1;5.7
stage 4   1;5.8 to 1;6.0
stage 5   1;6.0 to 1;7.10
stage 6   1;7.11 to 1;8.3
stage 7   1;8.4 to 2;2.0

There is, of course, some overlap from one stage to the next. Some changes that took place in one stage had their beginnings in the previous stage. The child was babbling at the start of the study and was still babbling in stage 6. He was also using a 'protolanguage' (Halliday 1975), communicating by a system of vocalizations accompanied by gestures and actions up to stage 3, when communication became more fully verbal, without dependence on non-verbal actions. The earlier stages of development are described in more detail than the later, as the latter followed along very much the same lines and it is felt that by stage 5 the way growth in complexity took place has been made clear. The description of the growth of complexity now follows.

Stage 1

The child's vocabulary was very small and was acquired very slowly over a long period of time; some of the words occurred only once. Plosives, nasals, and vowels were the only sounds used, apart from the one example of a labial glide. These are sounds that were familiar from babbling and their perception and production were thus well-practised. At this time the child used only one-word utterances of both one and two syllables and these had few consonantal contrasts. Syllable structures of one-syllable words were CV, VC and CVC, the last being the only ones with contrasts within the syllable. Systems at C were P and N, i.e., PV [baː] 'Bob', NV [nəu] 'no', VP [ʌp] 'up', VN [æn] 'Anne', PVP [gud] 'good', and PVN [bəun] 'bone' and [bæŋ]. Two-syllable words had open, CV, syllables only, and were mostly of a reduplicated structure (i.e., the whole or part of the syllable was repeated), (CV)², so that there were no contrasts at C within the structure. The possibilities were (PV)², [dada] 'Dada', [kukuː] 'cuckoo', and (NV)², [mama] 'Mama'. There was one word of CVCV structure, with a contrast of P and N, PVNV: [biːnə] 'Bina'. Two-syllable words had one accent but there was one two-syllable utterance with two accents, ['gɔ 'weɪ] 'go away', and it had the same intonation as the two-word adult model. The child did not use 'go' or 'away' separately so his ['gɔ 'weɪ] was intermediate between a one-word sentence and his first two-word sentences which had two accents.[2]

The only words of the CVC structure, [gud], [bəun], and [bæŋ], had a contrast at onset and ending, as in the adult models. In [gud] there is no contrast of manner of articulation, onset and ending both being plosive, but there is a place contrast: velar [g] and alveolar [d]. Features of voice and voicelessness are treated prosodically as relating to the syllable and not as part of consonantal contrasts, and so are not included in the discussion (see Waterson 1971b). [bəun] has a place of articulation contrast of bilabial [b] and alveolar [n], and there is also a manner contrast, oral [b] and nasal [n]. [bæŋ] has the same oral-nasal contrast but a different place contrast: bilabial [b] and velar [ŋ]. There was one three-syllable utterance, [pɔppɔppɔp] 'pop pop pop', (PVP)³, with no place or manner contrasts. This was used onomatopoeically.

At this time, when language use was infrequent and words were acquired with long intervals between each, the child was able to manage the place and manner contrasts in the few words used. This may be compared with the situation later on in stage 3, when the rate of vocabulary growth was faster and new words of the CVC structure had no place or manner contrasts—nor did two-syllable words, the only ones acquired being of the (CV)² structure. Thus at the start the child's learning seemed to be on the basis of individual items, whereas later it appeared to be mostly by pattern (see stage 3).

Stage 2

The rate of growth of vocabulary and of amount of language use increased and a number of new vowel sounds were acquired so that the child now had most of the vowels but not all the diphthongs and triphthongs (cf. Jones 1962). Plosives, nasals, and the labial glide were still

---

[2] The question of whether one-word utterances are sentences or not is irrelevant to this paper; they are referred to as sentences for convenience of exposition, but see Dore (1975) for a discussion of the problem.

the only consonants. There was one new syllable structure, V, and two new word structures, V and VCV, in neither of which were there any consonantal contrasts involved.

Examples: V   [uː] the letter *u*
           [ɑː] the letter *r*
      VCV [ɪtɪ] Kitty
           [æpʉ] apple

The first increase in utterance length from one word to two took place at this time. Two-word utterances are analysed as two-word sentences on account of their accentuation (i.e., by virtue of having two accents as opposed to one, which was the case in one-word utterances), by intonation contour, and by their relation to the context (cf. Bloom 1973).

The structure of these first two-word sentences was similar to those of other English children (e.g., Bloom 1970; Clark 1974) and was either (a) repetitive or (b) differentiated. The repetitive type consisted of a repeated one-word utterance, e.g., ['gɔn, 'gɔn] 'gone, gone', with the structure {gɔn}². The differentiated types were of two kinds: a sequence of one-word utterances, such as ['daun, 'ʌp] 'down, up', {{daun}{ʌp}}, or a sequence of two words expressing a semantic relation, such as ['æpʉ 'gɔn] 'apple's gone', {æpʉ gɔn}. The only functions of the two-word sentences were comments (declaratives), requests, and vocatives. As would be expected from the fact that only plosives and nasals were involved (the labial glide was still used only in 'go away'), there were few contrasts relating to place and manner within the two-word utterances. Such contrasts as occurred are shown below phonologically in relation to the C systems in the structure of the sentences.

Examples: Contrasts at C (relating to manner) are P and N.

Utterance	Sentence structure	Maximum contrasts
[gɔn, gɔn] Gone, gone	{PVN}{PVN} = {PVN}²	{P—N}² i.e. P—N—P—N
[gud, gud] Good, good	{PVP}{PVP} = {PVP}²	P
[nau, nau] Now, now	{NV}{NV} = {NV}²	N
[ʌp, daun] Up, down	{{VP}{PVN}}	P—N
[daun, ʌp] Down, up	{{PVN}{VP}}	P—N—P
[mama, popo] Mama, potty	{{(NV)²}{(PV)²}}	N—P
[æpʉ gɔn] Apple's gone	{VPV PVN}	P—N

Contrasts at P and N (relating to place) are p, t, k (see table overleaf).

From the above and the table overleaf it may be seen that the greatest number of contrasts, P—N—P—N and k—t—k—t, occurred in a repeated-word utterance, in {gɔn}². Where there was no repetition, the maximum contrast was less: P—N—P and t—p in {daun, ʌp} and P—N and p—k—t in {æpʉ gɔn}. In the other cases there were fewer contrasts.

At this time there were two longer utterances in use with accentuation and intonation as in the adult models: ['ɔː 'gɔn, 'nəu 'mɔː] 'All gone, no more' and [gu'naɪ, 'nəu, 'nɔt 'nau] 'Goodnight, no, not now.' Both were used as indivisible units and with specific functions, so they were intermediate between a one-word and a four-word sentence (cf.

94   Prosodic phonology

Utterance	Sentence structure	Maximum contrasts
[gɔn, gɔn]	$\{kVt\}\{kVt\} = \{kVt\}^2$	$\{k-t\}^2$ i.e. k—t—k—t
[gud, gud]	$\{kVt\}\{kVt = \{kVt\}^2$	$\{k-t\}^2$ i.e. k—t—k—t
[nau, nau]	$\{tV\}\{tV\} = \{tV\}^2$	t
[ʌp, daun]	$\{\{Vp\}\{tVt\}\}$	p—t
[daun, ʌp]	$\{\{tVt\}\{Vp\}\}$	t—p
[mama, popo]	$\{\{(pV)^2\}\{(pV)^2\}\}$	p
[æpu̜ gɔn]	$\{VpV\ kVt\}$	p—k—t

['go 'weɪ] in stage 1). Interestingly, these longer utterances are no more complex in terms of consonantal contrasts than the two-word sentences; no new contrasts are involved and the maximum contrast is P—N—P—N and k—t in {{ gunaɪ} {nəu} {nɔt nau}}, as shown below.

Examples: Contrasts at C are P and N.

Utterance	Sentence structure	Maximum contrasts
[ɔ: gɔn, nəu mɔ:] All gone, no more	$\{\{V\ PVN\}\{NV\ NV\}\}$	P—N
[gunaɪ, nəu, nɔt nau] Good night, no, not now	$\{\{PVNV\}\{NV\}\{NVP\ NV\}\}$	P—N—P—N

        Contrasts at P and N are p, t, k.

| [ɔ: gɔn, nəu mɔ:] All gone, no more | $\{\{V\ kVt\}\{tV\ pV\}\}$ | k—t—p |
| [gunaɪ, nəu, nɔt nau] Good night, no, not now | $\{\{kVtV\}\{tV\}\{tVt\ tV\}\}$ | k—t |

    The child was thus using the same sort of contrasts in his planning and production of these longer utterances as in the shorter ones and this may be one of the reasons why he was able to use these sentences, which were so much longer than those in his general usage.

Stage 3
    There was a big increase in vocabulary size and in amount of language use. No further instances of actions instead of words were recorded so there was obviously greater reliance on language for communication. There were no new syntactic functions and no increase in utterance length other than the appearance of the first three-syllable word. There was, however, an appreciable increase in the number of two-word sentences and more of the non-repetitive, differentiated type began to be used. The word 'gone' was very productive, being combined with 'Mama', 'Dada', 'car', and 'Bob'. Apart from a few new sounds in some isolated words (viz., [br] in [bre:] 'bread', [f] in [fɔ:] 'four', and [l] in [deɪl] 'tail'), plosives and nasals were still the only consonants that were used and there was little that was new in syllable or word structure. The biggest expansion in the vocabulary was in words of the familiar PV, (PV)², and PVP structures in which there were no consonantal contrasts: e.g., [gu:] 'goose', [dɔ:] 'door', [bə:] 'bird', [gau] 'cow'; [pæpæ] and [bæbæ] 'Patrick', [beɪbɪ] 'baby', [bæbu:] 'birdie'; [gʌk] for 'truck', 'jug', 'cake', [dɪk] and

then [gʌk] for 'stick'.

In stages 1 and 2 nearly all the adult models of the words the child attempted had only plosive and nasal consonants. Now the child was attempting words in which the models had other sounds as well but he continued to use only plosives and nasals and this resulted in his attempts being less like the models than was the case earlier. He was still responding only to what was auditorily most salient in the models. For instance, 'cheese' (adult [tʃi:z]) was [di:] and 'rope' (adult [rəup] was [əup]. The CVC structure words acquired during this period had no contrast at the C places. Thus 'truck' (adult [trʌk]) and 'jug' (adult [dʒʌg]) were both [gʌk], PVP and kVk, and 'moon' (adult [mu:n]) was [mu:m], NVN and pVp. Homonyms, resulting from the child's production of words based on the same sets of salient features in the models, appeared in the child's speech at this time: e.g., [di:] for 'cheese', 'tea'; [bɔ:] for 'ball', 'paw'. New two-syllable words were of a reduplicated structure, mostly (PV)² (see the examples above). The first three-syllable word, 'banana', had open syllables only and consisted of a single syllable followed by a repeated syllable, CV(CV)². It had alternative forms with one syllable, [ba], PV, and two syllables, [nana], (NV)². The three-syllable form was a combination of these: PV(NV)², [banana].

The two-word sentences had the same sort of contrasts as in stage 2. Only the differentiated types are examined here as the repeated types had no contrasts: e.g., { mɔ· }²'moth, moth', {gɑ:}² 'car, car', {ɑ:}² 'ah, ah', { nəu }²'no, no'.

Examples: Contrasts at C are P and N. Contrasts at P and N are p, t, k.

Utterance		Sentence structure		Maximum contrasts	
[dada gɔn]	Dada's gone	{(PV)² PVN}	{(tV)² kVt}	P—N	t—k—t
[mama gɔn]	Mama's gone	{(NV)² PVN}	{(pV)² kVt}	N—P—N	p—k—t
[ba: gɔn]	Bob's gone	{PV PVN}	{pV kVt}	P—N	p—k—t
[gɑ: gɔn]	Car's gone	{PV PVN}	{kV kVt}	P—N	k—t
[mɔ: di:]	More cheese	{NV PV}	{pVtV}	N—P	p—t
[mama ʌp]	Get up, Mama	{(NV)² VP}	{(pV)² Vp}	N—P	p

In these differentiated, non-repetitive two-word sentences, the maximum contrast is N—P—N and p—k—t, in { mama gɔn}; this is less than the maximum in the repetitive example in stage 2 but more than the maximum in the differentiated types.

Of the three longer utterances used, one was repetitive, with four accents, and had no contrasts, ['ɑ: 'ba:, 'ɑ: 'ba:] 'Ah Bob, ah Bob', and the other two were composed of combinations of familiar words: 'dirt' and 'oh' with the old-established 'go away', i.e., ['də:t, 'gu: ə'wʌ:] 'Dirt, go away' and ['əu, 'gəu ə'wei] 'Oh, go away', with simple contrasts of plosives and labial glide. The last two examples had three accents, as in the adult models, but were intermediate between two-word and three-word sentences since 'Go away' was still used only as a single indivisible unit, i.e., as a word.

The acquisition of CVC structure words in a simpler form in this stage than in stages 1 and 2 (i.e., without a contrast at onset and ending) cannot be explained as being due to motor constraints, as the child had already shown himself able to produce and use words of this structure with a contrast, for instance, [gud] 'good', [bæŋ] 'bang' and [bəun] 'bone' in stage 1, and [gɔn] 'gone', [kot] 'coat', [dəːt] 'dirt' and [daun] 'down' in stage 2. Nor can it be said to be due to a limited memory span, as he was producing utterances that were longer than a one-syllable word with several contrasts, for instance, in the differentiated two-word utterances, such as [dada gɔn] 'Dada's gone', P—N, t—k—t, and [mɔː diː] 'More cheese', N—P, p—t. The reason for it may well be that, aside from increase in complexity taking place at other levels of language, there was a change in the way the child was coding language. The evidence shows that he was now responding to adult models in a patterned way (cf. the homonyms and the expansion of the vocabulary by the acquisition of words of established structures, PV, (PV)[2] and PVP), and this would suggest that he was learning by pattern recognition and was developing a coding system by classification in addition to coding by individual item, which appeared to be the earlier strategy. The absence of contrast in CVC structure words would thus be explained as a processing constraint. The child had to handle the storage, retrieval, and planning of a growing number of items with ever-increasing frequency as the vocabulary and language use continued to expand. He was also producing more two-word utterances. He thus had to develop a new organization, or new coding systems, in order to be able to handle the more complex language he was needing to use, as his cognitive and social development was advancing, and it seems that he had not yet acquired a complex enough system to handle a large number of words of anything but the simplest structure. It seems his working capacity was stretched to the full and he was therefore not able to cope with consonantal contrasts in the words he was now acquiring, nor with any increase in the number of syntagmatic contrasts in two-word utterances, as shown above, nor indeed with an increase in utterance length, apart from the three simple examples already described.

Stage 4

Although there was still no increase in utterance length (apart from the use of two four-word utterances of very simple structure), a great change took place during this stage, the shortest of all the stages. Not only was there a further big increase in amount of language use and in vocabulary growth (again especially in words of established structure) but a new range of sounds—continuants—came in and was used in several words. These continuants were sibilants and fricatives, sounds that are less salient in the adult models than the plosives and nasals to which the child had been responding earlier. This means that for some time before, he must have been discriminating more in his perception and recognizing more, and was now ready to attempt these new sounds. He was obviously aware of the contexts in the models in which they occurred because he was producing them appropriately in several words. The production of these less salient sounds of the models is in line with the acquisition of plosives and nasals. Thus, the first to be produced were those in contexts in which they had the greatest auditory salience in the models, the less salient being produced later (in stage 6), showing that the non-production in such contexts was not due to an inability to produce the particular sounds but rather because they had not been given attention.

The continuant sounds the child was now attempting required more skill, not only in perceptual discrimination, but also in production. The articulators have to be in a posture of close approximation to achieve friction, neither completely in contact (as in plosives and nasals), nor well clear of each other (as in vowels). The appearance of sibilants and fricatives in stage 4 is not seen as resulting primarily from a production difficulty which had been overcome but as arising from the child's increased perceptual discrimination, the need for their production not having arisen until the child was able to discriminate them and recognize them as functional. As the child's babbling was not recorded, it is not known whether these sounds formed part of the babbling repertoire but they do not appear to have been well-practised, as their production was not always successful. However, the inaccurate production may well have reflected inaccurate identification of the sounds as well as difficulty in production.

Another factor that points to the child's increased perceptual discrimination is that whereas before this stage, very few words changed in form from the one in which they were first acquired, now they began to get more variable in form as the child changed his productions to match the models more closely (see Paper 4), and the instability of the form of words which has often been noted in the speech of young children appeared in his speech. His established words began to change and some of his homonyms diverged: e.g., 'stick' changed from [gʌk] to [gɪk], 'cake' from [gʌk] to [gek]. However, new ones continued to be acquired: e.g., 'duck' was acquired as [gʌk], like his 'truck' and 'jug'. Words in simple form changed more quickly to a more differentiated one: e.g., [beɪp] (for 'plate' and 'grape') quickly diverged to [bleɪt] and [geɪp] respectively.

Attempts at the friction and sibilance of the models were made with varying degrees of success. Friction was achieved at several places, i.e., bilabial, labio-dental, dental, and velar; and sibilance was produced at the palatal, palato-alveolar, and alveolar places. Attempts in initial position tended to be affricated.

Examples:

Fricatives

	Initial	Final
bilabial	[bβæ] fly	[gu:Φ] goose
	[βɔ:] four	[kauΦ] cow/calf
labio-dental	[fɔ:] four	[bɪf/bəf] beef
dental	-	[gu:θ] goose
velar	[ɣɔn] gone	-

Sibilants

	Initial	Final
palatal	[dʑu:/ɟʝu:] shoe	-
palato-alveolar	[dʒeɪn] chain	[dɪʃ] dish
		[uʃ] vest
		[uʃ/ɪʃ] fish
alveolar	-	[geɪps] grapes
		[dadaz] Dada's

The new sounds were used mostly in one-syllable words and brought new consonantal contrasts into use so that a higher level of complexity was reached in monosyllables before disyllables which continued to be mostly of the reduplicated type with no consonantal contrasts, e.g., [bebe] 'biscuit', [tɪtɪ] 'Kitty', [ɡyʲaɡyʲa/ɟjjaɟjja] 'Geoffrey', [mɛmɔ̃] 'lemon'. The first few examples of non-reduplicated two-syllable words appeared, each having a closed syllable: [bəu:n] 'balloon' and [pebl/bʌbl] 'table'. The labial glide [w] was now used more widely: for instance, [wæ], an alternative form of 'fly', [wæ], one of the forms of 'eye' (the others were [ʌ], [jæj], [æj], and lastly [aɪ]), and [wæwæ] 'barrow'. The use of new contrasts resulted in new word structures. For instance, in addition to the established structures with P and N, such as PV, PVP, PVN, VP, VN, NVN, there were now PVS: [dɪʃ] 'dish'; VS: [ɪʃ] 'fish', [uʃ] 'vest'; PVF: [bɪf/bəf] 'beef', [kauɸ] 'cow/calf', [ɡu:θ/ɡu:ɸ] 'goose', and P͡SVN: [dʒen] 'chain'. The few new disyllabic structures were PVVN: [bəu:n] 'balloon', PVPVL: [pebl/bʌbl] 'table', and P͡LVSVS: [prəʃəʃ] 'precious'. One new three-syllable word, [pe:toto] 'potato', came into use. It was of the same structure, viz., CV(CV)^2, as the one acquired in stage 3 but the systems at C places were different, PV(PV)^2 of [pe:toto] contrasting with PV(NV)^2 of [banana]. The increase in the number of different word structures meant that the whole phonological system had increased in complexity.

The use of differentiated, non-repetitive two-word sentences became even more frequent and for the first time they greatly outnumbered the repetitive type. The consonantal contrasts in the majority of the two-word sentences were still of the familiar plosives and the nasals but there were a few that contained words with the new continuant sounds, for example:

[dadaz yʃ] Dada's wash	{(PV)^{2}S VS}	P—S
[dʒen ba:p] Bob's chain	{P͡SVN PVP}	P͡S—N—P
[prəʃəʃ beɪbɪ] precious baby	{P͡LVSVS (PV)^2}	P͡L—S—P

The phonological structure of two-word sentences was thus beginning to grow more complex with new contrasts involving S, P͡S, and P͡L.

At the syntactic level several new relations were expressed in two-word sentences, for instance: the possessive relation: { mama ɛə} 'Mama's hair', {dada dau} 'Dada's towel'; the use of a qualifier of quality: { puə ba:} 'poor Bob', { prəʃəʃ beɪbɪ}; and listing: { bʌbl, bɛə} 'table, chair'.

One three-word utterance and two four-word utterances were recorded. The three-word utterance was of the listing type: [du:, dḷi:, fɔ:] 'two, three, four'. The four-word utterances were repetitive; one had no consonantal contrasts and the other had only one, as shown below.

Utterance	Sentence structure		Maximum contrasts	
[dada di:, dada di:] Dada's tea, Dada's tea	{(PV)^2 PV}^{2}	{(tV)^2 tV}^{2}	P	t
[aɪ, aɪ, nəu, mʌ] eye, eye, nose, mouth	{V}^{2}{NV}{NV}	{V}^{2}{tV}{pV}	N	t—p

This is consistent with the earlier stages where the few longer utterances contained no more contrasts than were found in general use.

By the end of this stage there was thus an increase in vocabulary size; an increase in the number of different sounds; and a consequent increase in the different kinds of syllable and word structures and in the degree of differentiation within two-word sentences. There was also an increase in the use of differentiated two-word sentences and in the syntactic structure of such sentences, and more language was used in general. However, there was no increase in word length or in sentence length. The child thus appeared to be learning to process speech at a more complex level in short utterances before starting the regular use of longer utterances.

Stage 5

This stage saw a sudden increase in utterance length. Several new three-syllable words were acquired and the first four-syllable word appeared. Three-word utterances began to be used relatively freely and several utterances of four and five words were recorded. This increase in utterance length coincided with a great deal of verbal play, during which the child used repetitive utterances of up to twelve words in length, although there were never more than six different words in any one such stretch: e.g., [dada ti: ɔ: gɔn, bʌbu: ti: ɔ: gɔn, mama ti: ɔ: gɔn] 'Dada's tea is all gone, Patrick's tea is all gone, Mama's tea is all gone', and [puə mama, puə dada, puə mæm, puə gɑ:, puə gagə] 'Poor Mama, poor Dada, poor man, poor car, poor tractor'. This verbal play lasted throughout the five weeks of this stage. The syntactic structures involved were of the type often used by the child in his everyday speech, as also were most of the word combinations, and the majority of the stretches of verbal play had only the well-established plosive and nasal consonants. It seems that this kind of play, with familiar articulations, familiar syntactic structures, and very familiar words (together with some more recently acquired) facilitated the planning and production of longer utterances by providing practice through the use of what was familiar. The verbal play is thus a further example of the use of the familiar in the production of something new (in this case longer utterances), and is reminiscent of babbling, during which children spend quite a lot of time repeating familiar patterns in sequences of relatively long stretches (cf. Tuaycharoen 1977). The verbal play was similar to one of the pre-sleep monologues described by Weir (1962) but took place during the day.

In this stage the vocabulary expanded at an even faster rate than before. There was not much in the way of new articulations. Alveolo-palatal affricates [tɕ] and [dʑ] began to be used: [tɕi:z] 'cheese' and [dʑæm] 'jam'. Sounds acquired earlier were now used in a wider range of contexts and the instability in the form of words noted in the previous stage increased; for example, the lateral began to be used in post-vocalic position: [aɫa], then [elən] 'Helen', [pi:ɭəu] 'pillow', [kxjaɪətlɪ] 'quietly'. The possibilities of syntagmatic contrasts within one-syllable words became greater, for instance, [pɪn] 'pin', [byʃ], then [buʃ/bəʃ] 'brush', [bi:s̠] 'piece', [geɪt] 'gate', [dʑæm] 'jam', [bred̠] 'bread', [gɭaf] 'glove'. The contrasts are evident from the transcriptions, and phonological representation is therefore not given. The first use of a word with complex onset and complex ending was recorded: [gɭeps] 'grapes'.

There were more examples of two-syllable words with a closed syllable and with a higher degree of syntagmatic differentiation, e.g., [βʌβaɪn] 'robin', [gærɪʃ] 'garage', [tɔ:təs] 'tortoise', [bʌʔn] 'button', and for the first time there were two-syllable words with abutting consonants,

-CC-. Examples are [aːntɪ] 'Auntie', [kxjaɪətlɪ] 'quietly', [aːkju] 'thank you'. Three-syllable words still had repeated syllables and there were some new structures: (CV)²CV, (CV)²CVC and C(V)²CV. The earliest three-syllable words had only the familiar plosives and nasals but now there were some with continuants: lateral continuant [l] and labio-dental fricative [v].

Examples:

Teddy-bear	[tedɪbɛə]	(CV)²CV	(PV)²PV
Marmalade	[mɑːmʌeɪd/mɑːmaleɪd/ meːmeːlot/mʌːmæleɪt]	(CV)²CV and (CV)² VC	(NV)²LVP and (NV)² VP
Cauliflower	[gahava]	C(V)²CV	P(V)² FV
Butterfly	[bʌʔəvæ/bæʔævæ]	C(V)²CV	P(V)² FV

The one four-syllable word was also repetitive, with simple contrasts, as was the case with the first two-syllable and three-syllable words. The example is [maːtotaːto] 'tomato', N(VPV)P(VPV), This was used in free variation with the disyllabic form [maːto], NVPV (cf. the first three-syllable word [banana], which had shorter alternant forms: monosyllabic [ba] and disyllabic [nana]).

As a result of the greater number of articulatory contrasts within words, and the increase in the number of such words, there was greater syntagmatic differentiation in the two-word utterances than before. Sometimes the form of words differed in two-word utterances from that used in isolation in a way that reduced the number of articulatory contrasts. For example, 'dog's eye' was [dœeɪ] (with frontness of articulation throughout instead of backness in 'dog' [dɔg] and frontness in 'eye' [aɪ]) but 'dog's nose' was [dɔʔ nəu] (with backness throughout); 'go on' [gəu ɔn] (with backness and rounding throughout) but [gœ bæ] for 'go back' (with frontness instead of backness in 'go'). 'Man' was usually [mæm] but 'The man's gone' was [mæ̃ gɔn] or [mæ̃ gɔm], with no place closure for the nasality at the ending of 'man' and sometimes with bi-labial place of articulation of the final nasal of 'gone' harmonizing with the bilabial place at the onset of 'man'; similarly, 'moon' was [muːm] or [muːɲ] but 'The moon's gone' was [mũː gɔɲ] or [muː gɔɲ], again with no closure at the end of the first word.

This stage saw the start of the use of inflections, though probably not as yet with grammatical function but rather resulting from attention being paid to less salient features, e.g.: [dadaz dauu] 'Dada's towel' (cf. [dada dauu] in stage 4); [dada ɪʃ] 'Dada's fish'; [mœ gḷeps] 'more grapes'. Function words too began to appear, again showing an increase in perceptual discrimination, the child now paying attention to the weak unstressed words in adult utterances.

Examples:

[baʔ gɔn ɪn gɑːdn]	Bob's gone in the garden
[bɪʔ æ gaga]	Bit of tractor
[dada ən mama]	Dada and Mama

The structure of three-word sentences was mostly a combination of a familiar two-word sentence and a one-word sentence: e.g.: {mama gḷa gɔn} 'Mama's glove's gone' was a combination of the previously used {mama gḷa} and {gɔn}; {əupu geit dædı} 'Let's open the gate for Daddy' was a combination of {əupu geit} and {dædı}. Four-word sentences were similarly combinations of shorter sentences, e.g.: {mɔ: bubaɪɲ ækju mama} 'More pudding, thank you, Mama' was a combination of {mɔ: bubaɪɲ} and {ækju mama}. The early use of combinations of ready-made utterances in the formation of longer utterances has been pointed out and illustrated by Clark in her study of her son's acquisition of English syntax (Clark 1974, 1978). The other possibility was repeating one or more items, as in: {{tu: æpl}{ʌn æpl}} 'Two apples, one apple'; {{bʌbu: ın}{bʌbu: ın}} = {bʌbu: ın}² 'Let Bobby in, let Bobby in'. The five-word sentences were very repetitive and of a stereotyped structure, such as was used by the mother when pointing out and naming objects in the environment or in picture books: {{mæm}{ɲaɲa mæm}{tu: mæm}} 'Man, another man, two men'; {{bɛə}{ɲaɲa bɛə}{tu: bɛə}} 'Bear, another bear, two bears'.

To begin with, mostly familiar sounds (plosives and nasals) and mostly familiar words were used in the three-word, four-word and five-word sentences and there were not many contrasts within them—that is to say, the degree of syntagmatic differentiation was not great.

Examples:

Three-word sentences:
{gəu bæc æn} Go back, Anne
{mama təu gɔn} Mama's toe's gone
{ɲo, ɲo, bʌbu:} No, no, Patrick

Four-word sentences:
{a:l gɔɲ, nc̃æ mɔ:} All gone, no more
{ba? gɔn ın gɑ:dn} Bob's gone in the garden
{pı·, pı·, gau, gau} Pig, pig, cow, cow

Five-word sentence
{pı·, ɲaɲa pı·, tu: pı·} Pig, another pig, two pigs
{mæm, ɲaɲa mæm, tu: mæm} Man, another man, two men

But at this time a few two-word sentences had the possibility of contrasts with liquids [l, r] and sibilants, for example: {hʌḷəu tʃi:z} 'Hello, cheese'; {tu: tsi:z} 'Two cheeses'; {əupm gærıʃ} 'Open the garage'. Once again it is seen that new, longer utterances were first produced with familiar articulations and a relatively low degree of syntagmatic differentiation compared with the level of differentiation possible in shorter utterances.

Increase in complexity of the child's phonetics and phonology in relation to growth in vocabulary, syntax and amount of language use has now been demonstrated and as development continued along much the same lines, the last two stages are considered only very briefly.

Stage 6

The rapid increase in vocabulary and amount of language use continued. Words were acquired in more differentiated form than before and those acquired earlier in reduplicated form became more differentiated. Some words were acquired in simple form but progressed rapidly to a closer match to the models, e.g.: 'saucer' started as [ohə] and [œhə] and changed to [dzodʐə], and then to [so?sə]. More of the less salient sounds of the models were produced—for instance, the lateral began to be used more freely and in several contexts: [el] 'the letter *l*', [tauəl] 'towel', [lʌk], then [lɔc] 'lock', [klɔk] 'clock', [ʌl̥ɪ] 'elephant', [ʌl̥ɪ] 'lovely', [ʔeləu] 'fellow', [buːlʊɲ] 'balloon'. The affricate [dʑ] became more common: [dʑan] 'John', [dʑan] 'swan'. The less salient nasals (those in unaccented intervocalic position) began to be produced: [eːnɪ] for 'Rooney' (previously [ẽhẽ]); [ʌnɪ] for 'honey' (previously [ahuː]); and [enɪ] 'any'.

In addition to the repetitive type of three-syllable words, such as PV(PV)² [baɪkuku] 'bicycle', NV(PV)² [maːtoto] 'tomato', there were now some examples in which the three syllables differed, e.g.: [pɪdʑama] 'pyjamas', [uːbrelə] 'umbrella' (based on '*u* for 'umbrella''), [bæcberɪ] 'blackberry' (which, however, soon changed to the simpler two-syllable [bætɪ]). By the end of this stage, the use of three-syllable words was beginning to increase but they were not yet widely used. A five-syllable word appeared in a highly repetitive form of 'tomato': [maːtotototo] NV((PV)²)². There was now a wide range of different word structures.

Sentences of two, three and four words were used freely in differentiated form. Five-word sentences were used in repetitive and in differentiated form, the latter being combinations of familiar shorter sentences.

Examples:

Repetitive: {{babɪ ɪə}{babɪ ɲaɲa ɪə}} Bobby's ear, Bobby's other ear

Differentiated: {mama, dəːtɪ ænd ɔː wet} Mama, dirty hand's all wet

This was made up of three units: {mama}, {dəːtɪ ænd} and {ɔː wet}, which had all been used before. Six-word sentences were repetitive only.

Repetitive:

{{ʌn bʌbuː buːt}{tuː bʌbuː buːt}} One Patrick's boot, two Patrick's boots

{{ mama nɪk}{mama nicɪ mama gaga}} Mama, look at Nick; Mama, Nicky is using Mama's tractor (grass-cutter)

A few more inflected forms began to be used: *-ing* forms, e.g.: [bəːdɪ ʔɪŋɪŋ] 'Birdie's singing'; [mama kʌmmɪŋ] 'Mama's coming'; plural *-s*: [tuː pɪns gɔn] 'The two pins have gone'; possessive *-s*: [mamas dɑːlɪ] 'Mama's darling'; third person singular *-s*: [ɪə kʌms dædɪ] 'Here comes daddy'.

More function words came into use, showing the child's increasing awareness of the weak unstressed words in the adult models. Some of the function words (those italicized in the examples) harmonized with the context, as can be seen from the transcription.

Examples:

[bɪʔ ɪ dʑæm pupu] A bit of jam for my pudding
[bɪʔ ɪ ɡæm] A bit of a stamp
[bʌbuː geʔ ʔə] Patrick will get it
[ɪŋk ek mama pɪn] Ink out of Mama's pen
[mama ɔʃ ɪt] Mama'll wash it

Stage 7

There was steady progress, with increasing complexity at all levels. Continuant sounds were used in a wide range of contexts and the child was now responding to the least salient and the least easily discriminable sounds in the adult models—for instance, the liquids [r] and [l], the semivowels [j] and [w], and the fricatives [θ] and [ð], but he was not always producing them correctly. The previous uses of [w] were mostly not in the contexts where they occurred in the adult models, for example, [wæwæ] for 'barrow', [wæ] for 'fly'. Now [w] was used where the model had [w] but it was sometimes omitted: [wɛəz flaɪ?] 'Where's the fly?', but [mamaz ɔʃɪŋ] 'Mama's washing'. [j] was used in initial position: [wɛə ɑ: ju en?] 'Where are you, n?', [jes] 'Yes'. Adult's [r] was variously [r], [j], [w] or [z], or nothing: [ri:d] 'read', [rʌn] or [ʌn] 'run'; [j] in [kjas] 'across', and in [kʌŋgɪju:] 'kangaroo'; and [w] in [wʌnɪŋ] 'running', [kwʌs̜] 'cross' and [dʒafwɪ] 'Geoffrey'; [z] in [zeɪzɪns] 'raisins'. Several clusters were now used: [pleɪɪŋ] 'playing', [ɡlasɪs] 'glasses', [bləu] 'blow', [kləus] 'clothes', [twɛəf] 'twelve', [flaɪ] 'fly', [stjʌc] 'struck', [ts̜i:] 'tree'. The child responded to adult [θ] and [ð] with sibilants, labio-dental fricatives and the glottal stop: [fu:] 'through', [wɪf] 'with', [zɪs] and [ʔɪs] 'this', [zɛə] 'there'.

Pronouns and the copula began to be used and the number of unstressed words per sentence increased; by the end of the stage more than one often occurred, for instance: ['ketu 'sɪŋɪŋ, ɪs 'ɡoɪn tu 'boɪu] 'The kettle is singing, it's going to boil'; ['kʌp 'ti: fɔ: 'bʌbu:, 'pɔ:ʳ ɪt ɪn 'bʌbu:s 'kʌp] 'A cup of tea for Patrick, pour it in Patrick's cup'; ['wɔt ə ju 'ɡɔt ɪn maɪ 'hænd?] 'What have I got in my hand?'; ['iəs maɪ 'tauzəz fə 'mʌmɪ] 'Here's my trousers for Mummy'; ['mænz nʌt̜ 'kwʌs̜, 'es i:?] 'The man's not cross, is he?'; ['zɪs ʌns vɔ: 'mama, 'zɪs ʌns vɔ: 'bʌbu:] 'This one's for Mama, this one's for Patrick'. As may be seen from the examples, utterance length increased to eight and nine words.

Some inflections with grammatical function were now used fairly regularly. For instance, the plural: [tu: βa:s] 'Two flowers', [tu: waɪs] 'Two flies', [ɪtɪ baɪ i:tɪŋ bʌbus zeɪzɪns] 'Little boy eating Patrick's raisins'; possessive -s: [beɪbɪz piɫəu] 'Baby's pillow', [bʌbu:s tʃɛə] 'Patrick's chair', [bʌbu: af mamas peɲ] 'Patrick wants to have Mama's pen'; third person singular present: [bʌbu: a:s mamaz ʔɔʃɪŋ] 'Patrick hears Mama's washing', [bʌbu: ɔnts pendɪl] 'Patrick wants a pencil', [ɔf mama ɡəus] 'Off Mama goes'. Past tense forms were also used, e.g.: [bʌbu: ɡɪt̜ blænkɪt] 'Patrick will get the blanket' (said when the child was going off to get the blanket) and [bʌbu: ɡɔt blænkɪt] 'Patrick got the blanket' (said when he came back with it), [mama du: ɪt] 'Mama'll do it' (a request for something to be done) and [mama du:d ɪt] 'Mama did it' (when it was done).

It was towards the end of this stage that the greatest increase in grammatical complexity took place and it is significant that it did not take place until the vocabulary was quite large, language use was quite fluent and the phonological system was well-developed, and the child was able to pay attention to and discriminate the weak, non-salient stretches of the adult models.

Summary

Growth in length and in complexity of syllable, word, and sentence is now summarized below.

Growth in complexity and length of syllable and word
The first words were mostly monosyllabic and the structure thus coincided with that of the syllable, so a separate account of syllable

structure is not given. The first monosyllabic words had the structure CV, VC, and CVC, the ones of greatest length being those of the CVC and some of the CV structures. The first few CVC words had a contrast at the onset and ending, e.g., [bəun] 'bone', but when the vocabulary was expanding rapidly, words of such structure had a sameness in place and manner of articulation at the onset and ending; this may be viewed as a repetition of a consonant within the syllable, i.e.:

CVC [gʌk]   C͜VP_k   [beɪp]   C͜VP_p   [muːm]   C͜VN_p

These later became differentiated, with contrasts at onset and ending: [trʌk], [greɪp], [muːn] ('truck', 'grape', and 'moon' respectively).

Two-syllable words at first had open syllables only and a repeated syllable, so no consonantal contrasts were involved, e.g., [beːbeː] 'biscuit'. The two syllables gradually became differentiated: [bebɪt], [bɪkɪʔ].

The first three-syllable words similarly had no closed syllables and had a repeated syllable. They consisted of a combination of a single syllable and a repeated one, e.g., [banana] $PV(NV)^2$, [peːtoto] $PV(PV)^2$. Gradually more complex structures came into use: $(NV)^2LVP$ [meːmeːlot], $P(V)^2FV$ [gahava], and these were followed by fully differentiated ones: P̂LVPVPVS [plætɪpus] 'platypus', PVSVPV [taɪsɪku] 'tricycle'.

The first four-syllable word was similarly repetitive: [maːtotaːto] C(VCV)C(VCV), and consisted of familiar syllables with a simple contrast of N and P: N(VPV)P(VPV).

The first five-syllable word was another form of 'tomato' and was also very repetitive: [maːtotototo] $CV((CV)^2)^2$, again with the familiar contrast of NV and PV: $NV((PV)^2)^2$.

It has been seen that one-syllable words and reduplicated syllable words were used before differentiated two-syllable words were acquired. Three-syllable words followed slowly until differentiated two-syllable words were being used freely, and it was some time before four-syllable and five-syllable words came to be used regularly—in fact, not until after the age of two. How greater differentiation took place within words over a period of time in the same child's phonological development has been described in separate studies (Waterson 1970, Paper 4), the phenomenon being essentially the same—a wider use of the familiar appearing to make possible the production of what was new (in this case, the use of more familiar features and a minimum of syntagmatic differentiation when a new contrast was being attempted).

Growth in complexity and length of sentence

Increase in length and complexity of sentence shows a parallel to that of syllable and word. Speech began with one-word sentences and the first two-word sentences were mostly repetitive:

[gɔn, gɔn] Gone, gone {gɔn}²   (cf. the structure of the first two-syllable words: $(CV)^2$.)
[gɑː, gɑː] Car, car {gɑː}²

Differentiated, non-repetitive two-word sentences, consisting of familiar words, began to be used more:

[mama gɔn] Mama's gone {mama gɔn}
[mɔː diː] More cheese {mɔː diː}

and when they outnumbered the repetitive type and were used freely, three-word sentences came into use. These mainly consisted of familiar shorter sentences—that is to say, they consisted of familiar ready-made units; for instance, {mama gʟa gɔn} 'Mama's glove's gone' consisted of the frequently used {mama gʟa} and the very common {gɔn}; and {mœ ge:k dada} 'More cake, Dada' was made up of {mœ ge:k} (the usual request for cake), together with the name of the person to whom the request was addressed (the familiar {dada}). These may be compared with the structure of the first three-syllable words, which were a combination of familiar syllables, PV and NV: PV(NV)[2] and PV(PV)[2].

Sentences of four or more words were also first repetitive in form:

Four-word sentences:
[ɑ: ba:, ɑ: ba:] Ah Bob, ah Bob {ɑ: ba:}[2]
[dada di:, dada di:] Dada's tea, Dada's tea {dada di:}[2]

Five-word sentences:
[bɛə, ɲaɲa bɛə, tu: bɛə] 'Bear, another bear, two bears
{{bɛə}{ɲaɲa bɛə}{tu: bɛə}}

Gradually, when more of the differentiated type began to be used, even longer sentences came into use, as seen in stage 7.

Conclusions

It has been shown that increase in length and in complexity of the syllable took place in a similar way to that of monosyllabic words. A parallel in the way one-syllable, two-syllable, three-syllable, four-syllable, and five-syllable words were acquired is evident in that increase in length first took place by the repetition of some part or by the use of what was familiar: CV syllables and P and N systems. This same kind of process was seen in the increase of sentence length and complexity, which was achieved by the repetition of words or by the use of a combination of familiar short sentences. There was thus a parallel in the way increase in length and complexity (syntagmatic differentiation) took place at the levels of syllable, word, and sentence. The similarity of this to Piaget's *vertical décalage* was pointed out to the writer by G. P. Ivimey of the Institute of Education, University of London (personal communication).[3]

Growth at the phonetic and phonological levels has been seen to be from the simple to the complex. When speech first began, the syllables, words and sentences were of very simple structure and were short in length. Increase in complexity first took place in single syllable words and sentences and when there was an increase in word and sentence length, there was no great increase in their complexity. Through the use of the familiar, sentences of greater complexity and greater length were produced than would otherwise have been possible at the particular stage of development; progress was thus closely related to the use of what was familiar. Words and sentences with repeated elements were used frequently to begin with, when the particular structure involved was becoming assimilated into the phonological system. The number of repetitive elements gradually decreased and the differentiated increased.

From the account given in this paper, it has been seen that increase in utterance length involves greater complexity not only in terms of the

---

3 For Piaget's *vertical décalage* see Sinha and Walkerdine (1978).

number of syllables within a word, or of words within a sentence, but also in relation to the degree of differentiation or number of contrasts within the syllable, word, and sentence—whether the articulations involved are new or familiar, whether the consonants at the beginning and ending of a syllable are the same or different, new or familiar, and whether there is a high or low degree of differentiation within the words concerned. This suggests that phonetic and phonological complexity brings its own constraints on utterance length.

The fact that new, longer utterances were first produced with familiar articulations and a relatively low degree of syntagmatic differentiation, compared with the level of differentiation possible in shorter utterances, leads to the speculation that as far as processes of planning and production are concerned, the overall complexity of longer utterances with a low level of syntagmatic differentiation does not greatly exceed that of shorter utterances consisting of fewer items but having a higher degree of differentiation. The selection of items from the memory store and their arrangement in a particular sequence must in itself involve quite complex operations, so the structure of longer utterances needs to be relatively simple at first. If this were not so, children would start using longer utterances much earlier than they do. Further support for this speculation comes from the fact that longer utterances are produced by repetition and by the combination of established units: either syllables, words, or short sentences; the use of repetition and of established, ready-made units must economize on planning. Further careful observations and testing are needed to assess the validity of this speculation.

This particular child's language development was especially patterned and systematic. Being highly intelligent,[4] he may have hit on a useful strategy early which enabled him to process speech efficiently. On the other hand, it is possible that this systematicity became evident because the child happened to be very vocal and was recorded daily, so that most phases of development were captured. Whatever the reason may be, the evidence suggests that similar neural processes were at work in his processing of syllables, words, and sentences. It is interesting that the same kind of growth in complexity at word level has been reported in the phonological development of a Spanish-speaking child (Marlys Macken, Stanford Child Language Project: personal communication); similar use of the familiar when learning the new has been reported in the emergence of language from babbling in a study of a Thai baby (Tuaycharoen 1977), and the use of ready-made units has already been demonstrated in the acquisition of syntax (e.g., Clark 1974). The same sort of repetitive and differentiated use of words in early sentences has been noted in the literature both for English (for instance, Bloom 1973) and for other languages (for example, for Dutch, cf. Schaerlaekens 1973). It is thus likely that this type of development is not idiosyncratic to the child reported on here.

It has been demonstrated that at first, increase in complexity does not take place at the same time at all the different levels of language. The semantic level and cognitive development have not been considered in this paper but it may well be that these are the levels at which

---

[4] The child has always been around two years ahead of his peers at school.

progress is fastest, as so much depends on the child's understanding of the world around him for his language learning (cf. Slobin 1973). Language learning is very individual. Some children may advance faster at one level than at another and it may be that not all advance at the phonetic and phonological levels so far ahead of syntax as the subject of this paper (cf. for instance, Joan Velten, whose phonetic and phonological development was relatively slow (Velten 1943)). A great deal more work needs to be done before general statements can be made.

The main conclusions that can be drawn from the observations presented in this paper may be summarized as follows. The evidence suggests that the principle of *vertical décalage* may apply at the level of language learning—further studies are needed to test this. The major constraints on utterance length (leaving aside the question of cognitive constraints) depend on structural complexity and non-familiarity at the various interrelated levels of language. Language experience makes familiar what has been acquired and hence enables progress to be made in the acquisition of what is new; thus experience of language is clearly an essential part of the process of language learning, just as experience is necessary for the acquisition of other human skills. The child's ability to process language is very limited at first and he operates within his limits, so that when there is a major advance at one level there may be little or no progress at others. The acquisition of word forms first takes place by processing each item as an individual unit, but later on, learning proceeds by pattern recognition, and classification is by pattern as well as by individual item, so that speech processing becomes more efficient and the rate of learning increases.

Longitudinal studies of a larger number of children in relation to different languages, showing the interrelations of development at the various levels of language, may show that what has been illustrated here is typical of language development. It may be that such studies could lead to a better understanding of how speech is processed. A practical advantage of this type of analysis is that it provides a means for assessing the relative complexity of words and sentences by taking into account the number of syntagmatic contrasts involved. Such an analysis is more complicated than MLU as a way of arriving at some kind of comparability in the language development of children, but it provides a more accurate means of comparing the level of attainment. It makes possible the assessment of an individual child's achievement and provides some indication of what is within his capacity at the particular time. This could be very important for the teaching of the deaf and those with language disorders.

6
A TENTATIVE DEVELOPMENTAL MODEL
OF PHONOLOGICAL REPRESENTATION

First published in: Myers, T., Laver, J., and Anderson, J. (eds.) (1981). *The Cognitive Representation of Speech*. Amsterdam: North-Holland. 323-33.

In the present state of knowledge, the postulation of an underlying representation for speech can only be very tentative but such attempts are justified, as they raise issues which provide new bases for discussion and research. It is hoped that the model proposed in this paper will serve such a function. The writer sees its main contribution as offering an alternative theoretical approach for work on speech perception and interpretation—namely, that of pattern recognition and pattern matching, based on prosodic phonology, a non-linear theory, as opposed to linear theories in which phoneme segment identification is involved. What is put forward is not purely speculative but is firmly data-based. It arises from naturalistic case studies of the acquisition of the phonological system of English.

It is now widely accepted that the phoneme is not useful as a unit for the study of speech perception (see Paper 7). It is also widely recognized that speech interpretation is not normally dependent solely and primarily on the use of auditory cues but is greatly assisted by factors such as knowledge of the language, gestures, knowledge of the subject matter, context, cultural backgrounds of speaker and hearer, and so on. These produce expectations and at the same time constrain the probabilities. A speech processing model must be compatible with this and should not place too heavy a dependence on phonetic and phonological cues. In the model presented here, speech recognition depends on a minimum of auditory cues (which comprise the 'pattern' of the word or larger unit) and leans heavily on knowledge of the language and the kind of non-verbal cues listed above. A developmental model needs to be universal in principle (that is to say, the principles must be applicable to speech processing in general), but it must also be able to handle the data of specific languages (i.e., the acquisition of the phonological system of a particular language). It is claimed that the model presented in this paper fulfils these conditions.

As the acquisition of the phonological system is gradual (Paper 5), a model needs to account for the development of levels of representation, whatever these may be, and changes in the form of a child's word in process of acquisition should be relatable to changes in the levels of representation. The developmental model proposed in this paper takes this into account.

The proposed model is grounded in prosodic phonology, which places an emphasis on whole units in speech and on the syntagmatic relations within and between the units. The theory thus takes into account co-articulations and overlapping, which are essential features of speech. Because of this syntagmatic character, there is a greater correlation between findings made in acoustic studies and the phonological elements of this theory than with those of phoneme-based theories.[1]

---

1 For prosodic phonology, see Palmer (1970); Robins (1964); Papers 1 and 2.

Those proposing models of underlying phonological representation in relation to child language are much concerned with the question of how many levels of representation are required and what their nature is (cf. Ingram 1976; Macken 1980; Menn 1979a, 1979b; Smith 1981). In this paper a case is made for two levels: a phonetic level, Level of Representation 1 (LR1) for speech reception and recognition, and a lexical-phonological level (the lexicon), Level of Representation 2 (LR2), which is concerned with interpretation and production.

A phonetic level of representation is necessary in order to relate the physical (acoustic) form of the utterance to its interpretation as a word or sentence of the language. From the rapidity with which utterances are interpreted, it is generally accepted that it is not possible to process the whole of the acoustic signal and that there can be no one-to-one relation between the input and its interpretation (Denes 1963). Segment by segment processing is, of course, quite out of the question. It seems that there must be some kind of analysis involving a restricted number of cues, and evidence from first-language acquisition of learning by auditory pattern recognition (Papers 3, 4 and 5) suggests the likelihood of serial *scanning* for *word* and *sentence patterns* as an essential part of the processing of an utterance.

If then, as suggested above, only a limited number of acoustic cues in the form of an auditory pattern is used for word recognition, this is added confirmation of there being no direct access from the auditory input to the word in the lexicon and a further justification for a phonetic level of representation. It is suggested that the acoustic signal is filtered so that only the essential cues remain: these, it is proposed, are mainly features that are auditorily salient for the child (Paper 4). It is proposed that they are then synthesized into possible phonetic patterns of the language and are matched with the phonological patterns in the lexicon for interpretation.

There is less controversy about a lexical level of representation. No one disputes that every speaker has a lexicon—that is to say, that there is a large number of words known to him which is recognized when heard and most of these words are used by him. There is thus a stock of words stored in some form in the memory. The phonological system at word level (leaving aside the phonology of larger units like word-group, clause, sentence) is part of the lexicon in that the latter incorporates the total set of different word structures, with their different distributions of a limited set of sounds. The lexicon and phonological system are thus inextricably linked, hence LR2 being labelled 'lexical-phonological'. As *whole* words are known and remembered (apparently, in auditory form), it may be deduced that each word in the lexicon has its full phonetic specification. It is suggested that the phonetic specifications may be organized in a 'network', such as shown in fig. 2 (see p. 112) in order that pattern matching between LR1 and LR2 can take place in the most economical way.

For ease of exposition, the final stage of the proposed developmental model is considered first. Fig. 1 (see overleaf) shows the functions of LR1 and LR2 in relation to input and output as suggested for the fluent speaker/hearer. The model applies to the monolingual speaker but it can also apply to the bilingual and multilingual speaker, in which cases each language will have its own section in LR1 and a separate LR2. As the title of the paper indicates, the model is tentative, and as all will appreciate, it is over-simple. It deals only with phonetics and phonology and hence must be seen as part of a larger processing system. Among other things, it should be linked to a component in which ideas are formulated for expression as speech. A syntactic component is also essential. This would be composed of syntactic patterns. In fact, multi-word utterances can be handled by the model if phrase, clause, and sentence patterns are included in LR1 and LR2. A semantic component is also necessary to link together words of similar meanings. The scope of this paper is restricted to the representation of phonology, so syntactic and semantic components are not considered.

Fig. 1: *Phonological processing model: fluent monolingual speaker/hearer*

INPUT:	Familiar language material.
Processing:	Analysis by abstraction of perceptually salient features. Synthesis of features into possible phonetic patterns of the language.
LEVEL OF REPRESENTATION 1:	Store of possible phonetic patterns of the language (no meanings).
Processing:	Reception and recognition of phonetic patterns. Matching patterns with LR2.
LEVEL OF REPRESENTATION 2:	Store of lexical-phonological patterns (meanings included) with full phonetic specification, i.e., words.
Processing:	Interpretation of phonetic patterns (through matching). Production of speech.
OUTPUT:	Phonetic form.

The model functions in the following way. The first analysis of the input is to distinguish between speech and non-speech (not shown in fig. 1); the latter includes bird-song, music, animal calls, thunder, noise of machines, etc., and will be analysed under a different heading from speech. Speech will be divided into (one or more) known languages, and other linguistic possibilities, e.g., unknown foreign languages, phonetic 'nonsense', and so on (also not shown in fig. 1). Fig. 1 illustrates the processing of familiar language material only. Firstly, utterances are scanned and broken up into chunks—say, into phrase, clause, sentence, on the basis of intonation patterns. Each chunk is scanned further for salient areas on which attention is then focused, for instance, on areas of stress and accent, which mark the high information points of the utterance; these are generally carried by content words as opposed to function words, which are usually unstressed. Auditorily salient features at these points are abstracted and synthesized into possible phonetic patterns of the language which are stored in LR1. These patterns have no lexical meaning. The synthesis of each pattern is constrained by the set of salient features abstracted at the particular points in the chunk and the sequence in which they occur. Many non-salient, redundant features are ignored. The synthesized patterns are then matched with the

A tentative developmental model of phonological representation

lexical-phonological patterns in LR2, which include meanings (that is to say, they represent words). This is done with the aid of the semantics and pragmatics of what the utterance is predicted most likely to mean, from the sequence of content words and the non-verbal cues. The scanning and the matching of patterns within the chunk is carried on simultaneously so that the interpretation of the words is considered together, and the scanning of the following chunk starts before the interpretation of the first is complete so that that too influences the interpretation (see Paper 7). It is at LR1 that words will be accepted or rejected as conforming to the phonological system of the language. For instance, 'fleek' and 'blit' can be matched against patterns of English: 'fleek' will match the F̂LVP pattern (to which 'flip', 'fright' and 'fleet' belong) and 'blit' will match the P̂LVP pattern (to which 'plate', 'bright' and 'creek' belong) so they will be accepted, but 'fsog' will be rejected because there is no F̂SVP pattern in English.

Salient auditory cues in certain arrangements comprise the phonetic patterns of words. These patterns are schemata only, not the full acoustic spectra, and are sufficient to enable known words to be recognized with the aid of non-verbal cues. The recognition of content words in a particular sequence in an utterance provides enough information to constrain the probabilities of how they relate to each other, and to enable the unstressed, non-salient function words to be filled in to fit the rhythmic pattern of the utterance—in other words, the syntactic pattern can be reconstructed, and the whole utterance can thus be interpreted. (For confirmation of this kind of interpretation from hearing errors see Waterson 1971a). The function words do not need to be given much attention in speech processing in the normal course of events as they are limited in number, and their use is often predictable from the sequence in which the high information content words appear. That words should be recognized by only part of their acoustic make-up is not surprising if there is a parallel between visual and auditory perception, as it seems there must be (Neisser 1967). The visual image of a familiar object can be reconstructed mentally from a viewing of a part of it. For instance, if one sees a corner of a tape recorder showing from under a pile of papers, one has no difficulty in recognizing it as a whole tape recorder— that is, in reconstructing a mental image of the whole. Similarly, it is highly probable that one needs only an auditory pattern or even part of a pattern of a familiar word in order to be able to recognize it—that is to say, to reconstruct the full phonetic form. That familiarity aids speech processing is well known.

As already indicated, LR2 is concerned with the storage of words in their full auditory phonetic form and provides for the identification of the input by pattern matching. It is also the basis for production. The way words and their phonetic specifications are organized (that is, the phonological system) is obviously crucial to the model, as it must be possible for whole or part phonetic patterns to be matched very rapidly with the appropriate phonological patterns. A possible organization of phonological patterns in the form of a network is illustrated from child language in fig. 2 (see overleaf). In the early stages a child's LR1 and LR2 are considered to differ considerably from those of an adult. As parents and those who have studied the language development of very young children know, children's vocabulary for comprehension and production is very small at first and great use is made of contextual cues; adult speech has to be adapted in various ways to their level of comprehension (Snow and Ferguson 1977). Children's limited experience of language at the start means that they do not control a sufficient number of different word structures to cover all the patterns and functional sound contrasts of the adult language, nor do they necessarily pay attention to and recognize all the sounds of the adult language when first beginning to speak (Paper 4; Fourcin 1978). They therefore cannot have the adult phonological representation at the time when speech begins, unless of course they are late starters, so they have to construct their own levels of representation. As learning progresses, they pay attention to more of what is functional in the adult phonological system, i.e., the less salient features (Papers 4 and 5) until eventually their representations match those of adults.

The examples used for illustrating the possible organization of phonological patterns are taken from a stage in language development when there was a sudden expansion in the vocabulary. At this time the child had mostly CV, VC, CVC, and CVCV words. As the intention is to illustrate the principle, only CVC examples are considered and the network for only one particular pattern is given. The child had the following patterns:

1) Plosive-vowel-plosive, e.g.: [bʌp] cup, [bɪp] bib, [gek] cake, [gɔk] clock, [gɪk] stick, [gʌk] duck, [dɔp] stop. In LR2 these are organized under PVP.
2) Plosive-vowel-nasal, e.g.: [gɔn] gone, [daun] down, [dʌn] stone. These are organized under PVN.
3) Nasal-vowel-nasal, e.g.: [mu:m] moon, [mæm] man. These are organized under NVN.

PVP, which has the largest number of examples, is selected for illustration.

Fig. 2: *Organization (network) of phonological patterns in LR2*

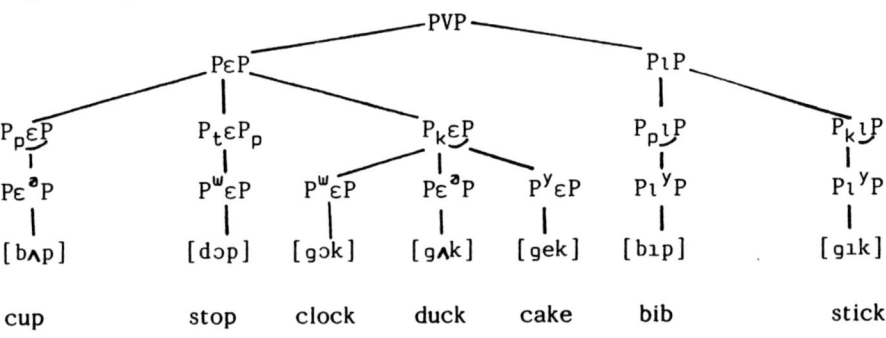

The symbols α, ɛ, ɪ, are used to represent the three functional contrasts at the V place of PVP. These function in conjunction with contrasting syllable prosodies which are represented by the symbols y, w, and ə. P stands for the plosive system which has the possibility of a contrast of three terms: p, t, and k. A fuller account of child English phonology in terms of prosodic theory is given in Paper 2.

A tentative developmental model of phonological representation

The organization of the child's PVP words shows a division by V grade into PɛP and PɪP. Under each of these headings further subdivisions are made by the terms at the onset, namely, p, t, and k, and by the prosodies y, w, and ə (see fig. 2 on opposite page). There are certain redundancies that can be by-passed in processing. Suppose a PVP phonetic pattern is matched with PVP → PɛP → P_pɛP: the contrast of ə and w of Pɛ^{ə}P and P^{w}ɛP is redundant, so can be by-passed, to go directly from P_pɛP to [bʌp] 'cup'. However, if the match is with P_kɛP, the w, ə, y contrast is important, as it carries the main distinction between [gɔk] 'clock', [gʌk] 'duck', and [gek] 'cake'. If the match is with PɪP, the contrast of p and k carries the main distinction, and y is redundant.

If the child next acquires 'cat' as [gæk], he will have a new V contrast in the PVP network, that of α:

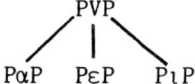

If he then acquires 'cart' as [gɑk], he will have a new prosodic contrast of y and w, and the network will expand again:

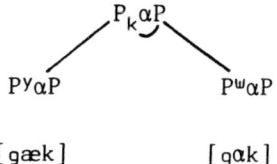

[gæk]   [gɑk]

Suppose the child then acquires 'cook' as [guk]. This will result in a new contrast of y and w with PɪP:

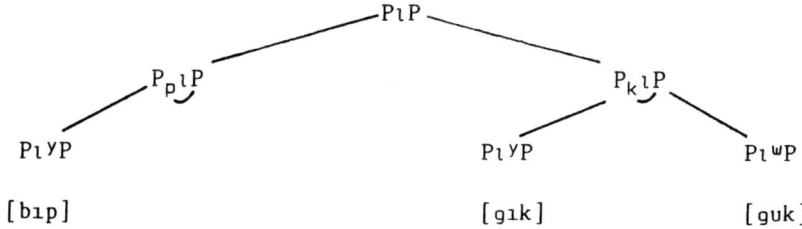

[bɪp]   [gɪk]   [guk]

In these ways the PVP network will expand and become more differentiated. When the child begins to make a contrast of place of articulation between onset and ending (for instance, velar-labial [kʌp] in 'cup', and alveolar-velar [dʌk] in 'duck', and so on), his network will become even more complex.

Only a very small sample of a very simple system has been shown. If one thinks of the adult system, with many thousands of words in the lexicon, the adult network must be extremely complex. However, this does not invalidate the model as the network of the human brain is very complex, and it is not impossible that it could handle such a processing system.

An example of how the interpretation of a word takes place in relation to the suggested network is given here. Context: the child is out with his mother. She draws his attention to a dog carrying a stick by saying 'Look, doggie got stick' ['luk, 'dɔgɪ 'gɔt 'stɪk]. 'Stick' is the intonation nucleus and has the strongest accent and is thus the most salient, and is also salient by recency. The child has the word 'stick' as [gɪk]. He sees the dog carrying the stick. He pays attention to the most salient part of the utterance, which is 'stick', but as [s] of [stɪk] is not auditorily salient, he identifies the phonetic pattern as plosive-vowel-plosive. He probably identifies this pattern by the sudden increase in acoustic energy on the release of the articulatory closure of the first plosive; the peak of intensity during the production of the syllabic element, which indicates a vowel, and the sudden cutting off of the syllabic phase which indicates a final plosive. The position of F1 shows a close vowel.[2] This restricted information enables him to make a match with PVP and then a further match with PɪP (see fig. 2). No further matching is necessary: the contrast of p and k is redundant as the context, the presence of the stick, provides enough information to identify what the child has heard as [gɪk] (his 'stick') and not [bɪp] (his 'bib'). Thus the few acoustic cues by which he recognizes a plosive-close vowel-plosive pattern, together with the visual cues of the context, are sufficient for the recognition of the word as 'stick'. Context assists in rapid speech processing without the necessity for detailed auditory analysis and matching.

In the case of PɛP words: [bʌp], [dɔp], [gɔk], [gʌk], and [gek], the hearer's knowledge that there is a wide range of possibilities no doubt ensures that more acoustic information is included in the scanning. The presence of the relevant object will, of course, constrain the probabilities very considerably. More processing will be needed in a situation where, for instance, a toy cup, clock, and duck are all present and the child is asked for one of them. In that event more scanning of the acoustic signal is needed to include, for example, F2 transitions to identify whether matching should be with p, t, or k.

At the stage of development of the network in fig. 2, the child's LR1 and LR2 patterns are unlike the adult's, and so is his production. At later stages, the child's LR1 patterns become like the adult's but his LR2 patterns may differ, depending on the constraints of his production ability and the level of development of the network. Later still, his LR1 and LR2 patterns will be like the adult's but his production may continue to differ for a time. This may be compared with the musical performance of a learner who knows how a piece should sound but does not have enough skill to achieve it. Of course not all the patterns are at the same stage of development at the same time. Some progress faster than others, and some match the adult pattern long before others. Eventually the child's LR1 and LR2 and production all match the adult's.

The processing involved in learning a new word must differ from that of recognizing a familiar one. Having looked at how familiar words may be recognized and interpreted in accordance with the model, consideration will now be given to how a new word is learnt, that is, how the patterns of LR1 and LR2 are constructed. In the case of a child

---

2 F1 is of lower frequency and greater intensity than F2 and F3 and children pay greater attention to the lower frequencies at first (Fourcin 1978; Paper 4).

A tentative developmental model of phonological representation 115

learning his first language, the patterns of LR1 and LR2 are constructed and then constantly restructured as perceptual and production skills develop. When a new word is being learnt, a great deal of analysis needs to be made in order to arrive at a phonetic specification for LR2. This means that there must be more detailed scanning of the acoustic signal in learning than in the recognition of a familiar word, for which only the pattern or part of the pattern generally suffices.

The construction of a child's forms for the word 'pudding' and its restructuring in relation to LR1 and LR2 will now be considered. The different recorded forms of the word provide an interesting case for trying to relate changes in form to changes in levels of representation. The forms are: age 1;6 [pupu]; early 1;7 [bubaɪɲ] and [bubuɪɲ]; later 1;7 [pupəɲ] and [bupəɲ]; 1;8 [budun]; then [pudun] and finally [pudɪŋ].

The child's productions are assumed to follow his perception, and patterns at LR2 are considered to be constructed on the maximum perceptual information available to the child. Production is based on LR2, so changes in patterns at LR2 result in changes in production.[3]

Age 1;6: [pupu].

The child's production suggests that most attention is given to the auditorily salient features of 'pudding' ['pudɪŋ], namely, the whole of the accented first syllable, and the plosive and close vowel grade of the second. The final nasal is short and weakly articulated and is thus non-salient, and is not produced by the child, nor are the features of frontness and spreading of the second syllable, which are associated with F2 and F3. The salient features listed above are considered to be the input.

The analysis for the construction of the LR1 pattern would involve the following:

1) number of syllables;
2) type of syllable, viz., open or closed onset and ending; breathy or non-breathy onset and ending;
3) type of closure: stop, oral or nasal;
4) place of closure: labial or non-labial;
5) type of syllabic phase: open, mid, or close vowel grade, long or short;
6) syllable features: backness and rounding; frontness and spreading, or neutrality as to those features.

Synthesis would follow the analysis and a pattern would be constructed on the basis of the features abstracted. Here the pattern consists of two open syllables, CVCV, the first with a breathy onset, ^{h}CVCV: both syllables with initial stop, PVPV, the first with labial place, P_pVPV, and both syllables with high V grade, $P_\iota P_\iota$; the first syllable with backness and rounding, $PV^{wr}PV$. The place of the stop, the type of onset, and the syllable features of the second syllable are left unspecified. A skeleton version of this pattern suffices for LR1, viz., $P_\iota P_\iota$, by which adult's 'pudding' [pudɪŋ] will be recognized. The pattern for LR2 requires more detailed specification as it is the basis for production, but it can only be constructed within the constraints of what the child is capable of producing and the degree of development of the network. As the specification for the second syllable is incomplete, all

---

[3] For a fuller discussion of the relation between perception and production, see Paper 4.

that the child can construct so far is PVPV—$^hP\iota^?P\iota$—$P_p\iota P_?\iota$. This incomplete pattern is sufficient for recognition of adult 'pudding' but as the LR2 pattern is the basis for production, the specification has to be completed in some way. The problem is overcome by using the same term for both syllable onsets, viz., p, $P_p\iota P_p\iota$, and the same prosodies, viz., h and w, as in the first syllable, $^hP\iota^hP\iota$ and $P\iota^wP\iota^w$, to complete the specification. This then is the basis for the child's [pupu], a reduplicated form, $(PV)^2$, such being the usual structure of the child's two-syllable words at the time. The form [pupu] was used for some time before it underwent a change.

Age 1;7 (early): [bubaɪɲ] and [bubuɪɲ].

These forms suggest that the child is now aware of features that he had not noted before and he is attempting to produce them. He now hears the word 'pudding' differently: he is aware of a final nasal and may or may not be aware of the velar place of closure.[4] He is also aware of the frontness and non-rounding of the second syllable as opposed to the backness and rounding of the first. There is thus some new information to add to the patterns of LR1 and LR2. LR1 will have a new pattern, PVPVN, instead of $(PV)^2$. The new specification for the LR2 pattern is as follows: it now has a final N, PVPVN, and a w-y contrast between the two syllables, $P\iota^wP\iota^yN$, thus getting closer to the adult LR2 pattern. The syllable onsets in the child's pattern are now different, h̲ instead of h, h̲PVh̲PVN (no longer involving the contrasts of voicelessness of consonants and voice of vowels) but the terms of the P systems are still p, P_pVP_pVN. The child's pattern lacks only the h-h̲ contrast at the syllable onsets, and the contrasts of p, t, k of P—P̄—N. h onsets of both syllables were more usual in the child's system at this time. They were apparently easier to produce because of familiarity, so what was less easy was reduced when attempting the new and unfamiliar. The attempts at frontness in the second syllable are conducive to the production of a palatal closure [ɲ] in final position. The points at which frontness starts in the child's two forms is probably related to production difficulties.

If at this stage an adult used [pupu] instead of [pudɪŋ] for 'pudding', it would not be recognized because it would not match the child's LR1 pattern (which is no longer PιPι but is now PιPιN) and so could not be matched with his LR2 pattern for recognition. This offers a possible explanation for children's non-recognition of their own forms when used by adults.

Age 1;7 (later): [pupəɲ] and [bupəɲ].

These two forms show greater skill in production; the child is now using breathy onsets with the recently acquired contrasts between the syllables, $^hP\iota^{wh}P\iota^yN$. He has also begun to make a contrast of non-breathy and breathy onsets, though in the wrong sequence, h̲PVhPVN. In view of the rapid progress of the child's forms at 1;8 (the changes took place within three days) it is likely that he was already aware of the contrast of breathy onset versus non-breathy onset of the two syllables of [pudɪŋ] at 1;7, and also of the different places at which the closures

---

4 The description is now given in articulatory terms instead of acoustic terms for reasons of simplicity.

are made, viz., labial, alveolar and velar. It is probable that the child's patterns at LR1 and LR2 are now like the adult's, the difference in his forms being due to some production difficulty.

Age 1;8: [budun], followed by [pudun] and then [pudɪŋ] within three days.

The child first attempts the labial-alveolar place contrast and while doing so, uses the familiar non-breathy syllable onsets and no contrast of syllable features; the final nasal is alveolar and harmonizes with the alveolar plosive. These articulatory simplifications make the production of the new contrast of labial and alveolar place easier to handle, $\underline{h}P_p V\underline{h}P_t VN_t$. In the second form, [pudun], the new labial-alveolar contrast is used with the contrast of breathy and non-breathy syllable onsets, $^hP_p V\underline{h}P_t VN_t$. Finally, these contrasts are used with the earlier acquired contrast of backness and rounding of the first syllable and frontness and spreading of the second, together with the new contrast of labial, alveolar, and velar places. The child's production is now like the adult's, as is his LR2 pattern, that is: PVPVN, $^hP_l\underline{h}P_lN$, $P_p l^w P_t l^y N_k$. The progress to the adult form within three days and by the use of articulatory simplification suggests that, as proposed above, the child's LR2 pattern was like the adult's at the start of 1;8 but that he still had production difficulties. At this time the child would certainly reject [budun] for 'pudding' from an adult, being well aware that the form was not correct, and he could well say, 'Not [budun]; [budun].'

To summarize, one may say that LR2 patterns are constructed with the maximum information available to the child. At first they are like or very like LR1 patterns—skeleton patterns of salient features fleshed out within the constraints of what the child can manage in relation to his production and organizational capabilities at the time. Later, LR2 has more detail added as the result of the child's increasing perceptual discrimination and attention span; he is able to give more attention to less salient features of the adult model. LR1 patterns remain as skeleton patterns to aid speedy recognition (see Summary). LR1 patterns do, however, undergo changes when the child's awareness of less salient features results in a different pattern; cf. [pupu] for 'pudding' and then the addition of a final nasal with a consequent change of pattern from $(PV)^2$ to PVPVN. Patterns at LR2 are specified in greater detail. Changes in patterns at LR1 and LR2 bring about a restructuring of the whole network. As the child's productions are assumed to follow his perception, changes at LR2 automatically bring about changes in his production, but always within the constraints of his capabilities.

The developmental model will now be outlined. It is proposed that a child starts with no LR1 and no LR2 but with an innate ability to recognize human vocalizations as different from other sounds, and with an ability to recognize auditory samenesses and differences. As the functions of LR1 and LR2 are now known to the reader, the account of the developmental model can be brief. The period from 3 weeks to 18 months is described; after 18 months development is as shown for 'pudding'.

Non-crying vocalizations start at around 3 weeks and from this time to about 4 months the vocalizations take the form of grunting, murmuring, cooing, shrieking, and unstructured babbling. There appears to be no voluntary production of same vocalizations, so it may be deduced that the child has no memory of his own vocalizations, nor probably of those of adults, though there may be direct imitations of adult vocalizations. At this stage the neural system may be tuning in to the recognition of different aspects of productions of the human vocal tract.

From approximately 4 months to 10 months, vocalizations include structured babbling, i.e., repetitive strings. The fact that the same repetitive strings are repeated on different occasions suggests that the child is able to remember and recognize his own babbling patterns. At this time also the child seems to recognize adult imitations of his patterns and imitates back. This production of same patterns means that there may well be some storage, i.e., that LR1 and LR2 have begun to develop. Although the child's output is still random in the main, there are some recognizable patterns, i.e., they are produced on the basis of LR2. LR1 and LR2 are not yet linguistically functional and at this time are universal in character. Some time around 8 months, a 'protolanguage' begins to be used, i.e., a limited set of simple functional vocalizations supplemented by gestures and used in relation to the context (Halliday 1975). These are the first linguistically functional phonological patterns and seem to be partly language-specific, so LR2 now has some rudimentary linguistic function.

Somewhere between 10 and 18 months the first words appear while babbling and the protolanguage continue. As the first words are often used only once or twice, it seems that they are forgotten, i.e., they are not stored at LR2, but gradually language-specific patterns begin to be stored at LR1, and lexical-phonological patterns at LR2. The network is very simple at this time, each individual word having its own fully specified pattern, as yet there being only one word per pattern. LR1 and LR2 now have linguistic function and are language-specific. When the vocabulary begins to expand by way of pattern recognition, the network begins to be organized by pattern in addition to being organized by individual item. Progress of child's forms to adult forms takes place in a similar way to that shown for 'pudding'.

The implications of this model are that the development of LR1 and LR2 is universal up to the protolanguage stage and acts as a preparation for language-specific development. The transition starts with the protolanguage. Thus a very simple non-linguistic network develops first; this changes to a more complex network for the proto-language, which is a necessary precursor for the more elaborate network of language.

Conclusions

The proposed model can handle the phonetic and phonological processing of the adult speaker/hearer (whether monolingual, bilingual, or multilingual) as well as the acquisition of the phonological system of a language. It is universal in that the principles apply to speech processing in general and it is language-specific in that the patterns are the patterns of the language of the environment. The model therefore fulfils the two essential conditions required of a theory of speech processing.

The theory behind the model, that of pattern recognition and pattern matching, is compatible with what is known at other levels of human perception. The phonetic patterns and the phonetic features used to describe them are compatible with much of the acoustic information available in relation to speech.

The model takes into account the importance of non-verbal cues and

119 A tentative developmental model of phonological representation

of the redundancy of speech, and shows why only a small part of the acoustic signal is sufficient for speech interpretation.

On the above grounds alone it seems that the model is worthy of further consideration and development. There are, however, certain further advantages, and these are given below.

As mentioned above, the processing of speech by pattern allows for a great deal of redundancy. As it is a pattern that is recognized, variation in the form of segments within it is unimportant since segments do not need to be identified; any such variation does not interfere with recognition and interpretation. This explains why normalization from one speaker to another across boundaries of dialect, age, sex, rate of speaking, and so on, is so easy, and why speech can be understood under noisy conditions. (For further discussion of this point see Paper 7.)

The model has a place for acceptable phonetic and phonological forms of words which do not happen to occur in the language, e.g., 'fleek' and 'blit' are acceptable in English as there are patterns for these types but 'fsog' is excluded, there being no pattern for this type.

Familiar words are shown to be processed differently from the new and unfamiliar.

The model can account for continuous development of speech processing from the pre-verbal stage to fluent speech, and allows for the growth and extension of the phonological system with the expansion of the vocabulary throughout adulthood.

Children's early simplified forms can be explained by limited linguistic perceptual discrimination, restricted articulatory skills, and the constraints of the developing phonological system in the form of a storage network. The network is organized by pattern and as it is being constructed on limited material, it must perforce be very simple at first. There may be some items which are relatively complex (e.g., [ʔevm̩] for 'heaven') which have individual entries, but the majority have to fit into patterned networks if speech processing is to be efficient and economical. Patterns change gradually as perceptual and articulatory skills develop, and the whole phonological system with its storage network (a network of networks) changes and becomes more complex. Such a view makes it plain why children do not have consonant clusters at first and why mostly one-syllable words are used and few words of two and three syllables. It also becomes clear why there is a minimum of consonant contrasts in their speech and why consonants in CVC words tend to harmonize (as in [gʌk]) and two-syllable words are reduplicated (as in [beːbeː]), especially at the time when the vocabulary begins to expand rapidly. Learning by pattern recognition can also explain many early forms that differ widely from the adult forms, there being individual differences in the way children create their patterns (e.g., Menn 1971; Paper 3; Priestley 1977; Macken 1978).

It has been noted in the literature that a child's direct imitation of an adult form is often more correct than his everyday usage. The model can explain this as the by-passing of LR2. In imitation, the adult form is given detailed analysis (as in the learning of a new word) and is then synthesized as for LR2, with its full phonetic specification, but it is produced directly as phonetic nonsense—that is to say, it is not stored in the network.

Finally, the model can account for a child's failure to recognize his own form of a word when used by an adult, and also earlier forms that have gone out of use. It can account too for a child's annoyance at an adult's use of his incorrect form, the *'fis* phenomenon'.

The phoneme-based approach has held sway in phonetic research for several decades but results in terms of insights into speech processing have proved disappointing. An alternative is offered in this paper which can explain aspects of speech processing for which answers have not been found previously. This suggests that it could provide a promising new line of research.

7
PATTERNS AS UNITS OF SPEECH PERCEPTION

First published in: Tuaycharoen, P., Chudananda, D., Sookgasem, P., Jackson, F., Hvitfeldt, R., and Hvitfeldt, C. (eds.) (1984). *Selected Papers from The International Symposium on Language and Linguistics, Chiang Mai, Thailand.* Bangkok: Thepmongkol Karnpim. 37-61.

Recognizing words does not normally present difficulties to the listener, and yet how it is done is one of the major problems facing speech perception research: it has still not proved possible to establish how we perceive speech, nor what the units are in terms of which we operate. The phoneme had been widely accepted as such a unit, but decades of careful acoustic research failed to find invariant cues to show a one-to-one correspondence between sound and phoneme, which is needed if we are to explain how speech is perceived in terms of phonemes. As Marslen-Wilson (1984: 101) has pointed out,

> Nontheless, it is clear that acoustic-phonetic research, for all its advances over the past thirty years, has failed to satisfactorily answer those questions that are most critical for researchers working on other aspects of language processing.

Many of those involved in speech perception research are now looking for units other than phonemes, as is evident from recent conference papers—for instance, Myers, Laver, and Anderson (1981), and van den Broecke and Cohen (1984). Vaissière summarizes some of the problems in relation to speech recognition programmes, and notes (Myers et al. 1981: 448) that it is 'still a matter of controversy whether speech perception by human listeners involves at a preliminary stage, or even at a later stage, the identification of an ordered series of units, such as phonemes'. Ladefoged (1984: 92) has argued quite strongly against phonemes: 'Perhaps the most startling conspiracy—one that seems to have deceived by far the majority of linguists—is the appearance of phonemes.' (See also Ladefoged 1980.)

The search has moved from speech sound segments to speech sound categories (i.e., the major classes of sound: for instance, plosives, fricatives, nasals), and diphones, demisyllables, syllables, words, and word groups are now being considered as candidates for units of speech perception. In common with several others working in the field, the writer believes that the concern should be with words and larger units: the question is whether invariant cues can be found for them. It seems that this must be possible, and the aim of this paper is to present the concept of an *invariant auditory word pattern* which functions within a framework of larger patterns, such as phrase, clause, and sentence. In such word patterns, the prosodic characteristics (i.e., the number of syllables, place of strong stress, syllable structure of the word, the relation of the syllables to each other within the word, the classes of sound in the syllables) are more important than the segmental. The concept of phoneme is not involved.

The concept of an invariant word pattern may be new but it should be seen as a logical development bearing in mind that intonation patterns of languages have long been recognized as invariant. The intonation patterns of English, for instance, have been described essentially as consisting of seven tunes (O'Connor and Arnold 1973). These are recognized as being the same for male, female, and child speakers, even though the actual pitches on which the contours are produced differ. Recognition depends on the contour (pattern), not on the actual frequencies, and similarly, the rhythm or stress patterning of the utterance depends on the relationship of strongly and weakly stressed syllables, not on actual degrees of intensity of syllabic peaks.

This concept of an invariant word pattern is an essential part of a theory of speech perception by pattern recognition, which will also be described here. The theory arose from the writer's work on child phonology; data of the speech development of the particular child studied are similar to those of other English children in very many respects, so it seems there is justification for generalizing the findings and formulating a theory of speech processing in early language development on the basis of such data. Supporting evidence was found in a study of a certain type of hearing error, and the theory will be illustrated from these sources, as well as by an example of some dialect forms of a word. It is hoped to show that the concept of an invariant pattern can go some way to help to explain some of the current problems of speech perception research, viz.:

1) the relationship between children's early speech perception and production;
2) the rapidity of speech perception, recognition, and interpretation by adults;
3) normalization from speaker to speaker across such variables as dialect, age, sex, and rate of speaking.

The theory still needs more work but it is hoped that even in its present stage it may contribute to thought on the subject and perhaps be the source of new ideas.

There seems to be general agreement in current theories of speech perception that the listener does not make use of the whole of the acoustic signal of an utterance, and that there is a great deal of redundancy in speech, and that speech perception is an active process in which the listener, as it were, constructs an interpretation: 'active hypothesizing concerning the intended message is clearly a part of the speech perception process' (Bond and Garnes 1980: 128). The listener has to abstract from the acoustic signal of the utterance, but he also has to make use of his knowledge of the language, the discourse context, the actual situation, and his knowledge of the world. All these produce expectations and constrain the possibilities, and so increase predictability. He thus makes his hypotheses and perceives what he expects to perceive. This is perhaps most easily demonstrated by misperceptions or hearing errors. An example is given on pp. 129-32. It would seem that any theory of speech perception and interpretation must not depend too heavily on acoustic cues and must allow for much use of other available information. The theory to be described here involves a minimum of acoustic cues: an auditory pattern of a limited number of such cues, which is interpreted in conjunction with discourse and other linguistic and non-linguistic information.

An account of the application of the theory follows. First, an indication is given of how it can be applied to speech perception in children. The same sort of processing is then suggested as a possible explanation of how normalization takes place: this is illustrated in relation to adult speech. Finally, the way speech processing can be shown to be very rapid is demonstrated in a discussion of a misperception.

The first account showing a child's learning of the phonology by pattern recognition is to be found in Paper 3. A few examples taken from there suffice for illustration. Data for the study of the particular child's language development were collected daily by means of phonetic transcription from the first recognizable word at around 10½ months to the use of multi-word utterances at around age 2 years. Notes on the context of use and on the child's general development were also made. No experiments were carried out. The data were not analysed until some time after collection was completed, so the transcription and data collection could not have been influenced by any ideas or preconceptions of how the development of the phonological system was taking place. The data in Paper 3 refer to age around 1;6. At this time a large number of the early words differed so greatly from the adult words that they would not have been recognized as such had their consistent usage not shown clearly what their intended referents were. Some examples are: [ɲeːɲeː] for 'window', [ɲiːɲi/ɲẽːɲẽ] for 'finger', [bæbuː] for 'bucket' and 'Bobby', [beːbeː] for 'biscuit', and [βæ, væ, bβæ] for 'fly'. The child appeared to be very inventive but when eventually the data were analysed, it was found that many of his words could be grouped into sets of patterns (for instance, NVNV, PVPV), and that there was a clear and easily statable relationship to the adult words on which they were based. This pattern relationship was describable mainly in terms of what was auditorily most salient in the adult words. An illustration is given below.

Two of the child's words of a PVPV pattern that were homonyms, viz., ['bæbuː], were used for 'bobby' and 'bucket'. Their structure is compared with that of adult's 'Bobby' ['bɔbɪ] and 'bucket' ['bʌkɪt]. The relationships between the syllables within the words are examined, first within ['bæbuː] and then within ['bɔbɪ], and then the relationship holding between the two words is considered. A similar analysis is made of ['bæbuː] and ['bʌkɪt].[1]

Structure of ['bæbuː]:

1) There are two syllables.
2) Both are open syllables: CVCV.
3) The first is strongly stressed, the second weakly stressed: 'CVCV.
4) Both syllables begin with a plosive: PVPV.
5) The plosives are bilabial: $P_p V P_p V$, and lax, with a degree of voicing: $^h P_p V ^h P_p V$.
6) The first syllable has a more open vowel, the second a more close: CACI.
7) The first syllable has no lip-rounding; the second has lip-rounding: $^r CV^r CV$.
8) The first syllable has frontness, the second backness: $^y CV ^w CV$.
9) The first syllable is shorter than the second: CV̆CV̄.

---

[1] The analysis is an advance on that in Paper 3, as the theory has been developed further.

Structure of ['bɔbɪ]:

1) There are two syllables.
2) Both are open syllables: CVCV.
3) The first is strongly stressed, the second weakly stressed: 'CVCV.
4) Both syllables begin with a plosive: PVPV.
5) The plosives are bilabial, $P_p V P_p V$, and syllable onsets are lax, with a degree of voicing: $\underline{b}P_p V \underline{b}P_p V$.
6) The first syllable has a more open vowel, the second a more close: CACI.
7) The first syllable has lip-rounding and the second has none: $^rCV^rCV$. ['bæbuː] has the reverse.
8) The first syllable has backness; the second has frontness: $^wCV^yCV$. ['bæbuː] has the reverse.
9) Both syllables are approximately of the same length. ['bæbuː] has a longer second syllable.

The relationships in (1) to (6) within the word ['bɔbɪ] are the same as in ['bæbuː] (i.e., six out of the nine), and these relationships are invariant. They represent a pattern common to both, which may be represented as $'\underline{b}P_p A\underline{b}P_p I$. The analysis thus suggests that the child was perceiving patterns in the adult words and responding by constructing his own patterns. The features that were produced by the child are those that are auditorily salient in the adult word. Some possible acoustic cues of this salience are suggested below.

1) Intonation: Fo (fundamental frequency).
2) Rhythm, i.e., the relation of strongly and weakly stressed syllables: peaks of intensity for number of syllables; greater or lesser intensity and greater or lesser duration for strong and weak stress respectively.
3) Plosives: salient by the burst (sudden release of energy), possibly also the silent interval in the case of the second plosive; low F1 locus.
4) The relationship of more open vowel to more close: this is salient by F1, which has greater intensity than F2 and F3—which are related to frontness, backness, rounding and non-rounding, features which the child did not produce accurately, as seen above.
5) The bilabiality is visually salient; the complete lip closures for [b] of ['bɔbɪ] can easily be seen. (For the importance of visual cues, see McGurk 1981.) A possible acoustic cue is low frequency locus of F2 (Massaro and Oden 1980).
6) VOT (voicing onset time) at the start of each syllable, which is consistent with English [b] rather than [p], which has delayed VOT.

The above cues appear to be available early to children, as infant speech perception research has shown that infants can discriminate many such features early (Bickley 1983; Crystal 1976; Trehub, Bull and Schneider 1981). The pattern common to the child's and adult's forms of 'Bobby' can thus be described as being represented by salient acoustic cues in a particular relationship—a pattern which represents the bare bones of the word spectrum and which is 'fleshed out' in different ways by adult and child. It has been shown that six out of the nine relationships within the child's and adult's forms of 'Bobby' are the same, so in spite of the apparent dissimilarity, ['bæbuː] is, in fact, quite a good match with ['bɔbɪ]. The child may not have produced all he perceived through lack of skill and he could not have perceived what did not match the adult form,[2] but it may be inferred that what is consistently common to his forms and to the adult words throughout his phonological system at this time was perceived by him and hence was produced.

A comparison between the child's ['bæbu:] for 'bucket' and adult's ['bʌkɪt] shows a similar relationship, but as the difference between the two forms is greater, it is perhaps even more revealing. The child again responds by matching the two syllables, with strong stress on the first. He matches plosives with plosives at the onset of each syllable but he does not respond to the final plosive. The final [t] is weakly articulated, having no audible release (Gimson 1964: 150-1), and is not salient. The onset of the first syllable of ['bʌkɪt] is lax and non-breathy ([b]), as opposed to the breathy onset of the second ([k]), but the child has lax non-breathy onsets in both syllables, with no place of articulation contrast. He was not yet making a contrast of non-breathy/breathy onsets in his two-syllable words. Instead he was reduplicating the plosive at the onset of his first syllable in most of his PVPV words at this time. This avoided the contrast of place as well as non-breathy and breathy syllable onsets.[3] Again the child does not match the actual vowel qualities but he has the same relationship of more open vowel in the first syllable to more close in the second. He was thus responding in the same way to the pattern of salient cues of the adult word, and his construction of his own form was similarly constrained by the limitations of his abilities.

It has been shown above how the child responded in a patterned way to particular types of adult words which may be described as PVPV and PVPVP words. He also responded in patterned ways to other types of adult words. Five different patterns are illustrated in Paper 3, so further exemplification need not be given here. The child does not have the full adult perception at the start. His perceptual discrimination develops gradually (Fourcin 1978; Trehub, Bull and Schneider 1981; Paper 5), so he uses fewer acoustic cues than an adult at the start. He also has to learn which of the many non-salient cues are relevant for the phonological system of the language he is learning, and in production he does not have the skill to make all the necessary articulatory contrasts within a

---

[2] The reasons for the differences in (7), (8), and (9) (pp. 123, 124) could be several: not paying enough attention to F2 and F3 which relate to backness and frontness, and rounding and non-rounding, and are less salient by lesser intensity than F1, which relates to degree of openness of vowel. The child may have been aware of F2 and F3 but not sufficiently to be able to place them in the correct sequence. Absence of lip-rounding in the first syllable may be due to the difficulty of producing lip-rounding with a fairly wide jaw-opening: [ɔ] is among the later acquired English vowels. Lip-rounding in the second syllable of ['bæbu:] may be due to a continuation of labiality after the production of the bilabial consonant. The lengthening of the second syllable of ['bæbu:] may have resulted from the parents' tendency to lengthen the second weakly stressed syllable of two-syllable words when talking to the child.

[3] It is possible that the child did not perceive the place difference but this is doubtful as it can be observed visually: it is more likely that he was not yet able to make the contrast, as evidenced by most of his CVCV words (Papers 4 and 5).

word even though he may be able to produce the particular sounds when they are not in contrast with others within the same word (Papers 3 and 5). In addition, he has to construct a storage system for the words he acquires as his language learning progresses; all this takes much time and effort. His patterns must thus be expected to be much simpler than the adult's, to begin with. Furthermore, because of the constraints of his capabilities, the words the child first constructs will mostly differ from what he perceives. They have to be constructed in a way commensurate with his abilities. It is these own stored constructions that are the basis for his productions and this will account for the differences between his forms and the adult's. (For a full discussion of this point, see Paper 6.)

The child's early patterns, as shown in relation to the PVPV patterns described earlier, are based mainly on the most salient features of the adult's words, i.e., those that are the most easily discriminable. He thus appears to attend selectively to such cues, paying less attention to the less salient, less easily discriminable; but as he gains more linguistic experience and his perceptual discrimination increases, his attention gradually extends to more, and he responds to more of what is less salient, finally matching the adult patterns and forms (Papers 4 and 5). He must, it seems, become aware that non-salient sounds have a function and they are therefore eventually incorporated into his system.

What about speech processing when the child becomes an adult? Can evidence be found for the same sort of pattern recognition in adult speech perception? It seems that it can. Adult words can be classified into patterns in a similar way to that described for the child but mostly with rather more complex patterns, and this will be considered below. If it can indeed be shown that adults perceive speech along the same principles as shown for the child, it will mean that in the normal course of events, the child starts to process speech along the same basic principles as he will when an adult, which seems a reasonable assumption, rather than that he should start in one way and then change course and follow different principles as he grows older. It is possible that if a child does not hit on the right strategy at the start, his language development will be delayed and he will need to change course in order to progress normally.

For the adult the main cues will, of course, include both the salient and less salient cues, as he has learnt which cues are relevant. It seems that among the cues will be those that discriminate the major classes of sounds of the phonological system of his language, i.e., the different cues for manner of articulation and those for the degree of openness of vowels. Other cues will be intensity, duration, and fundamental frequency. Position of loci and formant transitions will also play a part, no doubt. Some of the cues are already known; others need further research. It is suggested that the adult uses the same kind of selective attention as the child when processing the acoustic signal of speech, viz., abstracting patterns of words and larger units. A major part of speech perception may thus be viewed as scanning an utterance for word patterns: this means that skeleton word spectra, not full word spectra, are involved.

A word pattern will consist of cues in a particular relationship. From an acoustic point of view, the main cues could be among the following:

1) Peaks of intensity for number of syllables.

2) Intensity greater in some peaks, lesser in others, marking strong and weak stress.
3) Duration: some syllables longer, some shorter.
4) Fo for pitch patterning.
5) F1 for the relationship of degree of openness of vowels; the vowel of one syllable may be more open, more close, or the same as in the next.
6) Cues for the different classes of consonants which will differentiate them from each other (for instance, a plosive from a nasal, from a fricative, etc.).

Such cues are relative and this means that the word pattern is invariant: the actual degrees of intensity, actual durations, actual frequencies, actual quality of consonants and of vowels are variable from speaker to speaker and vary with rate of speaking, but do not normally affect the pattern.

A few examples of some simple English word patterns will now be given, using prosodic phonology as the theoretical basis. Only a partial analysis will be given—i.e., only as much as is needed to show words as belonging to different sets of patterns; this means that not all the contrasts will be given. In accordance with the theory, there are five classes of consonant in English: P; N; F; S (this includes the affricates [tʃ] and [dʒ]); and L. Vowels are classed by degree of openness into three grades: α; ε; and ι. Some two-syllable words are selected as examples, all with the structure CVCV, and with stress on the first syllable: 'pepper', 'kipper', 'barter', 'naughty', 'mighty', 'needy', 'ladder', 'wicker', 'rigour', 'vigour', 'shudder', and 'sugar'. The vocalic element of the first syllable carries the main contrast, so it is analysed as V, and the one in the second syllable is analysed as a syllabic, ə.

'Pepper', 'kipper', 'barter' belong to the PVPə pattern. Further subdivision is by vowel grade. 'Barter' ['bɑːtə] will have low V grade in the first syllable, PαPə, and there is a contrast of labial and apical terms at onsets: $P_p VP_t ə$. 'Pepper' ['pepə] will have middle V grade, PεPə, with labial terms in both syllables: $P_p VP_p ə$. 'Kipper' ['kıpə] will have high V grade, PιPə, with a contrast of dorsal and labial at the onset of the syllables: $P_k VP_p ə$.

Words like 'naughty' [nɔːtı], 'mighty' ['maıtı], 'needy' ['niːdı] have the pattern NVPə, and will be further subdivided by vowel grade. 'Vigour', 'shudder', and 'sugar' will be of the FVPə pattern, and so on.

Having introduced the concept of an invariant word pattern, the way in which it can help to explain normalization of inter-speaker variability will now be considered. Three different dialect forms of the word 'pocket' will be examined and it will be suggested that the three acoustically different forms share an invariant pattern which enables them to be recognized as the same word. The forms to be examined are ['pɔkıt], ['paːkıt], ['poʔəʔ]. In addition to the difference in acoustic form, they also differ in voice quality but as this is not relevant to the pattern other than placing them in the appropriate dialect, it will be excluded from discussion. When used in context, the native speaker of RP English will have no problem in recognizing these forms as the same word. Their shared invariant pattern is shown in fig. 1 (see overleaf). On the left are mostly articulatory features, in the centre the structure of the pattern, and on the right the possible acoustic cues. These are relative, i.e., not actual frequencies, actual durations, actual intensities, etc., and their relationships are the same in all three forms of 'pocket'; hence the invariance.

Fig. 1: *Normalization: Samenesses in some forms of 'pocket', viz.,* [ˈpɔkɪt], [ˈpaːkɪt], [ˈpoʔəʔ]

Syllable structure	CVCVC	Two relatively high intensity peaks bounded by plosive bursts.
Stress; pitch	ˈCVCVC	Fo involved.
Length of syllables	C̄VCVC	Relatively greater duration of first syllable, shorter of the second.
Stop at each consonantal position	PVPVP	Period of silence; no energy; noise of plosive burst; increase of intensity with the following vowel; low F1 locus.
Labial place of initial stop and non-labial of the other two	P_pVPVP	Low frequency locus for F2 transition of the first stop, the others relatively higher. (The first sound of a word is generally considered to be important for recognition.)
First vowel relatively more open than the second	CACI	F1 involved. It has greater intensity than F2 and F3 which are not relevant here, as contrasts of backness, rounding, frontness, and non-rounding are not common to all three forms.
Breath at the onsets of both syllables and at the end of the last syllable	$^hCV^hCVC^h$	Delayed VOT. This may not be important, as use of immediate onset of voicing would not cause unintelligibility.

The acoustic correlates of samenesses are mostly relatively low frequency, relative intensity of syllables, duration of syllables, and plosive bursts. These cues are relatively salient and occur in a particular arrangement, forming the basis for the pattern of the word 'pocket'. Interestingly, they are also cues much used in the early stages of language acquisition. The cues show the relationship between the two syllables within the word, i.e., the interrelationships within the whole word, and represent the word pattern which is shared by the three forms of 'pocket', thus enabling the listener to interpret these three forms as the same word, regardless of their acoustic differences—given, of course, an appropriate context.

The way the invariant pattern functions in continuous speech needs to be examined under natural conditions, as context and knowledge of the world play a very important role in speech perception and interpretation. In such a situation a great deal of the acoustic signal is redundant, as context constrains the possibilities and increases predictability. One may expect that the more support there is from the context and other information, the fewer the acoustic cues needed for interpretation. The whole pattern, or only part of the pattern, or more than the pattern (i.e., the full spectrum), may be used in the recognition process, depending on how much support there is in the form of information from other sources and how much masking there is of the acoustic signal by noise.

It is proposed that speech perception involves scanning an utterance for patterns which are then interpreted as is most appropriate to the context. It is suggested that there is first a rapid scanning to break up the acoustic signal into manageable chunks—into phrases, clauses and sentences. For this the suprasegmental (prosodic) features have to be processed ahead of the segmental and there is some evidence for this in the information processing model of Wood (1975) and in the experiments of Miller (1978). Further support comes from the view that the suprasegmental features are processed in different hemispheres in the brain— the suprasegmental normally in the right and the segmental in the left (Blumstein and Cooper 1974) and also from the fact that suprasegmental features are acquired earlier than the segmental (Crystal 1976), which suggests the primacy of prosodic features for speech processing.

Intonation patterns are used to recognize the limits of the chunks and also to identify the position of high information words which stand out by pitch and stress. In speech, 'words are pointed out by means of what we shall call accent' (O'Connor and Arnold 1973: 7). (Here 'accent' refers to strong stress.) Bond and Garnes (1980: 129-30), on the basis of their study of misperceptions, suggest four possible heuristic strategies for speech perception: pay attention to stress and intonation patterns; find a phrase; find a word; pay attention to stressed vowels. The rhythm of the utterance is noted by the relationship of strongly and weakly stressed syllables. The main focus will be on the strong stresses, as these indicate the presence of high information words. Some attention will be given to syllable length, as this can give an indication of whether a stressed syllable is a monsyllable or part of a larger group. For instance, in a stretch like 'man' in 'the *man laughed*' and 'the *manager laughed*', 'man' differs in length, being longer in 'man' and shorter in 'manager', as the two utterances take up roughly the same amount of time (O'Connor 1973: 197-8). Length of weakly stressed syllables gives an indication of whether these syllables precede or follow a strong stress, as those preceding are generally shorter (O'Connor 1973: 198). The sequence in which the high information words appear plays a part in the interpretation of the syntax. The interpretation of the weakly stressed parts of the utterance will be greatly influenced by that of the strongly stressed and by the context in which the utterance is made, as well as by the requirements of syntax as indicated by the high information words. This should become clearer from the example discussed below. The example is taken from hearing errors in Waterson (1971a).[4] Other examples of the same type of error may be found in Garnes and Bond (1980) and Browman (1980).

The context in which the misperception to be considered was made was a discussion about the fishing industry in Great Britain. There were two speakers, A and B, and the discourse was as follows:

A: Is Harwich a fishing port?
B: No, all kinds of fish.
 (A looks surprised, so B realizes he has made a mistake):
B: Oh, I thought you said was it herrings they were fishing for.

Once the topic of discourse is set, the participants operate within a

---

4 The analysis is updated in the light of the development of the theory.

circumscribed context and thus have certain expectations of what may be involved—for instance, in this case: fishing, the sea, ports, ships, trawlers, nets, various kinds of fish, the weather, landing fish, preparation for market, transport. Speech perception will be geared to a high expectation that this semantic field will be represented and the word patterns that are abstracted will first be checked against this part of the lexicon for interpretation. This is, of course, more economical on processing time and effort than if the search had to spread over the whole of the lexicon every time. On recognizing a word pattern, the hearer will try to interpret it, making use not only of the relevant part of the lexicon and the discourse context but also of his knowledge of the world, of the language, and of the actual situation in which the utterance is made—i.e., any information that may afford further cues. So, with knowledge of what is going to be talked about, there is a high expectation of the kind of vocabulary that will be involved; this means that a minimum of acoustic cues is needed to identify words: hence the possibility of rapid recognition and interpretation of word patterns. The interpretation will be one that seems most apt in relation to the discourse. It is suggested it will take place along the following lines: the nucleus (the last strongly stressed word—or syllable of a word (O'Connor and Arnold 1973: 14)) will be given attention first. It usually represents the key word in the utterance and is the most salient by pitch, as well as being the most recent in the memory. The other salient points will be examined for patterns next. Patterns that cannot be recognized and interpreted quickly may be skipped, so as not to hold up what can be processed rapidly, and once the majority of patterns have been interpreted, the rest become more predictable. When the strongly stressed words have been identified, the grammatical relations between them become predictable, and function words are filled in accordingly. The hearer makes his hypothesis on the basis of all the information available to him. If his interpretation proves inappropriate, he has to re-process the pattern or patterns which appear to be the cause of incompatibility. He may have to re-process only one pattern, or the lot.

The way the misinterpretation of A's utterance was made by B is now considered in terms of the proposed theory. The two versions are the question:

Is Harwich a fishing port?   ['ɪz   'hærɪdʒ ə 'fɪʃɪŋ pɔːt]

and the misperception:

Is it herrings they're fishing for?   ['ɪz ɪt 'herɪŋz ðə 'fɪʃɪŋ fɔː]

Scanning the pitch contour to break up the utterance into chunks reveals an intonation pattern which marks the utterance as a single unit:

a high start, stepping down, followed by a low rise, which is recognized as a question. The rhythm is noted by the relationship of strongly and weakly stressed syllables. The main focus will be on the three strong stresses, as these will indicate the presence of high information words. The last strongly stressed syllable of the utterance (the nucleus) will mark the key word and will be processed first. It will be considered in relation to the weakly stressed syllables for the reasons given, and on the basis of the cues described earlier, the pattern will be recognized as FVSVN (fricative-vowel-sibilant-vowel-nasal), with the same close degree of vowel in both syllables, viz., FISIN. Breathy onset of the pattern may be noted, ʰFISIN, as breathy/non-breathy type of onset is a functional contrast with fricatives in English. Attention then shifts to the beginning of the utterance. The first syllable will be treated separately from the second because both have strong stress and must therefore represent two separate words. (There is only one main stress per word in English.) The pattern of the first syllable is IS (close vowel-sibilant). The second strongly stressed syllable, together with the following weakly stressed syllable, has the pattern VLVS (vowel-approximant-vowel-sibilant), with breathy onset, ʰVLVS, with a more open vowel in the first syllable and a more close in the second, ʰALIS. The last syllable of the utterance has a degree of salience of vowel: not only is the vowel [ɔː] relatively more sonorous than the preceding [ɪ] but it also has salience by recency; it is most recent in the memory and nothing follows to detract attention from it: the pattern is ʷʳE̅, mid grade vowel with backness and rounding. The pattern of the utterance will thus have been perceived as something like the following:

IS ʰALIS ʰFISIN ʷʳE̅?[5]

with an unstressed syllable between ʰALIS and ʰFISIN.

The context of the fishing industry gives a high expectation of reference to fishing and the pattern ʰFISIN predicts it. The first pattern in the sequence, IS, together with the question intonation and knowledge of the language that such questions may start with 'is', will predict 'is'. As the last pattern of the utterance which immediately follows what is predicted as 'fishing' is compatible with the vowel [ɔː], 'for' is highly predictable. 'Port' would of course have been highly predictable but the plosive [p] in the weakly stressed position was weakly articulated and unaspirated, and was missed, as was the non-salient final [t]. The first hypothesis will thus predict:

Is ʰALIS fishing for?

In view of the context of the fishing industry in Great Britain and the above tentative hypothesis, the most likely prediction for ʰALIS would probably be the name of some kind of fish found around the coasts of Great Britain. A search for a name of such a pattern would produce one that is similar but not identical, i.e., ʰALINS 'herrings'. As the utterance was not heard clearly (or it would not have been a misperception), the hearer would be prepared to supply elements of a pattern that may have been missed, and a non-salient nasal in a weakly stressed syllable could easily have been missed, so that the pattern ʰALINS in place of ʰALIS would be acceptable. The sequence of the predicted words in the skeleton sentence: 'Is herrings fishing for?'[6] suggests what the appropriate syntactic structure of the utterance should be, and the function words

5 Spaces are left between the salient words to indicate possible places where non-salient function words can be filled in to provide a suitable syntactic structure for the utterance.
6 The question mark here shows that the utterance is predicted to be interrogative.

required by the syntax are then filled in, the final interpretation being:

Is ·it herrings they're fishing for? ['ɪz ɪt 'herɪŋz ðə 'fɪʃɪŋ fɔ:]

instead of:

Is Harwich a fishing port? ['ɪz 'hærɪdʒ ə 'fɪʃɪŋ pɔ:t].

The hearer thus constructed an interpretation to fit what he had managed to abstract from the acoustic signal with the help of other information available to him. He even supplied an unstressed word, 'it', where there was none, and there was no perceptual justification for it, as there was in the case of the interpretation of 'they're' [ðə], where there was an [ə] in the utterance. As Bond and Garnes (1980: 126) have noted: 'unstressed function words and grammatical morphemes are most often perceived as required by the sense of the sentence'. There is no one-to-one correlation between the acoustic signal and the interpretation of speech. The interpretation is created on the basis of selection from the acoustic signal and what the hearer thinks was intended by the speaker.

The computations in the proposed perception and interpretation of the utterance would be very much more rapid than the written description would suggest: plainly, it would be much faster than if the whole spectrum of the utterance had to be processed. Less time is needed to scan for patterns of a selection of words made up of a limited number of acoustic cues than if the whole spectrum of each word in the utterance had to be processed. Also, because the first scan is very rapid, there is time to re-scan the acoustic signal for further cues if required before it fades from the memory, and such re-scanning of different points in the signal should still prove more economical in time than processing the full spectrum of the whole utterance in the first place.

According to the theory outlined above, pattern recognition is an essential factor in speech perception and interpretation. Judging by the large number of homonyms, examples of harmony, and other patterned forms found in the speech of English children at an early stage of their language development, it seems that they adopt this strategy early. It may be that the sooner they do so, the faster their vocabulary grows and the more fluent their speech becomes—and it may be that if they do not, their language development would be delayed. More longitudinal studies of language development involving a wide range of languages should provide insights which could support or refute the theory presented here.

It is planned to test the theory by the use of synthetic speech experiments. It should be possible to synthesize word patterns and put them within the framework of utterances in given contexts. If, for instance, three words of the same pattern are selected and the pattern is placed in three separate normal speech utterances, each with a context suitable for one of the three words, the same pattern should be interpreted in three different ways as appropriate to the different contexts. Some form of masking over the whole utterance would be necessary so that the use of a pattern instead of the full spectrum would not be too evident. Care would also need to be taken that the context does not constrain the probabilities to such a degree that prediction could be made before the pattern is heard, i.e., without the use of any acoustic cues. The problem would be to find the minimal cues necessary. As stated earlier, less or more than the pattern may be needed, depending on the amount of other information available and how much background masking there is.

The view of scanning an utterance for chunking into smaller units by intonation and then for salient points at which the patterns of high information words are located for the rapid interpretation of meaning may be likened to fluent reading. In English, the fluent reader is guided by punctuation for chunking; he recognizes words by their general shape; he does not spell out each letter of each word; nor does he necessarily read each word. His eyes move back and forth, not in one long progression forward. He seeks out the high information words and uses his knowledge of the language, of the context, and of the world, to help him arrive at the meaning. Similar processes thus appear to be involved in reading so that reading may be seen as a visual parallel to the auditory processing of speech proposed here.

Conclusions

It seems that the theory can provide certain insights into speech processing. As the patterns described are invariant across several variables, it is possible to suggest an explanation of how the variability of productions from different vocal tracts, old and young, male and female, does not prevent them from being recognized as same; how some dialectal differences are normalized, and why rate of speaking does not affect speech recognition unduly.

The theory works equally well for the word in isolation as for the word in continuous speech, and can account for the fact that single words said in isolation are less easily identified than words in a longer utterance, even though the former may be articulated more clearly. This is because the word pattern needs the support of context for rapid interpretation and if there is none, the whole spectrum has to be processed, which takes more time.

Problems of explaining recognition in relation to word boundary cues (i.e., the acoustic differences at the beginning and end of a word in different phonetic contexts which change the acoustic shape of the word) do not arise, as attention is shown to be focused on the gross acoustic cues which constitute the word pattern, which are not affected by changes in context.

A further advantage of the theory which is not considered here but is outlined in Paper 6 is that the relationship between the acoustic signal and the matching of the pattern with the inner lexicon is direct, so that the amount of computation that needs to be presumed is greatly reduced. How the pattern relates to storage is suggested in the same paper.

The theory also has relevance to language processing in reading and suggests a parallel between visual and auditory perceptual processing of a particular kind.

This theory of speech perception has been illustrated with examples taken from several areas of language: the acquisition of phonology, hearing errors, and dialect examples. It has an empirical basis and can be tested experimentally. It has suggested explanations for certain aspects of speech perception which have been difficult to explain in the past. It would therefore seem to merit wider consideration.

8
SUMMARY

Papers 1 and 2 are introductory to the rest of the papers in that the principles of the theory of prosodic phonology, which is the theoretical basis for Papers 3 to 7, are explained and examples are given of how the principles are applied. Papers 3 to 7 represent the gradual evolution of two theories: a theory of the acquisition of phonology and a theory of speech perception. The two theories are interrelated in that the child is shown to start to process speech in the same way as he will continue to do as an adult. The theories are based on data from observational studies and thus have the natural use of language as their foundation. No experimentation was involved so there is no possibility of the influence of any artifacts such as may arise in experimental studies. As the theories are based on only one language, English, it cannot be assumed that speech processing will necessarily proceed in the same way for all languages.

New concepts are involved in the two theories with regard to the proposed units and processes of speech perception. Some supporting evidence for these concepts is given in the papers—from acoustic phonetics and from the field of psychology. Here a brief summary of the theories will be given and additional evidence from experimental studies and from related disciplines will be presented to provide further justification for the theories and the concepts involved on grounds other than the linguistic ones on which they are based.

In the theory of the acquisition of phonology, it is suggested that the development of the phonetic/phonological processing system starts with the early vocalizations and babbling which lay the foundations for two levels of representation: a phonetic level and a lexical-phonological level. The infant is exposed to auditory patterns quite early in the pre-verbal period, for instance, in the simplified and very salient intonation contours of motherese and the kind of babbling nonsense that adults frequently address to babies. The infant thus learns to recognize and to expect auditory patterns, and he himself makes use of patterns quite early in his productions, for example, in babbling, where there are not only consonant-vowel syllable patterns but also rhythmic and pitch patterns. A number of intonation patterns are also produced relatively early in the first communicative linguistic utterances as well as in jargon utterances (utterances which sound speechlike but are unintelligible). The 'protolanguage' (a system of a small set of forms, usually supplemented by gestures, used for a limited set of functions) is seen as the beginnings of a functional linguistic system. As the protolanguage is a functional system, protowords must be organized in a way that they can be retrieved when required by the child to express his intentions in relation to the situations in which he finds himself. They must therefore have an internal representation. First words are shown to be constructed not on the basis of segments but on patterns resulting from selective attention being paid to auditorily salient cues of the acoustic signal of whole words or word groups. Such selective attention results in skeleton patterns which are then fleshed out within the constraints of the child's current processing capabilities. Patterns are constructed at two levels of representation: the first, a phonetic level of representation (LR1), and the second, a lexical-phonological level of representation (LR2). In the construction of LR1, patterns are synthesized on the basis of auditorily salient features of the acoustic signal of speech as noted above, and are stored at LR1 for future matching when other such patterns are again synthesized in the process of speech recognition. The patterns of LR1 are more fully specified at LR2, and meaning is included there. LR2 patterns are the basis for production; hence the child's productions are constrained by the form of the pattern at LR2 as well as by motor constraints.

Speech processing takes place by synthesizing phonetic patterns from the acoustic signal and trying to match them with patterns at LR1. If a pattern is found to match, it is then paired with a pattern at LR2 and the word is recognized. If there is no match at LR1, a new pattern has to be constructed at both levels of representation. The patterns are very simple at first but change and become more complex as the child's processing abilities increase with the gradual maturation of his neural and motor abilities, and as his experience of language widens. As perceptual discrimination increases, more attention is paid to more of the less salient features of the acoustic signal, and the patterns at LR1 are therefore re-constructed. This means that LR2 patterns no longer match so they too are changed accordingly. As production is based on LR2, the child's productions also change and move closer to the adult forms of the words.

The auditory patterns constructed by the child on the basis of salient cues in a particular sequence are *invariant* because what constitutes the pattern is the *relationship* of the cues comprising it and not the *actual* frequencies, intensities, durations, etc. of the various cues. Thus recognition of words is possible regardless of variables such as men's voices on relatively low frequencies and children's voices on relatively high frequencies.

When one or two words of the same pattern have been acquired, others of the same pattern do not need detailed attention for recognition and are therefore acquired in quick succession, and fit into a ready-made network. Those that do not fit already established patterns need more detailed attention in order that a pattern can be created, and hence are acquired more slowly. The patterns at the two levels of representation are organized in an economical and efficient storage system in the manner proposed in Paper 6, which makes retrieval quick and easy (see also Waterson 1986 for fuller discussion and illustration). The two levels of representation are constantly being restructured to accommodate an ever-increasing number of patterns of the growing vocabulary. Some patterns subsume many words, others just one or two.

Content words addressed to the child are auditorily, semantically and functionally salient for him and are learnt before function words, which are non-salient. The child makes much use of context in his interpretation of speech. Phonetics, phonology and semantics develop first, and apart from word order and intonation, syntax lags behind.

The child's acquisition of the phonetic and phonological systems (the two levels of representation) is shown to be an active, creative process, and the way the levels of representation function in speech perception and interpretation is essentially the same as proposed for adult speech processing but at a much lower level of complexity at the start.

Much of the proposed theory of the acquisition of phonology hinges on the immaturity of the child's perceptual discrimination for speech and its gradual development as evidenced in his selective attention to and production of mainly auditorily salient features of the acoustic signal of speech at the start, followed by the gradual acquisition of less salient features. Some evidence for gradual development of perceptual discrimination has already been given from acoustic studies (Fourcin 1978) and from naturalistic evidence (Paper 6). Piaget's view of children's development from syncretism (perception of unanalysed wholes) to analysis and synthesis, and his belief that children perceive in terms of general schemata (Piaget 1959) have been noted as supporting evidence for the holistic perception of auditory patterns of words (Paper 4). Vernon's 'figure from ground' differentiation which she said is fundamental to perception is cited (Paper 4) as support for children's attention to auditorily salient cues as standing out from the less salient (Vernon 1971). Neurology provides further support through evidence of the infant's neural and anatomical immaturity for speech. A review of neural development in infants may be found in Netsell (1981), and Kent (1981) gives an account of the immature vocal tract and how it develops. There is also neurological evidence for the child's early holistic perception, such as is assumed in the theory of phonological development; this is indicated below.

It has been found that brainstem or subcortical mechanisms develop earlier than cortical mechanisms in visual and auditory systems (Whitaker 1976) and that the infant at first uses primarily subcortical auditory processing, which involves holistic analysis—analytic processing coming later with cortical maturation. Evidence of holistic processing would thus be expected to be present in the child's early productions. This has indeed been found to be the case in child language studies in that intonation and rhythm are learnt early and words as wholes are the focus of attention, not the segments of which words are said to be constituted. Fernald (1984), in her study of the salience of mothers' pitch patterns as contributing to the development of infants' auditory processing, considers early neural development in relation to early auditory processing and emphasizes that motherese intonation contours are exceptionally well-suited to the infant's early holistic processing capabilities (Fernald 1984: 18). Basing herself on Whitaker (1976), she notes:

> The young infant relies primarily on subcortical auditory processes which are adequate for the 'holistic' analysis of certain acoustic signals. The development of auditory processes that are more 'analytic' in nature, those ultimately specialized for decoding speech, depends on later cortical maturation.
>
> (Fernald 1984: 13-14)

Fernald also refers to Warren (1976) as making a distinction between holistic and analytic processing modes. She mentions his 'Holistic Pattern Recognition' as involving 'global recognition of complex acoustic sequences independent of the identification of constituent sounds' (Fernald 1984: 14), such holistic processing allowing for 'same/different discrimination of two auditory patterns, as well as recognition of a particular pattern, whereas the identification of individual units in a sequence of sounds requires the analytic processing mode'. All this accords well with the proposal that when he acquires his first words, the child makes greater use of the earlier established holistic processing in his learning and less of the later developed, less familiar analytic processing mode; his word patterns are based on auditorily salient cues reflecting a holistic representation of the word but as an auditory skeleton—the cues based on less salient features, which are needed to complete the shape of the word and which require a greater degree of analytic processing to match the adult form, are added later.

The electrophysiological experiments of Molfese (1983) provide interesting evidence which has relevance to the question of attention being given to different cues at different phases of development. His experiments show that various cues for speech are processed by different mechanisms and that these mechanisms develop at different times and mature at different rates.

The theory proposed for adult speech processing will now be outlined and its similarity to that suggested for the child will become evident.

Speech processing by adults takes place by means of invariant auditory patterns and pattern recognition by way of two levels of representation. The adult's LR1 and LR2 are highly complex but they function in the same way as explained for the child, viz., pattern synthesis and then pattern matching at the two levels of representation with interpretation aided by knowledge of the language, context, and knowledge of the world, all of which constrain the possibilities and provide a high degree of predictability. Although the adult's patterns are more complex than the child's, they are still skeleton patterns based on skeleton word spectra and thus take less time to process than would the full spectra of the acoustic signal of words.

In processing continuous speech, the adult listener breaks up the spoken text into chunks on the basis of stress, rhythm and intonation, as it is in course of being produced; the processing of these prosodic (suprasegmental) features takes place ahead of the internal analysis of the chunks. The first chunk is then searched for patterns at points which are salient by stress and pitch which mark the positions of high information content words. The acoustic signal at these points is synthesized into skeleton patterns which are matched with patterns at LR1. These are then matched with patterns at LR2 to identify the words. The matching is aided by the constraints imposed by the context and listener's use of all and any information available to him. This process takes place before the function words are considered. A start on the analysis of the second chunk is made before the interpretation of the first is complete as it may influence the way the first chunk is interpreted. The sequence in which the patterns of content words appear in the utterance, and their meaning, enables the syntax to be predicted, and function words are then filled in to complete the interpretation of what the listener supposes was the intended message. Speech interpretation is thus shown to be an active, creative process: the listener constructs an interpretation on the basis of scanning the acoustic signal for word patterns (and in fact also sentence patterns, but this is not considered here) and making use of other available information in order to arrive at something that makes sense in relation to the context. The interpretation of speech is thus not based on a one-to-one relation to the acoustic signal but rather on abstractions being made at salient points in the acoustic signal, which are then synthesized into patterns and matched with LR1 and LR2 patterns, the interpretation being aided by the listener's own expectations.

The view that the spoken text is broken up into chunks for processing on the basis of prosodic features is not new. For instance, Nooteboom et al. (1974) suggested that the speech signal is structured by prosody into 'perceptually coherent configurations of auditory events' which form 'perceptual wholes suitable for further perceptual analysis' (Nooteboom et al. 1974: 40).

Units that have been proposed as the most likely to be used as chunks are clauses, and there are studies which support this view, e.g., Bond (1981) in her study of misperceptions found no errors involving perceptual metathesis or word boundaries occurring across clause boundaries.

The proposal that the prosodic features of intonation, stress and rhythm are processed ahead of word patterns implies that different processes are used from those used in word pattern recognition. There is some evidence for this in neurology. Of the two hemispheres of the brain, one (usually the left) is more commonly dominant for speech but it is now recognized that the non-dominant hemisphere is also concerned with some language function. One of its functions is the processing of the prosodic features of speech (Ross and Mesulam 1979). As the processing of intonation, stress and rhythm is in a different hemisphere from that concerned with other aspects of speech, it follows that different mechanisms will be employed for word patterns, and therefore it should be possible for the processing of intonation patterns for chunking the speech signal into appropriate units for analysis, to take place in parallel but a little ahead of the processing of the word patterns, as has been suggested in the theory.

Evidence of the primacy of prosody for speech interpretation may be taken from Oakeshott-Taylor (1980), who reviews various studies and cites the tape-splicing experiments of Wingfield (1975), and Wingfield and Klein (1971), in which sentences were created which were grammatically acceptable but prosodically anomalous. Such utterances were found to be more difficult to understand than normal utterances and when syntax and prosody conflicted, prosody was given priority in interpretation, and syntax and lexis were made to suit the prosody. Oakeshott-Taylor also makes reference to the work of Martin (1975). Martin was concerned with the timing and rhythm of speech and proposed that the perceived rhythm of an utterance enables the listener to predict the occurrence of stressed (i.e., high information) words in real time so that the perceptual mechanism is prepared for decoding them. He suggested that one of the main functions of prosody is to 'enable the listener to expect or anticipate the rough outlines of speech not yet heard' (Martin 1975: 161). This fits well with the suggestion of prosodic processing in advance of word pattern processing which requires that attention be given first to the stressed words in the utterance.

It is well known that in the normal speech perception situation, articulation is often imprecise and portions of the speech signal are frequently masked by noise, and yet, in general, listeners do not have difficulty in understanding speech in such circumstances. It is therefore clear that information other than just the acoustic signal is used. It is well documented that words in context are more intelligible than when spoken in isolation. Experimental studies in the 1950s, of Miller et al. (1951) and O'Neill (1957), demonstrate this.[1] It is therefore plain that

---

[1] The experiments showed that words heard in context were recognized more quickly

Summary

any theory of speech perception must take into account that context, knowledge of the language and non-linguistic information play an important role in speech perception and that reliance is not placed purely on the acoustic signal. The theory of speech perception presented in this book is compatible with this in that it is proposed that a minimum of acoustic cues is used for word recognition, viz., a skeleton auditory pattern, aided by other non-acoustic information. Recognition of a word in isolation, with no support from context or other information, will require more of the spectrum for identification and will therefore require more time and effort before recognition is achieved.

It seems that most of the sensory information humans have to deal with is in the form of patterns; as Bruner says:

> Perception involves the act of categorization...We stimulate an organism with a suitable input, and the organism reacts by sorting the input into a class of things or events. (Bruner 1957: 123)

Visual perception is recognized as functioning in terms of patterns, so auditory perception for speech may also be expected to be in the form of patterns. Neisser (1967) has already been cited in this connection (Paper 4). The concept of auditory salience has been justified acoustically in that features described as auditorily salient have been shown to have acoustically salient correlates, and the concept of invariant auditory pattern has been justified similarly. It is of interest that several experimental studies, not aiming to demonstrate invariant auditory word patterns, nevertheless provide useful evidence in support of the concept.

Investigations by Ladefoged and Broadbent (1957) aimed to find out whether identification of vowels depended on the absolute values of their formants (what was the generally accepted view) or if it depended on the relationship of the formant values of the particular vowel to the values of the other vowels of the same speaker. The conclusion was that

> linguistic information conveyed by a vowel sound does not depend on the absolute values of its formant frequencies but on the relationship between the formant frequencies for the vowel and the formant frequencies of other vowels pronounced by the speaker. (Ladefoged and Broadbent 1957: 98)

Another relevant experiment is that of Oakeshott-Taylor on the intelligibility of vowels in a fixed syllable, /pVps/. Fourteen vowels were examined and were spoken in isolation and in different frames. The acoustic characteristics of the syllables, viz., duration of syllables, duration of vowels, and temporal structure all varied with the context in which the syllables were spoken. Formant frequencies, fundamental frequency modulation and peak intensity were all affected by the different contexts. The important finding from the point of view of the proposed invariant

---

and easily than when heard in isolation. It was also found that words were recognized more easily than in isolation when in a context that gave no clues to meaning. This may be because some 'tuning-in' or readiness for perception is needed to enable processing of the word to begin at the start of its production. When a word is presented in isolation, there is no indication when the acoustic signal will begin so there may be some backtracking in perception which takes time but which is avoided when there is even a simple introduction such as 'The next word is...'.

auditory pattern is that

> Within each context condition,...the relative duration, formant locations, intensities and Fo modulations were by and large maintained.
> (Oakeshott-Taylor 1980: 207)

That is to say, the relationships between the major cues were maintained —precisely what the theory of invariant pattern would predict. Other experiments also show that variation in the temporal structure of speech does not greatly affect intelligibility. Lehiste's experimental work on the duration of words in isolation and within utterances (Lehiste 1972, 1974) shows that greater length of utterance results in shortening of duration of the test words. This happened both when the preceding and when the following context was increased; thus words in different contexts were shown to have different temporal structures. The experiments of Foulke and Sticht (1969) show that speech can be compressed to a high degree without losing intelligibility. Where subjects were permitted to familiarize themselves with the relevant word lists in advance, in the experiments of Fairbanks and Kodman (1957), the intelligibility rate was 90%, with speech compressed to as little as 15% of its original length. Lengthening of speech, as in drawling, is also understood easily and it seems that temporal reorganization of words in context does not result in difficulty in recognition. The concept of invariant auditory pattern explains why words should be intelligible under such different conditions. The pattern is made up of cues in a specific relationship which remains constant whether the pattern is compressed or expanded—it remains recognizable because the relationship of the cues stays unchanged.

As mentioned earlier, one of the claims of the proposed theory is that the listener scans the acoustic signal for content words first and fills in function words later in order to complete the syntax of his own interpretation of the utterance. Bond's work on misperceptions provides useful supporting evidence for the proposal that the speech signal is scanned for content words at the start of the speech perception process:

> Some perceptual errors suggest that listeners are scanning the speech signal and attempting to make a lexical identification as quickly as possible. (Bond 1981: 389)

Some experimental work on the effect of context supports the view that in processing speech, the listener supplies what he thinks is appropriate. Bond reports experiments by Warren (1976), Ganong (1978) and Garnes and Bond (1975) on the effect of context on speech perception. In Warren's experiment some sounds were omitted in sentences and the gaps were filled with noise of various sorts. The result was completely intelligible to the subjects, who were unable to say which sounds were missing even when asked to look out for them (Bond 1981: 381). This shows how much information the listener supplies himself when listening to speech. The experiments of Ganong (1978) and Garnes and Bond (1975) with synthetic speech showed that where acoustically ambiguous items were presented in context, they were interpreted as appropriate to make sense for the particular context. As Bond concludes, these experiments 'strongly suggest that semantic and lexical information affects the classification of acoustic events' (Bond 1981: 383). This observation adds support for the view that content words are processed first, ahead of function words, and influence the interpretation of the utterance, and that function words are filled in later.

Summary.

That content words and function words should be processed in different ways is supported by studies of misperceptions and by experimental work as well as by work on aphasias. Bond and Garnes (1980) find that content and function words behave differently—misperceptions take place within word classes and in words of similar phonological shape. This suggests that it is words of the same auditory pattern that are confused. Bond and Garnes also found that errors were not made between content and function words, and that function words were inserted or omitted to suit the listener's interpretation. This kind of evidence confirms that speech is not processed word by word but rather, as suggested in the proposed theory, that content words are processed first and the function words are filled in later. Bradley and Garrett (1980), in experiments using lexical decision tasks, find evidence for separate routes for lexical access of content words and function words, content words being accessed by a frequency sensitive route (that is, the more frequently the word appears in the language, the faster is it identified), but function words, not being subject to a frequency effect, must therefore be accessed by a different route.

Evidence from Broca's aphasia and Wernicke's aphasia is particularly interesting in demonstrating the separate processing of content and function words. In Broca's aphasics content words are preserved but function words are either not used or are used incorrectly, and the comprehension of Broca's aphasics is relatively good. In Wernicke's aphasics content words are lost but function words are preserved, and although their speech may sound relatively fluent, it is not intelligible and the patient's comprehension is poor. Cooper and Zurif (1983) refer to detailed literature as being in agreement that the ability for comprehension of Broca's aphasics

> is largely based on their ability to utilize semantic and pragmatic cues independent of sentence structure. They understand a sentence primarily by sampling from it in terms of what each of the major lexical items—that is, the nouns and verbs—refers to and by combining these referential meanings in terms of what makes factual sense. (Cooper and Zurif 1983: 228)

This kind of processing is, in fact, what is proposed in the theory as the first phase in processing speech by normals; the second phase, that of constructing a syntactic structure for the utterance, appears not to be possible for Broca's aphasics, who seem to lose the mechanism for processing function words. Cooper and Zurif point out that the inability for syntactic analysis in Broca's aphasics is not a simple matter of omitting function words or not attending to unstressed words (function words are usually unstressed) but that 'the problem seems tied to a disruption of the specialized mechanism that accesses function words for their structure-building relevance' (Cooper and Zurif 1983: 230). The poor comprehension of Wernicke's aphasics, who have an inability to process content words, further supports the view of the proposed theory that the patterns of content words are of primary importance in speech processing.

In the discussion of levels of representation (Paper 6) it was suggested that bilinguals may have separate levels of representation for each language. There is some experimental evidence which suggests that this could be so. Ojemann (1983), in his electrical stimulation mapping experiments in naming with bilinguals, finds that:

> Not only are individual language functions discretely localized, but also the same functions expressed in different languages are often localized at least in part in different cortical areas. The study of effects of stimulation on naming in bilingual patients provides particularly good examples of this. (Ojemann 1983: 137)

The work of Albert and Obler (1978) on the bilingual brain is also relevant:

> There is no special reason to assume...that the second language sits in the brain of a bilingual in exactly the same manner as does the first and only language in the brain of a monolingual. (Albert and Obler 1978: 12)

And in the same work (p. 243) they also say: 'Bilinguals demonstrate not only the left hemispheric role in language but also a major right hemispheric contribution.'

The above findings are compatible with the view that each language has its own levels of representation. One must assume, however, that the two separate systems will be linked to a common semantic level of representation in view of situations where a bilingual, in a code-switching situation, may not remember in which of the two languages a particular piece of information was given.

The similarity of what has been proposed for auditory perception in speech processing to the processing of language through visual perception in reading has been pointed out in Paper 7.

Experimental evidence and evidence from related disciplines has shown that there is some justification for the units and processes proposed for the theory of the acquisition of phonology and the theory of speech processing. The theories have prosodic phonology as their theoretical basis: it seems, therefore, that prosodic phonology, the first of the non-linear phonological theories, has a useful contribution to make in the field of speech processing. The theories are not yet fully developed but they seem to rest on a reasonably firm foundation. They need to be linked more clearly to the planning of production and they need to be integrated into a unified speech processing theory which includes semantics, syntax and pragmatics. It is nevertheless hoped that these theories will prove useful for further research in speech processing and language acquisition, and for the study of language disabilities and their remediation.

REFERENCES

Albert, M. and Obler, L. (1978). *The Bilingual Brain*. New York: Academic Press.
Bar-Adon, A. and Leopold, W. F. (eds.) (1971). *Child Language: A Book of Readings*. Englewood Cliffs: Prentice-Hall.
Bell, A. and Hooper, J. B. (eds.) (1979). *Syllables and Segments*. Amsterdam: North-Holland.
Bellugi, U. and Brown, R. (1964). *The Acquisition of Language*. Monograph of the Society for Research in Child Development, serial no. 92, 29, 1. Lafayette, Indiana: Child Development Publications.
Bendor-Samuel, J. T. (1960). 'Some problems of segmentation in the phonological analysis of Terena'. *Word 16*. 348-55. (Reprinted in Palmer 1970: 214-21.)
Berry, M. (1975). *Introduction to Systemic Linguistics. Vol. 1: Structures and Systems*. London: Batsford.
Bickley, C. A. (1983). 'Acoustic evidence for phonological development of vowels in young children'. In Cohen and van den Broecke (1983: 624).
Bloom, L. (1970). *Language Development: Form and Function in Emerging Grammars*. Cambridge: M.I.T. Press.
Bloom, L. (1973). *One Word at a Time: The Use of Single-word Utterances before Syntax*. The Hague: Mouton.
Blumstein, S. E. and Cooper, W. E. (1974). 'Hemispheric processing of intonation contours'. *Cortex 10*. 146-58.
Bond, Z. S. (1981). 'From an acoustic stream to a phonological representation: the perception of fluent speech'. In Lass (1981: 375-410).
Bond, Z. S. and Garnes, S. (1980). 'Misperceptions of fluent speech'. In Cole (1980: 115-32).
Bradley, D. C. and Garrett, M. (1980). 'The lexical component and sentence processing'. Unpublished manuscript. M.I.T. Quoted in Cooper and Zurif (1983).
Braine, M. (1971). 'On two types of models for the internalization of grammars'. In Slobin (1971: 153-86).
Browman, C. P. (1980). 'Perceptual processing: evidence from slips of the ear'. In Fromkin (1980: 213-30).
Brown, R. (1958). 'How shall a thing be called?'. *Psychological Review 65*. 14-21. (Reprinted in Brown 1970: 3-15.)
Brown, R. (1970). *Psycholinguistics: Selected Papers by Roger Brown*. New York: The Free Press.
Brown, R. and Fraser, C. (1964). 'The acquisition of syntax'. *Monographs of the Society for Research in Child Development 29*. 43-79.
Bruner, J. S. (1957). 'On perceptual readiness'. *Psychological Review 64*. 123-52.
Bruner, J. S. (1975). 'The ontogenesis of speech acts'. *Journal of Child Language 2*. 1-19.
Buffery, A. W. H. and Waterson, N. (1980). 'Neuropsychological assessment and modification of cerebral asymmetry: implications of brain function therapy (B.F.T.) for clinical psychology and developmental neurolinguistics'. In Ingram, Peng, and Dale (1980: 337-80).
Burling, R. (1959). 'Language development of a Garo and English-speaking child'. *Word 15*. 45-68. (Reprinted in Bar-Adon and Leopold 1971: 170-85.)
Carroll, J. B. (1961). 'Language development in children'. In Saporta (1961: 331-45).
Chomsky, N. (1965). *Aspects of the Theory of Syntax*. Cambridge, Mass.: M.I.T. Press.
Chomsky, N. (1966). *Current Issues in Linguistic Theory*. The Hague: Mouton.
Chomsky, N. (1967). 'The formal nature of language'. In Lenneberg (1967: 397-442).
Clark, R. (1974). 'Performing without competence'. *Journal of Child Language 1*. 1-10.
Clark, R. (1978). 'Some even simpler ways to learn to talk'. In Waterson and Snow (1978: 391-414).
Cohen, A. and Nooteboom, S. G. (eds.) (1975). *Structure and Process in Speech Perception*. Proceedings of the Symposium on Dynamic Aspects of Speech Perception Held at Eindhoven. Berlin: Springer Verlag.
Cohen, A. and van den Broecke, M. P. R. (eds.) (1983). *Abstracts of the Tenth*

International Congress of Phonetic Sciences. Dordrecht, Holland: Foris Publications.
Cohen, M. (1969). 'Sur l'étude du langage enfantin'. *Enfance 3-4.* Paris.
Cole, R. A. (ed.) (1980). *Perception and Production of Fluent Speech.* New Jersey: Lawrence Earlbaum.
Cooper, W. E. and Zurif, E. B. (1983). 'Aphasia: information-processing in language production and reception'. In B. Butterworth (ed.) *Language Production. Vol. 2.* New York: Academic Press. 225-56.
Crystal, D. (1970). 'Prosodic systems and language acquisition'. In Leon (1970: 77-90).
Crystal. D. (1976). *Child Language, Learning and Linguistics.* London: Edward Arnold.
Denes, P. (1963). 'On the statistics of spoken English'. *Journal of the Acoustical Society of America 35,* 892-904.
Denes P. and Pinson, E. (1972). *The Speech Chain.* New York: Bell Telephone Laboratories.
Dore, J. (1975). 'Holophrases, speech acts and language universals'. *Journal of Child Language 2.* 21-40.
Fairbanks, G. and Kodman, F. (1957). 'Word intelligibility as a function of time compression. *Journal of the Acoustical Society of America 29.* 636-41.
Faust, M. (ed.) (1983). *Allegemeine Sprachwissenschaft, Sprachtypologie und Textlinguistik. Festschrift für Peter Hartman.* Tübingen: Narr.
Ferguson, C. A. and Farwell, C. B. (1973). 'Words and sounds in early language acquisition: early initial consonants in the first 50 words'. *Papers and Reports on Child Language Development 6.* Stanford: Stanford University. 1-60.
Ferguson, C. A. and Garnica, O. (1975). 'Theories of phonological development'. In Lenneberg and Lenneberg (1975: 153-80).
Ferguson, C. A. and Slobin, D. I. (eds.) (1973). *Studies of Child language Development.* New York: Holt, Rinehart & Winston.
Fernald, A. (1984). 'The perceptual and affective salience of mothers' speech to infants'. In L. Feagans, C. Garvey, and R. Golinkoff (eds.) *The Origins and Growth of Communication.* Norwood, New Jersey: Ablex Publishing Corporation. 5-29.
Firth, J. R. (1935). 'The technique of semantics'. *Transactions of the Philological Society.* (Reprinted in Firth 1957: 7-33.)
Firth, J. R. (1948). 'The semantics of linguistic science'. *Lingua 1, 4.* 393-404. (Reprinted in Firth 1957: 139-47.)
Firth, J. R. (1950). 'Personality and language in society'. *The Sociological Review 42, 2.* (Reprinted in Firth 1957: 177-89.)
Firth, J. R. (1951). 'Modes of meaning'. *Essays and Studies.* (Paper presented at a meeting of the English Association. In Firth 1957: 190-215.)
Firth, J. R. (1957). *Papers in Linguistics 1934-1951.* Toronto: Oxford University Press.
Flores d'Arcais, G. and Levelt, E. (eds.) (1970). *Advances in Psycholinguistics.* Amsterdam: North-Holland.
Fodor, J. A. and Katz, J. J. (eds.) (1965). *The Structure of Language.* Englewood Cliffs, New Jersey: Prentice-Hall.
Foulke, E. and Sticht, T. (1969). 'Review of research on the intelligibility and comprehension of accelerated speech'. *Psychological Bulletin 72.* 50-62.
Fourcin, A. J. (1978). 'Acoustic patterns and speech acquisition'. In Waterson and Snow (1978: 42-72).
Francis, H. (1971). 'An investigation into the structure and development of speech, reading and writing of a young child'. Ph.D. thesis, University of Leeds.
Fraser, C., Bellugi, U. and Brown, R. (1963). 'Control of grammar in imitation, comprehension and production'. *Journal of Verbal Learning and Verbal Behavior 2.* 121-35. (Reprinted in Oldfield and Marshall 1968: 48-69.)
Fromkin, V. A. (ed.) (1980). *Errors in Linguistic Performance: Slips of the Tongue, Ear, Pen, and Hand.* New York: Academic Press.
Fry, D. B. (1966). 'The development of the phonological system in the normal and the deaf child'. In Smith and Miller (1966: 187-206).
Ganong, F. A. (1978). 'A word advantage in phoneme boundary experiments'.

Journal of the Acoustical Society S20 (A).
Garnes, S. and Bond, Z. S. (1975). 'Slips of the ear: errors in perception of casual speech'. In R. E. Grossman, L. J. San and T. J. Vance (eds.) *Papers from the Eleventh Regional Meeting of the Chicago Linguistic Society.* Chicago, Illinois: Chicago Linguistic Society. 214-25.
Garnes, S. and Bond, Z. S. (1980). 'A slip of the ear: a snip of the ear? A slip of the year?'. In Fromkin (1980: 231-9).
Gimson, A. C. (1964). *Introduction to the Pronunciation of English.* London: Arnold.
Gray, T. (1970). 'Effects of filtering and vowel environment on consonant perception'. *Journal of the Acoustical Society of America* 48. 993-8.
Grégoire, A. (1937). *L'Apprentissage du Langage: Les Deux Premières Années.* Paris: Librairie E. Droz.
Halliday, M. A. K. (1975). *Learning How to Mean: Explorations in the Development of Language.* London: Arnold. **(For Halliday (1973) see Addendum on p. 149.)**
Henderson, E. J. A. (1949). 'Prosodies in Siamese'. *Asia Major (New Series)* 1. 189-215. (Reprinted in Palmer 1970: 27-53.)
Henderson, E. J. A. (1951). 'The phonology of loan words in some South-East Asian languages'. *Transactions of the Philological Society.* 131-58. (Reprinted in Palmer 1970: 54-81.)
Hulst, H. van der, and Smith, N. (1983). *The Structure of Phonological Representations (Part 1).* Dordrecht-Holland: Foris Publications.
Ingram, D. (1971). 'Phonological rules in young children'. *Papers and Reports in Child Language Development* 3. Stanford University. 31-49.
Ingram, D. (1976). 'Phonological analysis of a child'. *Glossa* 10. 3-27.
Ingram, D. (1978). 'Language development during the sensorimotor period'. In Waterson and Snow (1978: 379-89).
Ingram, D., Peng, F. C. C., and Dale, P. (eds.) (1980). *Proceedings of the First International Congress for the Study of Child Language.* Lanham: University Press of America.
Ingram, T. T. S. (1966). 'Syntactic regularities: general discussion'. In Lyons and Wales (1966: 214-19).
Jakobson, R. (1941). *Child Language, Aphasia and Phonological Universals.* Translated by A. R. Keiler (1968). The Hague: Mouton.
Jakobson, R. and Halle, M. (1961). 'Phonemic patterning'. In Saporta (1961: 346-58).
Jones, D. (1962). *An Outline of English Phonetics.* Ninth edn. Cambridge: Heffer.
Katz, J. J. (1966). *The Philosophy of Language.* New York & London: Harper & Row.
Kent, R. D. (1981). 'Articulatory-acoustic perspectives on speech development'. In Stark (1981: 101-26).
Kirk, U. (ed.) (1983). *Neuropsychology of language, Reading and Spelling.* New York: Academic Press.
Labov, W. (1972). 'On the use of the present to explain the past'. *Preprints of the Eleventh International Congress of Linguistics.* 1110-35.
Ladefoged, P. (1967). *Three Areas of Experimental Phonetics.* London: Oxford University Press.
Ladefoged, P. (1980). 'What are linguistic sounds made of?'. *Language* 56, 3. 485-502.
Ladefoged, P. (1984). 'Out of chaos comes order'. In van den Broecke and Cohen (1984: 83-95).
Ladefoged, P. and Broadbent, D. E. (1957). 'Information conveyed by vowels'. *Journal of the Acoustical Society of America* 29, 1. 99-104.
Lass, N. J. (ed.) (1980). *Speech and Language: Advances in Basic Research and Practice. Vol. 3.* New York & London: Academic Press.
Lass, N. J. (ed.) (1981). *Speech and Language: Advances in Basic Research and Practice. Vol. 6.* New York & London: Academic Press.
Lass, N. (1984). *Phonology: An Introduction to Basic Concepts.* London, New York & Sydney: Cambridge University Press.
Laver, J. (1970). 'The production of speech'. In Lyons (1970: 53-75).
Lehiste, I. (1964). *Acoustical Characteristics of Selected English Consonants.* The Hague: Mouton.
Lehiste, I. (1972). 'Timing of utterances and linguistic boundaries'. *Journal of the*

Acoustical Society of America 51. 2018-24.
Lehiste, I. (1974). 'Interaction between test word duration and length of utterance'. *Ohio State University Working Papers in Linguistics 17.* 160-9.
Lenneberg, E. H. (1965). 'The capacity for language acquisition'. In Fodor and Katz (1965: 579-603).
Lenneberg, E. H. (1966a). 'A biological perspective of language'. In Lenneberg (1966c: 65-88).
Lenneberg, E. H. (1966b).'The natural history of language'. In Smith and Miller (1966: 219-52).
Lenneberg, E. H. (ed.) (1966c). *New Directions in the Study of Language.* Cambridge, Mass: M.I.T. Press. (Paperback edn.)
Lenneberg, E. H. (1967). *Biological Foundations of Language.* New York, London & Sydney: Wiley.
Lenneberg, E. H. and Lenneberg, E. (eds.) (1975). *Foundations of Language Development. Vol. 1.* New York: Academic Press.
Leon, P. (ed.) (1970). *Prosodic Feature Analysis.* Montreal-Paris: Didier.
Leopold, W. F. (1939). *Speech Development of a Bilingual Child. Vol. 1.* (1954 reprint.) Evanston: North Western University Press.
Leopold, W. F. (1947). *Speech Development of a Bilingual Child. Vol 2.* North Western University Press.
Leopold, W. F. (1961). 'Patterning in children's language'. In Saporta (1961: 350-8).
Lewis, M. M. (1936). *Infant Speech: A Study in the Beginnings of Language.* (1968 reprint.) London: Routledge & Kegan Paul.
Liberman, A. (1961). 'Some results of research in speech perception'. In Saporta (1961: 142-53).
Lyons, J. (ed.) (1970). *New Horizons in Linguistics.* Harmondsworth: Penguin Books.
Lyons, J. and Wales, R. J. (eds.) (1966). *Psycholinguistics Papers: The Proceedings of the Edinburgh Conference 1966.* Edinburgh: Edinburgh University Press.
Macken, M. A. (1978). 'Permitted complexity in phonological development: one child's acquisition of Spanish consonants'. *Lingua 44.* 219-53.
Macken, M. A. (1980). 'The child's lexical representation: evidence from the "puzzle-puddle-pickle" phenomenon'. *Journal of Linguistics 16.* 1-17.
Marslen-Wilson, W. D. (1984). 'Perceiving speech and perceiving words'. In van den Broecke and Cohen (1984: 99-103).
Martin, J. G. (1975). 'Rhythmic expectancy in continuous speech perception'. In Cohen and Nooteboom (1975: 161-77).
Massaro, D. W. and Oden, G. C. (1980). 'Speech perception: a framework for research and theory'. In Lass (1980: 129-65).
McGurk, H. (1981). 'Listening with eye and ear'. In Myers, Laver and Anderson (1981: 336-7).
McNeill, D. (1966). 'The creation of language by children'. In Lyons and Wales (1966: 99-132).
Menn, L. (1971). 'Phonotactic rules in beginning speech'. *Lingua 26.* 225-51.
Menn, L. (1979a). 'Phonological units in beginning speech'. In Bell and Hooper (1979: 151-71).
Menn, L. (1979b). 'Towards a psychology of phonology: child phonology as a first step'. Paper for the *Proceedings of the Third Annual Michigan State University Conference on Metatheory: Applications of Linguistic Theory to the Human Sciences.*
Menyuk, P. (1971). *The Acquisition and Development of Language.* Englewood Cliffs: Prentice-Hall.
Miller, G. A., Heise, G. A. and Lichten, W. (1951). 'The intelligibility of speech as a function of context of test materials'. *Journal of Experimental Psychology 41.* 329-35.
Miller, G. A. and Nicely, P. E. (1955). 'An analysis of perceptual confusions among some English consonants'. *Journal of the Acoustical Society of America 27.* 338-52. (Reprinted in Saporta 1961: 153-75.)
Miller, J. L. (1978). 'Interactions in processing segmental and suprasegmental features of speech'. *Perceptions and Psychophysics 24.* 2. 175-80.
Miller, M. (1978). 'Pragmatic constraints on the linguistic realization of "semantic

intentions" in early child language'. In Waterson and Snow (1978: 453-67).
Molfese, D. L. (1983). 'Neural mechanisms underlying the processing of speech information in infants and adults: suggestions of differences in development and structure from electrophysiological research'. In Kirk (1983: 109-28).
Mowrer, D. E. (1980). 'Theories of phonological development'. In Lass (1980: 1-33).
Myers, T., Laver, J. and Anderson, J. (eds.) (1981). *The Cognitive Representation of Speech*. Amsterdam: North-Holland.
Neisser, V. (1967). *Cognitive Psychology*. New York: Appleton-Century-Crofts.
Netsell, R. (1981) 'The acquisition of speech motor control: a perspective with directions for research'. In Stark (1981: 127-56).
Nooteboom, S. G., Eggermont, J. P. M., Hart, J., van Katwijk, A. F. V., and Slis, I. H. (1974). 'Time in speech perception'. *I.P.O.* (Annual Progress Report, Instituut voor Perceptie Onderzoek, Eindhoven.)
Oakeshott-Taylor, J. (1980). *Acoustic Variability and Its Perception: The Effects of Context on Selected Acoustic Parameters of English Words and Their Perceptual Consequences.* Frankfurt am Main: Verlag Peter D. Lang.
O'Connor, J. D. (1973). *Phonetics*. Harmondsworth: Penguin Books.
O'Connor, J. D. and Arnold, G. F. (1973). *Intonation of Colloquial English*. London: Longman.
Ohnesorg, E. (1959). *Druhá Fonetická Studie o Dětské Řeci.* Brno: Spisy University v Brně Filosofická Fakulta. No. 57.
Ojemann, G. A. (1983). 'Interrelationships in the brain organization of language-related behaviors: evidence from electrical stimulation mapping'. In Kirk (1983: 129-52).
Oldfield, R. C. and Marshall, J. C. (eds.) (1968). *Language*. (Penguin Modern Psychology.) Harmondsworth: Penguin Books.
Olmsted, D. (1971). *Out of the Mouth of Babes*. The Hague: Mouton.
O'Neill, J. J. (1957). 'Recognition of intelligibility test materials'. *Journal of Speech and Hearing Disorders 22.* 87-90.
Palmer, F. R. (1955). 'The "broken plurals" of Tigrinya'. *Bulletin of the School of Oriental and African Studies 17.* 548-66. (Reprinted in Palmer 1970: 133-51.)
Palmer, F. R. (ed.) (1970). *Prosodic Analysis*. London: Oxford University Press.
Peters, R. (1963). 'Dimensions of perception for consonants'. *Journal of the Acoustical Society of America 35.* 1985-9.
Piaget, J. (1959). *The Language and Thought of the Child*. Translated by M. Gabain and R. Gabain. (1967 reprint.) London: Routledge & Kegan Paul.
Piaget, J. (1971). *Structuralism*. London: Routledge & Kegan Paul.
Priestley, T. M. S. (1977). 'An idiosyncratic strategy in the acquisition of phonology'. *Journal of Child Language 4.* 45-65.
Reddy, D. (1967). 'Computer recognition of connected speech'. *Journal of the Acoustical Society of America 42.* 329-47.
Robins, R. H. (1957). 'Aspects of prosodic analysis'. *Proceedings of the University of Durham Philosophical Society. Vol. 1.* Series B (Arts). No. 1 (1957). 1-12. (Reprinted in Palmer 1970: 188-200.)
Robins, R. H. (1964). *General Linguistics: An Introductory Survey*. London: Longman.
Robins, R. H. (1983). 'J. R. Firth: a reconsideration of his place in 20th century linguistics'. In Faust (1983: 259-67).
Robins, R. H. and Fromkin, V. A. (1985). *Linguistics and Linguistic Evidence: The LAGB Silver Jubilee Lectures 1984.* Newcastle upon Tyne: Grevatt & Grevatt.
Ross, E. D. and Mesulam, M.-M. (1979). 'Dominant language functions of the right hemisphere? Prosody and emotional gesturing'. *Archives of Neurology 36.* 144-8.
Saporta, S. (1961). *Psycholinguistics: A Book of Readings*. New York: Holt, Rinehart & Winston.
Schaerlackens, A. M. (1973). *The Two-word Sentence in Child Language Development*. The Hague: Mouton.
Schiefelbusch, R. L. and Bricker, D. D. (eds.) (1981). *Early Language: Acquisition and Intervention*. Baltimore: University Park Press.
Sinha, C. and Walkerdine, V. (1978). 'Conservation: a problem in language, culture, and thought'. In Waterson and Snow (1978: 357-78).
Slobin, D. I. (1966). 'Comments on "developmental psycholinguistics"'. In Smith and Miller (1966: 85-91).

Slobin, D. I. (1970). 'Universals of grammatical development in children'. In Flores d'Arcais and Levelt (1970: 174-80).
Slobin, D. I. (ed.) (1971). *The Ontogenesis of Grammar*. New York & London: Academic Press.
Slobin, D. I. (1973). 'Cognitive prerequisites for the development of grammar'. In Ferguson and Slobin (1973: 175-208).
Smith, F. and Miller, G. (eds.) (1966). *The Genesis of Language*. Cambridge, Mass.: M.I.T. Press.
Smith, N. V. (1981). 'On the cognitive representation of developing phonology'. In Myers, Laver and Anderson (1981: 313-21).
Snow, C. E. and Ferguson, C. A. (eds.) (1977). *Talking to Children: Language Input and Acquisition*. Cambridge: Cambridge University Press.
Stark, R. E. (ed.) (1981). *Language Behavior in Infancy and Early Childhood*. New York: Elsevier/North-Holland.
Trehub, S. E., Bull, D. and Schneider, B. A. (1981). 'Infant speech and nonspeech perception'. In Schiefelbusch and Bricker (1981: 9-50).
Tuaycharoen, P. (1977). 'The babbling of a Thai baby: from early communication to speech'. Ph.D. thesis, University of London.
Vaissière, J. (1981). 'Speech recognition programs as models of speech perception'. In Myers, Laver and Anderson (1981: 443-57).
van den Broecke, M. P. R. and Cohen, A. (eds.) (1984). *Proceedings of the Tenth International Congress of Phonetic Sciences*. Dordrecht, Holland: Foris Publications.
Velten, H. V. (1943). 'The growth of phonemic and lexical patterns in infant language'. *Language 19*. 281-92.
Vernon, M. (1971). *The Psychology of Perception*. Harmondsworth: Penguin Books.
von Raffler Engel, W. (1967). 'The auditory perception of distinctive features in a six year old child'. *Proceedings of the Sixth International Congress of Phonetic Sciences (Prague)*. 751-4.
von Raffler Engel, W. (1970a). 'The LAD, our underlying unconscious and more on "Felt Sets"'. *Language Sciences 13*. 15-18.
von Raffler Engel, W. (1970b). 'The function of repetition in child language as part of an integrated theory of developmental linguistics'. *Bullettino di Psicologia Applicata 97, 98, 99*. 27-32.
Warren, R. M. (1976). 'Auditory perception and speech evolution'. In S. R. Harnad, H. D. Steklis, and J. Lancaster (eds.) *Origins and Evolution of Language and Speech*. New York: New York Academy of Sciences.
Waterson, N. (1970). 'Some speech forms of an English child: a phonological study'. *Transactions of the Philological Society*. 1-24.
Waterson, N. (1971a). 'Some views on speech perception'. *Journal of the International Phonetic Association 1*. 81-96.
Waterson, N. (1971b). 'Child phonology: a comparative view'. *Transactions of the Philological Society*. 34-50.
Waterson, N. (1978). 'Language acquisition: a learning process'. *Revue de Phonétique Appliquée 46-47*. 183-92.
Waterson, N. (1986). 'The role of patterns in language acquisition'. (In a volume based on selected papers from the Second International Conference on Language Acquisition, Language Contact and Language Conflict, Hamburg. Tübingen: Gunter Narr Verlag. Forthcoming, summer 1986. Book title and page numbers unavailable at the time of going to press.)
Waterson, N. and Snow, C. E. (eds.) (1978). *The Development of Communication*. Chichester & New York: Wiley.
Weir, R. H. (1962). *Language in the Crib*. (Janua Linguarum. Series Maior 14.) The Hague: Mouton.
Whitaker, H. A. (1976). 'Neurobiology of language'. In C. E. Carterette and M. P. Friedman (eds.) *Handbook of Perception. Vol. 7*. New York: Academic Press.
Wichelgren, W. (1965). 'Distinctive features and errors in short-term memory for English vowels'. *Journal of the Acoustical Society of America 38*. 583-8.
Wichelgren, W. (1966). 'Distinctive features and errors in short-term memory for

English consonants'. *Journal of the Acoustical Society of America* 39. 388-98.

Wingfield, A. (1975). 'The intonation-syntax interaction: prosodic features in perceptual processing of segments'. In Cohen and Nooteboom (1975: 146-60).

Wingfield, A. and Klein, J. P. (1971). 'Syntactic structure and acoustic patterns in speech perception'. *Perception and Psychophysics* 9. 23-5.

Wood, C. C. (1975). 'Auditory and phonetic levels of processing in speech perception: neurophysiological and information processing analyses'. *Journal of Experimental Psychology: Human Perception and Performance* 1. 3-20.

Addendum

Halliday, M. A. K. (1973). *Explorations in the Functions of Language.* London: Arnold.

INDEX OF PERSONAL NAMES

Albert 142, 143
Anderson 121, 146, 147, 148
Arnold 122, 129, 130, 147, 161
Bar-Adon 143
Bell 143, 146
Bellugi 25, 51, 143, 144
Bendor-Samuel 7, 12, 143
Berry 8, 143
Bickley 124, 143
Bloom 54, 93, 106, 143
Blumstein 129, 143
Bond 1, 122, 129, 132, 138, 140-1, 143, 145
Bradley 141, 143
Braine 69, 73, 143
Bricker 147, 148
Broadbent 139, 145
Browman 129, 143
Brown 25, 49, 51, 54, 143, 144
Bruner 88, 139, 143
Buffery 23, 143
Bull 124, 125, 148
Burling 71, 143
Butterworth 144

Carroll 25, 143
Carterette 148
Chomsky 52, 143
Clark 88, 89, 93, 101, 106, 143
Cohen, A. 121, 143, 145, 146, 148, 149
Cohen, M. 25, 144
Cole 143, 144
Cooper 129, 141, 143, 144
Crystal 53, 124, 129, 144

Dale 143, 145
Denes 57, 109, 144
Dore 88, 92n, 144

Eggermont 147

Fairbanks 140, 144
Farwell 91, 144
Faust 144, 147
Feagans 144
Ferguson 2, 14, 91, 112, 144, 148
Fernald 136, 144
Firth 1, 2, 4-8, 14, 144, 147, 160
Flores d'Arcais 144, 148
Fodor 144, 146
Foulke 140, 144
Fourcin 89, 112, 114n, 125, 136, 144
Francis 54, 144
Fraser 51, 54, 143, 144
Friedman 148
Fromkin 8, 143, 144, 145, 147
Fry 25, 26, 48, 54, 64, 70, 144

Ganong 140, 144
Garnes 122, 129, 132, 140-1, 143, 145

Garnica 2, 14, 144
Garrett 141, 143
Garvey 144
Gimson 42, 125, 145
Golinkoff 144
Gray 57, 62, 145
Grégoire 25, 145
Grossman 145

Halle 25, 26, 145
Halliday 8, 118, 145
Harnad 148
Hart 147
Heise 146
Henderson 1, 5, 11, 12, 145
Hooper 143, 146
Hulst 1, 145

Ingram, D. 65, 88, 109, 143, 145
Ingram, T. T. S. 25, 145

Jakobson 25, 26, 42, 50, 145
Jones 28, 40, 92, 145

Katz 52, 144, 145, 146
Kent 136, 145
Kirk 145, 147
Klein 138, 149
Kodman 140, 144

Labov 62, 145
Ladefoged 25, 41, 42, 121, 139, 145
Lancaster 148
Lass, N. J. 143, 145, 146, 147
Lass, R. 14, 145
Laver 53, 121, 145, 146, 147, 148
Lehiste 57, 140, 145, 146
Lenneberg, E. 144, 146
Lenneberg, E. H. 25, 52, 143, 144, 146
Leon 144, 146
Leopold 25, 26, 42, 43, 46-8, 51, 68n, 143, 146, 153
Levelt 144, 148
Lewis 25, 26, 43, 46, 53, 54, 146
Liberman 57, 146
Lichten 146
Lyons 145, 146

Macken 109, 119, 146
Marshall 144, 147
Marslen-Wilson 121, 146
Massaro 124, 146
Martin 138, 146
McGurk 124, 146
McNeill 52, 146
Menn 67, 69, 109, 119, 146
Menyuk 53, 146
Mesulam 138, 147
Miller, G. A. 57, 58, 62, 138, 144, 146, 147, 148
Miller, J. L. 129, 146

Index of personal names

Miller, M. 88, 146
Molfese 137, 147
Mowrer 2, 14, 147
Myers 121, 146, 147, 148

Neisser 70, 73, 111, 139, 147
Netsell 136, 147
Nicely 57, 58, 62, 146
Nooteboom 138, 143, 146, 147, 149

Oakeshott-Taylor 138, 139, 140, 147
Obler 142, 143
Oden 124, 146
O'Connor 122, 129, 130, 147, 161
Ohnesorg 25, 26, 147
Ojemann 141-2, 147
Oldfield 144, 147
Olmsted 62, 147
O'Neill 138, 147

Palmer 7, 14, 108n, 143, 145, 147
Peng 143, 145
Peters 57, 147
Piaget 48-9, 61, 66, 70, 73, 105, 136, 147, 152
Pinson 57, 144
Priestley 119, 147

Reddy 61, 147
Robins 8, 14, 108n, 147
Ross 138, 147

San 145
Saporta 143, 145, 146, 147
Schaerlackens 106, 147
Schiefelbusch 147, 148
Schneider 124, 125, 148

Sinha 105n, 147
Slis 147
Slobin 54, 64, 68, 107, 143, 144, 147, 148
Smith, F. 144, 146, 147, 148
Smith, N. 1, 145
Smith, N. V. 109, 148
Snow 112, 143, 144, 145, 147, 148
Stark 145, 147, 148
Steklis 148
Sticht 140, 144

Trehub 124, 125, 148
Tuaycharoen 99, 106, 148

Vaissière 121, 148
van den Broecke 121, 143, 145, 146, 148
van Katwijk 147
Vance 145
Velten 25, 26, 31, 71, 107, 148
Vernon 53, 54, 57, 63, 71, 73, 136, 148
von Raffler Engel 53, 54, 58, 148

Wales 145, 146
Walkerdine 105n, 147
Warren 136, 140, 148
Waterson 15, 23, 27, 28, 54, 55, 61, 62, 63, 64, 89, 90, 92, 104, 111, 129, 135, 143, 144, 145, 147, 148
Weir 25, 99, 148
Whitaker 136, 148
Wickelgren 58, 148
Wingfield 138, 149
Wood 129, 149

Zurif 141, 143, 144

INDEX OF SUBJECTS

accent: *see* stress
accommodate; accommodation (in Piaget's sense) 70, 73, 135
acoustic
  characteristics of syllables varying with context 139; cues: *see* cues, acoustic; correlates of features 23, 58ff; correlates of forms of 'pocket' 128, exx. in fig. 1, 128; correlates of phoneme segments 1; effects in relation to articulation 2; effects, production of 65, 69, 73; energy as cue to recognition of plosives 114; events, classification affected by semantic and lexical information 140; evidence for greater and lesser salience 3; *see also* mingograms; spectrograms; facts, more easily relatable to prosodies and phonematic units than phonemes 1, 108, 118; form, different in the same word 127; information, in relation to scanning and in relation to patterns and features 114, 118; make-up and word recognition 111; salience: *see* salience; salient; signal: *see* signal; *see also* spectrum/spectra
acquisition 2; of grammar, and similarity to acquisition of phonology 51-2; of other human skills 107; of phonetic and phonological systems, a creative process 35; of semantics 55; of syntax 69, 101, 106; of words of established structure 96; *see also* child language data; *see also* level(s) of representation
acquisition of language 14, 26, 88; and insights for linguistic theory 2; as a slow process 64; role of phonology in 54;
acquisition of phonology 52, 53, 55, 61, 62, 66, 89, 133, 135; child's capacity for 52; hypothesis of 72-3, 136, 142; of English 9, 15ff, 108; summary of theory of 134-5; summary of developmental model in 117-8; theories of 2;
  see also level(s) of representation
analysis
  and synthesis for construction of patterns, examples of 115-7; articulatory feature 25, 29 ff (*see* exx.); *see also* features; auditory 114; child's early holistic 136; chunking speech into units in perception for 138; detailed, in imitation and in learning new words 119; discourse 8; *see also* syncretism; distributional 25;

features involved in, for construction of LR1 pattern 115; first, of input 110; first level of, in terms of C and V 19; holistic, of words, pieces and sentences 4; involving restricted number of cues 109; of chunks 137; of homonyms 38, 123-4 (*see* exx.); *see also* stages in phonological development; of irregularities unexplainable by assimilation, metathesis and substitution 43-8; of words, into structure and systems, prosodies and phonematic units/C and V systems 5, 18, 19, 17-23 (*see* exx.), 123-4; partial 8, 13-14; perceptual 138; phonological 7, 9, 10, 14, 28; polysystemic 23; prosodic 8, 15, 19, 23, 25, 46; prosodic, practical advantages of 107; *see also* prosodic
aphasia; aphasics
  Broca's 141; Wernicke's 141
articulation(s)
  complex 40; difficulty in 64; familiar 99, 106; forceful 41; of nasal stops, weak in some contexts 35; new 11, 99; rapid changes in 64
assimilation (in Piaget's sense) 66, 73
attention
  detailed, not required for familiar patterns 66, 135; increase in 89, 117; more detailed, for new and unfamiliar 66, 68, 71, 135; not paid to everything 56, 71; not paid to weak sounds 66, 126; selective 126, 134, 136; to auditorily salient features/cues 115, 136; *see also* salient; features; cues, auditory; to auditorily salient parts of words, utterances, chunks 2, 110, 114, 130; to different cues at different phases of development 129, 137; to gross acoustic cues 133; to less salient features 72, 89, 100, 117, 135; to less salient parts of utterances 65, 103; to places of articulation 63; to speech 42, 53; to stressed vowels 129; to weak, unstressed words 100, 11; *see also* features, auditorily less salient; to words as wholes 136
babbling
  as preparation for language 64, 72, 118; early, unstructured 117; in emergence of language of a Thai baby 106; in overlap between stages of phonological development 91; in overlap with protolanguage and first words 118; later, structured 118; patterns 118, 134; role of, in construction of internal representation of phonology 3,

117-18, 134; sounds from 92, 97;
verbal play reminiscent of 99
basic features: *see* features
bilingual(s)
  experiments with 141-2; basic features of English and German 47-8; *see also* German and English bilingual; in English and German 46
brain
  different hemispheres of 129, 138; cortical maturation of 136; function for speech and need for theory to be viable in relation to brain function 1; language in monolingual's and bilingual's 142; mechanisms in relation to speech development, subcortical and cortical 136; network of 113; roles of left and right hemispheres of 142; subcortical auditory processing in 136
breathy: *see* prosodic (h element)

C system(s): *see* system(s)
child language data (examples):
  comparison of child's $(NV)^2$ words with adult models 27; comparison of child's PVP and PVN words with adult models 56, 68; homonyms 31, 68, 87; PV, PVP and $(PV)^2$ words 87; PVP words in network 112, 113; selected from Leopold (1939) and reinterpretation of 46-8; sentences 93, 94, 95, 98, 100, 101, 104-5; stage 1: 19-20, stage 2: 22, 93, 94, stage 3: 94-6, stage 4: 96-8, stage 5: 99-101, stage 6: 101-2, stage 7: 102-3; trisyllabic words 100; words of different structures: continuant 29f; fricatives 97, labial 29, nasal 32, sibilant 30, stop 31
child language data, longitudinal
  for 'Patrick' 63-4, 70-1; for 'pudding' 15-16, 115-17; for taught words 'please' and 'thank you' 68-9
children's early vocabulary
  basis for 54; limited patterns of 68; slow rate of acquisition of 92
chunk(s)
  analysis and interpretation of 137; as processing unit in continuous speech 110-11, 129, 130
chunking by intonation 133, 137
class(es)
  grammatical, separate phonological systems for 9; of consonants, cues for, in speech processing 127; of sounds, five in English 127; of sounds, major 121, 126; word, misperceptions within 141
clause(s)
  as chunk(s) in speech processing 110,
129; as likely units in speech processing 138; evidence from misperceptions 138
coding
  by classification 96; by individual item 96; change in 96; new system of 96
cognition
  of categories and processes of human experience linked to advances in language development 68; visual and auditory, as constructive processes 70, 73
collocation
  conditioning lexical probabilities 42; meaning by 16
complexity
  avoidance of 67; degree of, in phonetic and phonological systems 9, 10, 13, 91ff; higher levels of, in monosyllables as opposed to disyllables 98; in language 3, 96, 106, 107; in planning and production 106; in perception and production, minimum of 63; increasing ability for 71; of planning, production, storage and retrieval 69; of word 90-1; relative, of word and sentence 107; sentence, related to development at other levels of language 88
complexity, growth of/increase in
  at all levels 89, 102; in grammar 103; in language 3, 67, 72, 88-9; of phonological system 10, 67, 92-103; in sentence 98, 104-5; in syllable and word 103-4, 105, 106
complexity, constraints of/limitations in
  dependent on structural complexity and non-familiarity at interrelated levels of language 107; in phonology 106; in planning and production of utterance 55, 64; in planning, production and perception 55; in syntax 64
  see also constraints
congruence
  absence of, in segmental comparison of child's early forms and adult's forms 27; between levels of analysis 4
consonant clusters
  absence of, in early speech 9, 11; presence of, in stage 7 103; reasons for 119
constraints
  contextual, aid to pattern matching and interpretation 61, 137; by sequence of context words 111; of developing phonological system 119; of probabilities due to non-linguistic cues 108, 137; on construction by limitation of abilities 115, 117, 125, 126, 134; motor, production of later simple forms not due to 95, 125

Index of subjects

see also complexity, constraints of/limitations in

content (vs. function) words
different phonological structure of, from function words 10; learnt before function words 135; obligatory V unit and non-obligatory a unit in 10; processing of, in speech interpretation 129-32; salience of 135; scanning for 140; separate processing of, from function words 137, 141; sequence of, an aid to interpretation 111; stress and accent (strong stress) carried by 110;
see also information; high information content words

context(s)
discourse 130, 131; effect of, on speech perception 140; importance of, for recognition of patterns 3, 133; linguistic elements in 6; of language development 88; of utterances, words in 10, 53; repetitive 72; role of, in speech interpretation 2; social 5; sounds in range of specific 10, 25, 35, 89, 96, 99, 102, 103

context of situation
as social component in prosodic theory 2; definition of 6-7; perception conditioned by 42

contextualization as a key concept 6

continuant structure
adult forms of 35, 42; compared with labial structure 30; comparison of child's and adult's forms of 35-6; description of 29-30; non-production of nasals in 42-3, 44-5; type 29

contrast(s) 11-14; articulatory 13, 88, 89, 90, 101, 125; paradigmatic 12, 19, 20-3, 67, 112; prosodic 20, 21-3, 113, 117; syntagmatic/differentiation 13, 16-19, 31, 62, 64, 88, 89, 90-101, 104-7, 108, 116, 117, 119, 125, 126

cues
contextual 112; essential 109; for interpretation of utterance 130-2 non-verbal 108, 111, 118; phonetic and phonological 108; selective attention to 134; semantic and pragmatic 141; word boundary 133

cues, acoustic 48, 61, 65, 109, 114, 122, 124, 125, 126, 127, 130, 132, 133, 135, 139, 140; main, for adult 126, 126-7 (see exx.)

cues, auditory 108; less salient/non-salient 61, 125, 126, 137; salient 108, 111, 124, 125, 126, 128, 134, 135, 137

development
auditory processing 136-7; cognitive 49, 73, 106; language 8, 9, 26, 68, 106, 107, 111, 122, 123, 126; neural 136; of child, general 26, 123; of levels of representation (LR1 and LR2) 117-8; see also level(s) of representation; network; of theories of development 2, 136; of words and sentences, parallel processing in 3, 94, 104-5; phonetic 88, 89; phonetic, longitudinal 15-16 (see exx.), 68-9, 115-17; see also perception; salient; phonological: see development, phonological; syntactic 3, 88, 91, 92-103

development, phonological 8, 9, 88, 89, 107; in relation to other areas of language development 3, 91-103; of a Spanish-speaking child 106; of word 63-4, 115

developmental model of phonological representation 117-20; its validity for monolingual, bilingual and multilingual speakers 109, 118; what it needs to account for 108

dialect:
three forms of the word 'pocket': see English; normalization across variables in speech

differential features: see features
differentiated: see repetitive; sentence
differentiation: see contrast(s); syntagmatic
discrimination: see perceptual discrimination

Dutch 106

English
acceptability and non-acceptability in word patterns of 111, 119; acquisition of phonological system of 9, 55, 108; acquisition of syntax in 101; analysis of child's 15ff, 28ff, 92ff, 123ff; [b] 124; breathy/non-breathy onset in, a functional contrast in fricatives 131; comparison of fluent reading with interpretation of speech in 133; development of V systems ahead of C systems in 14; five classes of consonant in 127; function words 10; see also function words; intonation patterns 121-2; see also intonation; late acquisition of [ɔ] in 125n; main stress 131; see also stress; past tense suffix 10-11; proposed theories based on 134; three dialect forms of 'pocket' in 127-8, 128 (fig. 1); see also normalization across variables in speech; word patterns of 127;
see also bilingual(s)

Index of subjects 155

experience, importance of, in language development 27, 55, 64, 65, 66, 67, 68, 69, 70, 71, 72, 89, 107, 112, 126, 135
exponence; exponents
as phonetic realizations of phonological units 7, 10, 14; of C systems 12; of prosodies 23; of terms within C systems 17; of V grades 20, 23
familiar
articulations 99, 101, 106; consonants 106; features 16, 104; items, combination of 89, 100-1; see also ready-made; language material 110; nasals 98; patterns 94, 99; phonological structures PV, (PV)^2 and PVP 94; plosives 98; production of voiced sounds 16; schemata 72; sentences 102, 105; sounds 92, 101; syllables 105, 117; syntactic structures 99; use of, when learning new material 16, 89, 99, 104, 105, 106, 107, 116; utterances 9; words 10, 95, 99, 101, 111, 114, 115, 119
features
basic 29-42, 43-51, 65; basic, definition of 29; coded in memory 58; combinations of 26, 64, 70; differential 29-42, 49, 65; differential, definition of 29; distinctive, of generative phonology 25, 57; familiar 16, 41, 104; in description 25, 28, 29ff (see exx.), 57, 58, 90, 127-8; in production not perceived in model 70; new 63, 71; phonetic 25, 57, 118; phonetic, perception of 42, 48; segmental 57, 61, 67; strong 41, 42, 44; strong, acoustic correlates of 58ff; syllable 57, 61, 67; treated prosodically, with contrastive function 11 et passim; weak, 44; weak, acoustic correlates of 58ff; with morphophonological value 12
features, auditorily less salient 65, 69, 70, 71, 72, 89, 100, 101, 112, 116, 117, 135, 136
features, auditorily salient 62, 63, 64, 65, 67, 69, 72, 109, 110, 115, 117, 124, 126, 135, 139; schema based on set of 72; set(s) of 50, 51, 65, 72, 85
function (vs. content) words 10, 54, 100, 102, 110, 111, 130, 132, 140; early omission of 8; learnt later than content words 135; separate processing of, from content words 137, 141
German and English bilingual 46; children, evidence from data of 47, 55;
data, reinterpretation of 46-8
grammar
acquisition of 51-2, 73; increase in complexity of 103
grammatical
deviances 26; inflections 100-3; morphemes, perception of 132; relations, predictable 130; structure, basic units of 51

h prosody and h̲ (non-h) prosody: see prosodic
harmony
articulatory 55, 72; in CVC monosyllables 9, 13, 56, 67-8, 100; in disyllables 29, 31, 32; in early stages 66; in relation to pattern recognition 132; of syllable onset and ending 64
hearing errors
analysis of 129-32; in auditory perception 61-2, 129; in visual perception and related storage and production 69; evidence of, for theory of speech perception 54, 111, 122, 133;
see also misperceptions
high information content words 111, 129, 130, 134, 137, 138; information from 111, 133, 140; patterns of 133;
see also content words
high information points of utterance 110;
see also information
holistic
and analytic processing models 136; approach of prosodic phonology 2, 3; pattern recognition 136; processing capabilities, early 136
homonyms
as evidence of pattern recognition 132; discussions and examples of 25, 31-2, 38, 65-8, 123-5; divergence of 67-8, 97; in relation to salience: acoustic 59-60, auditory 61; recognition of schema resulting in 67, 96
individual
development 26; linguistic biographies, need for 2
individual items/units
coding by 96, 118, 119; learning by 67, 92; processing of words as 107, 136
individual language functions 142; localization of, in bilingual brain 142
information
acoustic 114, 118; grammatical 4; linguistic 139; new 116; non-linguistic 122, 130, 132, 137, 138, 139; semantic and lexical 140; supplied by hearer 132, 140;
see also high information content words; high information points of utterance

interpretation
  content words processed before function words in 140; influence of content words on 111, 133, 140; minor role of syntax in 3, 108, 109, 119, 132, 135; of phonetic patterns 110; of PVP pattern words in relation to LR2 113-4; of speech as an active, creative process 122, 137; of speech without too much dependence on acoustic cues 122; of strongly stressed parts of utterance and influence on weakly stressed parts 129; of syntax, influence of content words on 129, 131; of word patterns 130; of words 111; on basis of selection from acoustic signal 132; proficiency in 70; rapidity of 109, 122, 132, 133; without a one-to-one correlation with acoustic signal 132, 137
intonation
  pattern(s) 110, 121, 124, 129, 130, 134, 138; pattern(s), learnt early 53, 124, 129, 136, 144; processing, ahead of word patterns 129, 138; role of, in breaking up text into chunks 129, 137-8

knowledge
  of context 133; of the language 61, 108, 122, 128, 130, 131, 133, 137, 139; of the subject matter 108; of the world 122, 130, 133, 137

labial structure
  adult words 32-3; compared with continuant structure 30; comparison of child's and adult's forms of 33-4; description of 29; non-production of labial stops in 45-6; production of labial continuant sounds in 43-4; type 29
language
  restricted 8, 9, 11; use, amount of 3, 63, 88, 89, 91, 92, 94, 96, 99, 101, 103
learning
  by individual item 67, 92, 107; by pattern recognition 2, 92, 96, 107, 109, 122, 123; early stages of 61; increase in rate of 89; language 2, 26, 50, 73; language, *vertical décalage* at level of 107; of a new word 114-17, 119; of syntax 88; perception at start of 41; processes, as for cognitive development 73; progress, giving more attention to functional items 112;
  see also acquisition; acquisition of language; acquisition of

phonology
length of sentence 99; increase in 99, 104-5
length of syllable 40; as prosody 20ff; increase in 103-4, 105
length of utterance 54, 88, 89, 94, 96; constraints on 54, 64, 106, 107; increase in 88, 89; no increase in 94, 96
length of word 99; increase in 99, 103-4, 105
length prosody: *see* prosodic
level(s) 1; acoustic 1, 10, 23; auditory 10; of linguistic description, autonomous 4; semantic 88, 106; sentence 105; social 6; syllable 105; syntactic 8, 89, 98
level(s) of analysis 7; congruence between 4; first 19; meaning at 6, 7; prosodic phonology as 7; *see also* phonological processing model; phonological theory; social 6
level(s) of language 63, 89, 96; different 106; growth at 105; increase in complexity at 96; interrelated 89, 107; progress at 3, 89, 107
level(s) of representation 109; adults' 137; child's construction of 112, 113, 114-18, 134-5; phonetic (LR1), phonological (LR2) 109-18, 119, 134; restructuring at 3, 115, 135
level, lexical 88, 89; of representation 109
level, phonetic 28, 88, 89, 107; correlation at, and at phonological level 27-8; exponent at 10; growth at 105; 'nonsense' 42, 119
level, phonological 88, 89, 107; growth at 105; statement of meaning at 7
lexical
  access to content and function words 141; decision tasks 141; identification 140; information 140; level 88, 89; meaning 110; phonological patterns: *see* level(s) of representation; probabilities 42
lexicon 50, 109, 130, 133

meaning
  as a complex of contextual relations 5-7; as function 5-6; at different levels of analysis 6; through contextualization 5-7
mingograms (cf. spectrograms) 74-8 (figs. 1-12); as acoustic evidence for salience 3; discussion of 58-62
misperception(s)
  as evidence of non-linguistic information in speech processing 122; discussion of 129-40; within word classes, in words of similar phonological shape 141
model of phonological representation: *see*

phonological processing model
multistructural 8; analysis, examples of 19ff; as key concept in prosodic phonology 8, 10; definition of 9
multistructuralism, principle of 20
nasal structure
   adult forms of 39; compared with continuant structure 42-3; comparison of child's and adult's forms of 39-41; description of 32; production of [n] and [ɲ] in 44; recognition of schema in 49; type 29
network
   adult 113; changes in 119; contruction of 117-18, 134-5; constraints of 114, 115; expansion of 113; imitations not stored in 119; interpretation of word in relation to 113-14; organization of phonological patterns in 109, 111-13, 119; restructuring of 117;
   see also organization
neural
   abilities 135; development 136; immaturity 136; messages 63; processes 88, 106; system, tuning in 118
neurology
   evidence of separate processing of prosodic features and word patterns in 138; viability of phonological theory in relation to 1, 2
neutralization 13
non-production of weak sounds:
   continuants 42; labial continuants 43; nasal stops 42-3; oral stops 45;
   see also non-salient; production; salient, less
non-salient:
   final nasal 115; final [t] 13; function words 111n; nasal 131;
   see also salient sounds
normalization across variables in speech 2, 3, 14, 119, 122, 123, 127-8, 133
organization
   developing new 96; for language 89; new responses bringing changes in 70; of phonological patterns in network 111; of PVP pattern words in LR2 112-14;
   see also network
overlapping
   acoustic and articulatory 1, 4, 5, 108; of phonological systems 9; of stages in phonological development 91, 118

paradigmatic (vs. syntagmatic)
   and syntagmatic contrasts and functions 11; and syntagmatic relations,
distinctions between 11; contrasts of C systems 14; contrasts of V systems 19-23
   see also system(s)
partial analysis 8, 13, 17, 18
pattern(s)
   abstracting 126, 130; basic, of sentence types 51; construction of 114-17, 124, 134-5; determined by input 50; early exposure to 134; early simple word 66, 126; early use of, in production 134, 136; familiar 94, 99; first functional linguistic, in protolanguage 118; interpretation of 3, 110, 130-2; intonation: see intonation; lexical-phonological 109-11; see also level(s) of representation; of content words: see content words; high information content words; information; of phrase, clause and sentence 110, 121; of some English words 111, 119, 127; pitch: see pitch; processing 111, 128; see also processing; relationship of child and adult forms 2, 123-5; re-processing 130; scanning utterance for 129, 130; schemata 111; syntactic: see syntactic; synthesis into: see processing; word 111, 119, 126, 132, 133, 138, et passim;
   see also babbling; schema/schemata; word pattern, invariant auditory
pattern matching 70, 101, 108, 109, 110-11, 113, 114, 116, 118, 125, 126, 133, 135, 137; at phonetic and phonological levels of representation 110-18, 134-5, 137; see also level(s) of representation;
   see also word pattern, invariant auditory
pattern recognition
   expansion of vocabulary through 118; in speech perception and interpretation 116, 119, 122, 126, 132, 136, 137, 138; learning by 2, 66, 73, 92, 96, 107, 109, 119, 123, 135; theory of 108ff;
   see also word pattern, invariant auditory
perception
   and production 2, 53, 55-66, 115, 117; change in, and change in production 70-3, 87, 117; child's auditory 49, 122-6; child's auditory, limitations in 42, 55, 62, 64, 125; child's linguistic 41, 69; early holistic: see holistic; in imitation and repetition 41; of acoustic cues 48 et passim; see also cues, acoustic; of phonetic features 41-2 et passim; of salient features: see features, auditorily salient; of strongly articulated features 41-5; see also perceptual discrimination; of what is functional 56; syncretic, non-analytic 73;

syncretistic 49, 51; visual and auditory 70, 111, 133, 139, 142;
   see also speech perception; speech perception theories; speech perception, units of
perceptual discrimination
   gradual development of 125, 136; immaturity of 136; increase in 49, 63, 69-70, 73, 89, 97, 100, 117, 126, 135; limited 119;
   see also perception
phonematic unit(s) 1, 5, 7, 11, 17; as key concept in prosodic phonology 8; description of 11-13;
   see also prosody/prosodies
phonetic
   and phonological processing system 134; context: see context; development: see development; level: see level(s); level(s) of representation; nonsense 42, 110, 119; realization of phonological units 7; similarity between exponents 13; specification 109, 110, 111, 115, 119; system, increasing differentiation of 90
   see also exponence; exponents; features; level(s) of representation
phonetic complexity 106; growth of 91-103; summary of growth of 103-5
phonetic form(s)
   as output 110; reconstruction of, from auditory pattern 111; relationship of, with those of adult system 25
phonetics
   acoustic 4, 134; articulatory 1, 4; as a level of analysis 7; in model of phonological representation 110ff; meaning in 6
phonological
   deviances 26; probabilities 42; selectivity 91; system: see system(s);
   see also level(s) of representation
phonological processing model 109-10; development of 134-5; developmental 117-18; evidence in support of 48-9, 57-8, 59-62, 73, 74-86, 89, 105, 111, 136-42; levels of representation in 109ff; organization of phonological patterns in 112-13; processing in, in terms of: continuous speech 129-32, 137, familiar word 113-14, 135, new word 114-17, 135; requirements of, 108-9; what can be accounted for by 108, 118-20;
   see also acquisition; acquisition of phonology; development; level(s) of representation
phonological theory
   linear: generative 1, 24, 25, 57, phonemic 1, 4, 24, segmental 108; non-linear 1; advantages of non-linear 8; autosegmental 1; metrical 1; prosodic: see prosodic
phonology, growth in complexity of: see complexity, growth of/increase in
phonology, theories of acquisition of: see acquisition of phonology; see also prosodic
phrase as a unit of speech perception 1, 110, 129
piece
   as a unit in prosodic phonology 1, 3, 4, 5, 11, 12; as key concept in prosodic phonology 8; definition of 10; structures 13
pitch
   contour, scanning of 130; of intonation contours 122; marking high information words 129; words prominent/salient by 54, 130, 134;
   see also stress; salient
pitch patterns 134; child's early response to 53, 134; salience of mothers' 136
planning
   child's limited capacity for 55, 64, 66; difficulties and limitations of 63, 64; economy in 106; greater efficiency in 72; in expansion of vocabulary and language 96; increasing ability for 69, 90; simple 62; skill: see skill(s)
plosive: see stop structure
polysystemic
   analysis 20; as key concept in prosodic phonology 8; definition of 10-11
processing
   by adults 118, 126-8, 137; by adults, first phase in 141; by pattern recognition 118-19; see also pattern recognition; by synthesizing phonetic patterns and matching at LR1 and LR2 109, 115, 135, 137; see also level(s) of representation; development of infants' auditory: see brain; function words in: see function words; greater efficiency of, through learning by pattern recognition 107; holistic: see holistic; importance of syntagmatic differentiation in 90ff; see also syntagmatic; in learning a new word 114-17; see also learning; insights into 133; misperception in 129-32; see also hearing errors; misperception(s); model: see phonological processing model; of continuous speech 137; parallel between visual and auditory: see perception;

Index of subjects 159

prosodic features in 129, 137-8;
see also prosodic; rapidity of 2,
14, 114, 123; research in, failure
of 121; segment by segment 107;
serial scanning in: see scanning;
theory of 3, 14, 118, 122, 142;
see also constraints; perception;
speech perception theories
production
ability 71; and perception: see perception; as match with adult's 114, 117; basis for, constructions at LR2 109, 110, 111, 116, 126, 135; changes in, from changes at LR2 115; child's 89ff; complexity in: see complexity; complexity, constraints of/limitations in; constraints: see constraints; contrasts in: see contrast(s); difficulty 63, 64, 90, 97, 116, 117; early use of patterns in: see pattern(s); familiar: see familiar; from different vocal tracts 133; greater efficiency in 72; less accurate, of words of more than one syllable 64; increasing ability for 69, 90; limited capacity for 55, 64, 66; of auditorily salient features: see features, auditorily salient; of longer utterances 99; processes 106; unlike adult's 114; variable, recognized as same 133; see also non-production of weak sounds
prosodic
analysis: see analysis; characteristics of word patterns 121; contrasts: see contrast(s); elements: y, w, ə and short length 18, y, w, ə and long length 20, h, h̲ and w 17, h̲, r, r̲, y, w, short length and long length 123, h̲, r, r̲, y and w 124; features of syllable 5; features in speech processing: see processing; function of function words 10; links: h, h̲ and ə 11; phonology, theory of 1, 2, 3, 4-14, 17, 108, 134, 142; processes 7
prosody / prosodies
analysis into: see analysis; and phonematic units, contrasts handled in terms of 17; as key concept in prosodic phonology 8; definition of 7, 11-13; for overlapping features 5; see also features;
see also phonematic unit(s)
protolanguage
and overlap with babbling and first words 118; as a functional system 134; first functional linguistic patterns of 118; in construction of internal representation of phonology 118, 134; start of 118; use of, up to stage 3 91
protowords 134
r prosody and r̲ (non-r) prosody: see prosodic
reading and perception 71, 133, 142
ready-made
network 135; units, in formations of three-word sentences 105, 106; utterances in formation of longer utterances 89, 100-1
remediation
assessment of relative complexity of utterances for, in teaching the deaf and language-disordered 107; insights of prosodic analysis for 23, 142
repetitive
and differentiated sentences 93-103; sentences of five and six words 102 et passim; strings in babbling 118; see also babbling; words in sentences 106; words of three, four, and five syllables 104 et passim
restricted language
as key concept in prosodic phonology 8; definition of 8-9; of language games 11
retrieval 69, 72, 90, 96, 135
rhythm
acoustic cues of 124; and timing in speech interpretation 138; early response to 53, 134, 136; of utterance 122, 129, 130; processed in non-dominant hemisphere 138; role of, in chunking 137

salience
acoustic 57ff, 74-8 (mingograms in figs. 1-12), 79-86 (spectrograms in figs. 13-28); acoustic, child's response to 95, 123; acoustic cues for auditory 124, 128; acoustic information included in 114; auditory 89, 96, 139; by recency 131; of vowel 131; of mothers' pitch pattern 131; semantic, child's response to 89
salient
acoustically 139; areas, chunk scanned for 110; auditorily 72; by recency 114; by stress and pitch 137; by strongest accent 114; content words 135; cues: see cues; features: see features, auditorily salient; intonation contours 134; part of utterances 72, 114, 130; plosives 10; points in acoustic signal 137; points in acoustic signal in chunk(s) 133, 137; sounds, least 102; see also non-salient; visually 124; words 131n;
see also cues, auditory; features; features, auditorily salient

salient, less
    F2 and F3, compared to F1 125n;
    nasals 102; parts of adult words 3;
    plosives 10; sounds 96, 101;
        see also features, auditorily less
        salient; non-salient; salience;
        salient
scanning
    and matching of patterns in chunks
    111; chunks for salient points 110,
    137; for chunks 110, 129, 133; for
    patterns of a limited number of
    acoustic cues 132; pitch contour
    130; serial, of sentence patterns
    109; utterance for word patterns
    126, 129, 137; word and sentence
    patterns 109;
        see also chunk(s); signal
schema/schemata
    ability for perception of 52; but not
    full acoustic spectra 111; child's
    perception of 49, 52; confusion of
    words of same 61; perception in
    terms of, as evidence for holistic
    perception of auditory patterns 136;
    familiar 72; of sentences 51; recog-
    nition of 67, 72; recognition of, in
    new words 66, 67; similarity in, of
    different words 65;
        see also word pattern, invariant
        auditory
schwa (ə) prosody: see prosodic
semantic
    and lexical information 140; and
    pragmatic cues 141; component,
    necessary for processing system 110;
    correlation of child's and adult's
    forms for identification 28; differ-
    entiation 38; field 130; level of
    language 88, 106; level of rep-
    resentation; theory of 7
semantics
    acquisition of 55; and pragmatics
    in speech interpretation 111; im-
    portance of 8; included with syntax
    and pragmatics in a unified theory
    of speech processing 142; place of,
    in linguistic theory 4
sentence(s)
    and syllable and word, growth in
    length and complexity of 103-5; as
    unit of speech perception 1; differ-
    entiated and repetitive 93-103;
    grammatically acceptable, prosodi-
    cally anomalous 138; prosodic pro-
    cesses within 17
sibilant structure
    compared with German sibilant
    structure 46; compared with labial
    structure 43; comparison of child's
and adult's forms of 37; type 29
signal, 55 et passim;
    acoustic/speech 55, 56, et passim;
    child's ability to perceive and recog-
    nize more of 70, 90; child's ability to
    use only a small part of 55; holistic
    analysis of 136; masking of 129,138;
    more than, used in speech interpret-
    ation 138, 139; no one-to-one corre-
    lation of, with speech interpretation
    132, 137; patterns synthesized from
    135, 137; redundancy of 128; scanning
    of 89, 114, 115, 129, 132, 137; see
    also scanning; selection from 55, 56,
    68, 72, 109, 119, 122, 126, 132, 136,
    137, 140
skeleton
    auditory 137; patterns 61, 115, 117,
    134, 137, 138, 139; sentence 131;
    word spectrum/spectra 126, 137, 139
skill(s)
    acquisition of 107; articulatory 16, 49,
    111, 119; lack of 124, 125, 126; per-
    ceptual 49, 97, 115; planning 72, 91;
    production 16, 25, 72, 91, 97, 115
social
    context, use of language in 5; com-
    municative function of language 8;
    environment related to language
    through context of situation 6; see
    also context of situation; level of
    analysis 6; roles in restricted languages
    8
society
    importance of man in 5; language in 5
sociolinguistics prefigured in Firth's
    linguistic theory 5
Spanish-speaking child, phonological devel-
    opment of 106
spectrograms (cf. mingograms) 79-84; as
    acoustic evidence for salience 3; dis-
    cussion of 58-62; linear scale 79-82
    (figs. 13-20); logarithmic scale 83-4
    (figs. 21-4)
spectrum/spectra
    skeleton word 126; skeleton word, pat-
    terns based on 124, 137
spectrum/spectra, full/whole 126, 132, 137;
    as more than the pattern of a word
    128; processed without contextual sup-
    port 133, 139
speech perception 42; by pattern recog-
    nition: see pattern recognition; in
    adult 42, 125, 126; research 121; re-
    search on infant's 89, 124;
        see also perception
speech perception theories 122; alternative
    108, 122, 133; insights of 133; sum-
    mary of 134-5;
        see also level(s) of representation;

pattern recognition; perception
speech perception, units of 1; invariant word pattern 7; see also word pattern, invariant auditory; phoneme as 108; phrase as 1, 110, 121; syllable, word, phrase, sentence as 1, 121;
  see also perception
speech processing: see processing
speech therapy, insights for 23; see also remediation
stage(s) in phonetic and phonological development:
  stage 1: 92, stage 2: 92-4, stage 3: 94-6, stage 4: 96-9, stage 5: 99-101, stage 6: 101-2, stage 7: 102-3; and ages 91;
  see also child language data
stop structure
  adult forms of 37-8; compared with labial structure words 45; comparison of child's and adult's forms of 38-9; description of 31-2; production of [b] in 45
storage
  beginnings of 118; construction of 126; greater efficiency of, with patterned processing 72, 135; how word pattern relates to 133; increasing ability for 69, 90; of expanding vocabulary 96; of words in full auditory form 111
stress
  marking high information words 129; role of, in breaking up text into chunks 137; salient by 137; strong (or accent), focus on 110, 114, 130; strong, referred to as 'accent' by O'Connor and Arnold (1973) 129; strong (or accent), used by child in syllable matching 125;
  see also pitch; salient
structure(s) (vs. system(s))
  and system, definition of 11-14; as key concept in prosodic phonology 8; C as 10-11; change in child's phonological, leading to changes in phonological system 35; changes in sentence, leading to changes in grammatical system 51; comparison of child's and adult's 32-40; composed of C and V units 7; continuant 29-30, 35-6; different types of word 29, 32; different phonological, of content and function words 10; labial 29, 32-5; nasal 29, 32, 39-41; of word, syllable as element of 4; phonological, of syllable, word and sentence 88; prosodies as units relating to whole or part of 7; reduplicated word 92 et passim; repetitive/differentiated, of sentences 93 et passim; sibilant 29, 30-7; stop 29, 31, 37-9; strategies and processes in child's creation of phonological 88, 106-7; see also patterns; syllable 29-41, 92, 94, et passim; syllable, closed 21-2; syllable, open 20-1; syllable, word, and piece 11-14 et passim; temporal, of speech 139-40; word 92 et passim
syllable(s)
  acoustic characteristics of, varying with context 139-40; as element of word structure 4 et passim; constituents of 4; in relation to word structure 3 et passim; increase in length and complexity of 103-4; need for, in linguistic description 8
syncretic/syncretistic perception 61, 73; see also holistic; perception
syncretism
  development from, to analysis and synthesis 49, 136; verbal 48-9
syntactic
  analysis, Broca's aphasics' inability for 141; component as part of processing system 110; familiar structures, in verbal play 99; functions, absence of new ones with increase at other levels 94; learning of patterns 88; level 89; level, new relations at 98; limitations in complexity 64, 88; pattern, reconstruction of 111; structure, predicted by skeleton sentence 131-2, 137
syntagmatic (vs. paradigmatic)
  and paradigmatic contrasts and functions 11; and paradigmatic relations, distinction between 11ff; character of prosodic phonology 108; contrasts: see contrast(s); differentiation: see contrast(s)
syntax
  acquisition of: see acquisition; as relatively late acquisition 54, 55, 135; integration of, with phonetics, phonology and semantics 4, 142; learning of 88; limitations in complexity of 64, 88; non-readiness for 69; phonetic and phonological development ahead of 107; production of: see syntactic; priority of prosody over 138; 'regression' in 64; role of, in interpretation of speech 54, 129, 132, 140; use of ready-made units in 101, 106
synthesis in prosodic phonology 5; see also processing
system(s) (vs. structure(s))
  as key concept in prosodic phonology 8;

at C and V places and their terms as phonematic units 12 et passim

terms
contrast of, within a system 12; contrast of, within a structure 13; examples of 17-18 et passim
Thai 106; see also babbling

universal(s)
and language-specific character of developmental model 108; character of early stages of LR1 and LR2 118; linguistic 7; possible application of principles of acquisition of phonology as 55
universalist 1; view of prosodic phonology 7

V grade(s)
acoustic correlates of 57, 59-60; change of 18; child's response to 57; contrast of three, required to describe child's systems 18, 20ff, exponents of 20, 23; function with prosodic contrasts 20, 23; in paradigmatic contrasts 19-23, 127; in syntagmatic contrasts 18
V system(s): see system(s)
vertical décalage 105n; in language learning 105, 107
vocabulary
expansion of, by pattern recognition 118; expansion of, in adulthood 119; for comprehension and production 111-12; harmony in CVC structures with rapid expansion of 104; increase in grammatical complexity in relation to size of 103; increase in rate of growth of 72, 92; increase of, in relation to development at other levels of language 3, 72, 88, 91, 92, 94, 96, 98-9, 101; lengthening of intervals between hearings of each word with increase in 71; restructuring of levels of representation with increase in number of patterns in 135;
see also children's early vocabulary

w (vs. y) prosody: see prosodic
word(s)
analysis of, as wholes 4; as focus of attention as wholes 136; boundary cues 138; differences in structure and usage of one-syllable, two-syllable and three-syllable 9; first, constructed on basis of patterns 134; in context 138; in continuous speech 133; in isolation 133, 138; instability of 97, 99; key, processed first 131; newly acquired, more complex and closer match to model 71; order: see content words; syllable as element of structure of 4; temporal reorganization of 140;
see also information; high information content words
word pattern, invariant auditory 3, 121-2, 133, 135, 139-40; acoustic cues of adult's, 126-8; construction of 114-17, 124, 134-5; function in continuous speech of 128-32; in normalization: see normalization; of acoustically different forms 127-8;
see also cues, auditory; level(s) of representation; pattern(s); pattern matching; pattern recognition; schema/schemata

y (vs. w) prosody: see prosodic

Also available from Grevatt & Grevatt

An Annotated Bibliography of Verbal Materials: For Use in Psycholinguistic and Neurolinguistic Experimentation by Ruth Lésser and Peter Trewhitt.
ISBN 0 9507918 2 2. £1.70 net (UK); £2.95 (overseas). 1982.

'...provides a guide to some published texts which may be of value to the worker who is embarking upon project work, research or clinical assessment and analysis in the fields of psycho- and neurolinguistics. It consists of a catalogue of books and journal articles dealing with studies of both spoken and written language. The range of language levels stretches from the phoneme and grapheme to texts and discourse. The booklet is organized to take into account such factors as frequency of usage; age of acquisition; meaning dependency; media dependency; and grammatical phenomena.'
British Journal of Disorders of Communication

Linguistics and Linguistic Evidence: The LAGB Silver Jubilee Lectures 1984 by R. H. Robins and Victoria A. Fromkin.
ISBN 0 947722 00 9. £3.50 net (UK); £4.55 (overseas). 1985.

'Robins' [essay] displays the breadth and depth of reading in the history of this discipline that one has come to take for granted in his work... Both contributions to this jubilee publication are appropriately authoritative; both are judicious and unlikely to raise eyebrows or arouse tempers.'
Language

The Grammatical Hierarchy of Malayan Cantonese by Siew-Yue Killingley.
ISBN 0 9508149 0 3. £6.30 (UK); £7.30 (overseas). 1982.

'...quite a broad study of the syntax of a form of Cantonese about which very little has been written, that spoken in Malaya...Also provides the reader with a brief summary of the linguistic situation in Malaya...The book contains a truly excellent index.'
Journal of Chinese Linguistics

'This work, a revision of Killingley's University of London doctoral thesis, is an extensive catalog of Cantonese sentence, clause, phrase, and word types, presented in a tagmemic model...The book will be extremely useful to anyone planning to undertake work on Cantonese syntax; typologists and students of Southeast Asian areal phenomena will find much of interest here...'
Language

Also available from Grevatt & Grevatt

A Short Glossary of Cantonese Classifiers by Siew-Yue Killingley.
ISBN 0 9507918 0 6. £3.35 net (UK); £4.85 (overseas). 1982.

'...a most useful little book...aimed less at the linguist and more at the language learner...particularly helpful are the carefully pointed differences between classifiers which share a noun in common.'
Bulletin of the School of Oriental and African Studies

Cantonese Classifiers: Syntax and Semantics by Siew-Yue Killingley.
ISBN 0 9507918 3 0. £6.00 net (UK); £7.80 (overseas). 1983.

'Dr. Killingley points out the inadequate and often misleading material on classifiers in the earlier literature, and sets out to clarify the situation.'
Bulletin of the School of Oriental and African Studies

'Classifiers have attracted considerable attention lately, and Killingley's monograph sets out to provide a detailed study of Cantonese classifiers in the light of current linguistic research on the topic...The monograph leaves 'few aspects of the topic untouched...'
Language

'Cette étude detaillée des classificateurs nominaux du cantonais rendra de grands services aux sinologues...aussi bien qu'aux généralistes...'
Bulletin de la Société de Linguistique de Paris

A New Look at Cantonese Tones: Five or Six? by Siew-Yue Killingley.
ISBN 0 9508149 1 1. £3.50 net (UK); £4.55 (overseas). 1985.

UK purchases must include 15% p & p (single-copy orders or orders below £3) or 10% (multiple-copy orders). Overseas prices quoted are post free. Overseas sales either by pro-forma account or cash with orders. Non-sterling payments must include an extra £1 for bank charges. National Girobank a/c no. 62 630 2609. Bank Sort Code 72-00-00. Orders and payments to:

Grevatt & Grevatt, 9 Rectory Drive, Newcastle upon Tyne NE3 1XT, England.